Carsten Wendt

A Common Tax Base for Multinational Enterprises in the European Union

GABLER EDITION WISSENSCHAFT

Bibliographic information published by the Deutsche Nationalbibliothek
The Deutsche Nationalbibliothek lists this publication in the Deutsche Nationalbibliografie; detailed bibliographic data are available in the Internet at http://dnb.d-nb.de.

Dissertation Universität Mannheim, 2008

1st Edition 2009

Editorial Office: Frauke Schindler / Stefanie Loyal

Gabler is part of the specialist publishing group Springer Science+Business Media.
www.gabler.de

Cover design: Regine Zimmer, Dipl.-Designerin, Frankfurt/Main
Printed on acid-free paper
Printed in Germany

ISBN 978-3-8349-1326-5

Carsten Wendt

A Common Tax Base for Multinational Enterprises in the European Union

GABLER EDITION WISSENSCHAFT

Preface

Die vorliegende Arbeit wurde im März 2008 von der Fakultät für Betriebswirtschaftslehre der Universität Mannheim als Dissertation angenommen. Die Arbeit entstand im Rahmen des Forschungsprojektes „Besteuerung von Konzernen in Europa“, das am Zentrum für Europäische Wirtschaftsforschung (ZEW), Mannheim in Kooperation mit der Universität Mannheim durchgeführt und von der Deutschen Forschungsgemeinschaft (DFG) finanziert wurde. Darüber hinaus befruchteten verschiedene weitere Forschungsprojekte, die am ZEW bearbeitet wurden, Inhalt und Fortgang der vorliegenden Arbeit.

Mein erster und besonderer Dank gilt meinem verehrten Doktorvater und akademischen Lehrer Prof. Dr. Christoph Spengel, der das Forschungsprojekt anstieß und wissenschaftlich leitete. Das von ihm entgegengebrachte Vertrauen, zahlreiche fachliche Diskussionen und viele wertvolle Anregungen sowie die motivierende Arbeitsatmosphäre und die hervorragenden Forschungsbedingungen trugen ganz wesentlich zum erfolgreichen Abschuss der Arbeit bei. Herrn Prof. Dr. Dr. h.c. mult. Wolfgang Franz danke ich für die ausgezeichneten Forschungs- und Arbeitsbedingungen am ZEW. Bei Herrn Professor Dr. Dr. h.c. mult. Otto H. Jacobs möchte ich mich für die sehr guten Forschungsbedingungen an seinem Lehrstuhl bedanken. Danken möchte ich auch Prof. Dr. Ulrich Schreiber, der das Zweitgutachten übernahm.

Gerd Gutekunst, Rico Hermann und Thorsten Stetter danke ich für die sehr gute Zusammenarbeit und Unterstützung in den ersten Jahren meiner Promotionszeit. Bei Christiane Malke, Jannis Bischof und Nils Manegold möchte ich mich für ihre wertvollen Anregungen und die Durchsicht von Teilen des Manuskripts bedanken. Carsten Sauerland danke ich für die fachlichen Diskussionen. Den Kolleginnen und Kollegen am Lehrstuhl und ZEW danke ich für die gute und konstruktive Zusammenarbeit.

Mein Dank gilt auch den wissenschaftlichen Hilfskräften Gabriela Grunewald, Heidi Heller und Thorsten Neumann für Ihren tatkräftigen Einsatz in den Forschungsprojekten und Ihre Mithilfe bei den formalen Korrekturarbeiten.

Besonders bedanken möchte ich mich bei meinen Eltern, die mich auf meinem bisherigen Lebensweg unterstützen und mir durch beständigen Rückhalt diesen Weg ermöglichten.

Carsten Wendt

Summary of Contents

Preface V

Summary of Contents VII

Table of Contents IX

List of Abbreviations XIII

List of Figures XV

List of Tables XVII

1 Introduction 1

2 Theory of Multinational Enterprises 9

2.1 Definitions 9
2.2 Some Facts about Multinational Enterprises 10
2.3 Dunning's OLI Framework 11
2.4 Horizontal Foreign Direct Investment 13
2.5 Vertical Foreign Direct Investment 15
2.6 Knowledge-Capital Model 16
2.7 Internalization 17
2.8 Summary 26

3 Guidelines for Income Taxation of Multinational Enterprises 29

3.1 Functions of Corporation Income Taxes 29
3.2 Equity 32
3.3 Efficiency and Neutrality 40
3.4 Administrative Aspects of Taxation 49
3.5 Summary 50

4 Company Taxation in the European Union – a Stocktaking 53

4.1 National Investments 54
4.2 Foreign Direct Investments 76
4.3 Summary 85

5 An Evaluation of the Prevailing Corporation Tax in the European Union 87

5.1 Separate Accounting Under the Arm's Length Principle 87
5.2 Residence and Source Based Taxation 91
5.3 Measures to Protect the Tax Base 93
5.4 Effects of Corporate Income Taxes on Business Behaviour 94
5.5 An Aside – Influence of Decisions of the European Court of Justice 99
5.6 Summary 101

6 A Common Tax Base for Multinational Enterprises in the European Union 103

6.1 Harmonisation of the Tax Rate 103
6.2 Harmonisation of the Tax Base 104
6.3 A Common Corporate Tax Base 109
6.4 Common Consolidated Corporate Tax Base 154

7 Conclusions 201

List of References 207

Table of Contents

Preface V

Summary of Contents VII

Table of Contents IX

List of Abbreviations XIII

List of Figures XV

List of Tables XVII

1 Introduction 1

2 Theory of Multinational Enterprises 9

2.1 Definitions 9
2.2 Some Facts about Multinational Enterprises 10
2.3 Dunning's OLI Framework 11
2.4 Horizontal Foreign Direct Investment 13
2.5 Vertical Foreign Direct Investment 15
2.6 Knowledge-Capital Model 16
2.7 Internalization 17
2.7.1 Theory of the Firm 17
2.7.2 Boundaries of the Multinational Enterprise 21
2.8 Summary 26

3 Guidelines for Income Taxation of Multinational Enterprises 29

3.1 Functions of Corporation Income Taxes 29
3.1.1 The Corporation Income Tax as a Withholding Tax 30
3.1.2 The Corporation Income Tax as a Benefit Tax 31
3.1.3 The Corporation Income Tax as a Tax on Economic Rents 31
3.2 Equity 32
3.2.1 Individual equity 33
3.2.2 Inter-nation equity 37

3.3 Efficiency and Neutrality 40
3.3.1 The National Perspective 40
3.3.2 The International Perspective 45
3.4 Administrative Aspects of Taxation 49
3.5 Summary 50

4 Company Taxation in the European Union – a Stocktaking 53

4.1 National Investments 54
4.1.1 Corporate Income Tax 54
4.1.1.1 Nominal Tax Rates 54
4.1.1.2 Tax Accounting Rules 55
4.1.1.2.1 Relationship between Financial and Tax Accounting 55
4.1.1.2.2 Taxable Income 56
4.1.1.2.3 Recognition of Assets 57
4.1.1.2.4 Determination of cost values 59
4.1.1.2.5 Amortization 60
4.1.1.2.6 Recognition of Liabilities and Provisions 63
4.1.1.2.7 Inter-Company Dividends 64
4.1.1.2.8 Capital Gains 65
4.1.1.2.9 Loss Relief 67
4.1.1.3 Group Taxation 69
4.1.2 Corporation Tax System 74
4.1.3 Local Taxes 75
4.2 Foreign Direct Investments 76
4.2.1 Taxation of Foreign Income 76
4.2.2 Allocation of profits – the arm's length principle 79
4.2.3 Deductibility of interest 82
4.2.4 Loss Relief 83
4.2.5 Group Taxation 83
4.2.6 Business Reorganisations 84
4.3 Summary 85

5 An Evaluation of the Prevailing Corporation Tax in the European Union 87

5.1 Separate Accounting Under the Arm's Length Principle 87
5.2 Residence and Source Based Taxation 91
5.3 Measures to Protect the Tax Base 93
5.4 Effects of Corporate Income Taxes on Business Behaviour 94
5.4.1 International Capital Allocation 94
5.4.2 International Profit Allocation 96

5.4.2.1 Thin Capitalization 97
5.4.2.2 Transfer Pricing 98
5.5 An Aside – Influence of Decisions of the European Court of Justice 99
5.6 Summary 101

6 A Common Tax Base for Multinational Enterprises in the European Union 103

6.1 Harmonisation of the Tax Rate 103
6.2 Harmonisation of the Tax Base 104
6.2.1 A Common Corporate Tax Base 106
6.2.2 A Common Consolidated Corporate Tax Base 108
6.3 A Common Corporate Tax Base 109
6.3.1 Elements of a Common Corporate Tax Base 109
6.3.1.1 Guidelines for the Design of the Tax Base 109
6.3.1.2 IFRS as a Starting Point for a Common Corporate Tax Base 113
6.3.1.3 Comparison of Selective Member States' Tax Accounting Rules and IFRS 116
6.3.1.4 Proposals of the Common Consolidated Corporate Tax Base Working Group (Common Consolidated Corporate Tax Base WG) 121
6.3.2 Effects of a Common Corporate Tax Base 127
6.3.2.1 Methodology – European Tax Analyzer 128
6.3.2.2 Economic Structures of the Model Firms 130
6.3.2.3 Comparison of International Tax Burdens Based on Domestic Accounting 131
6.3.2.3.1 Base Case 132
6.3.2.3.2 Industry Specific Effective Tax Burdens 135
6.3.2.4 A Comparison of International Tax Burdens in Case IFRS Serves as a Starting Point for the Tax Bases 139
6.3.2.4.1 Scenario of a Common Corporate Tax Base 139
6.3.2.4.2 Base Case 141
6.3.2.4.3 Sensitivity Analysis: Effects in Different Industries 148
6.3.2.4.4 Dispersions of Effective Tax Burdens across Industries 149
6.3.3 Summary 153
6.4 Common Consolidated Corporate Tax Base 154
6.4.1 General Attributes of a Common Consolidated Tax Base 154
6.4.2 Implementation Issues 160
6.4.2.1 Definition of the Taxable Unit 160
6.4.2.1.1 Legal Ownership 160
6.4.2.1.2 Additional Criteria 162
6.4.2.1.3 Personal Scope of the Common Consolidated Corporate Tax Base 164
6.4.2.1.4 Territorial Scope 166

6.4.2.2 Consolidation 171
6.4.2.2.1 Intra-group Loss Relief 172
6.4.2.2.2 Adjustment of Intra-group Transfers 174
6.4.2.2.3 Other Adjustments 178
6.4.2.2.4 Distinction between Different Types of Income: Business and Non-business Income 178
6.4.2.2.5 Consolidation in Case of Less than 100%-owned Affiliates 179
6.4.2.2.6 Income arising on cross-border investments in third countries 181
6.4.2.2.6.1 Necessity of Common Rules 181
6.4.2.2.6.2 Outbound Investments 183
6.4.2.2.6.3 Inbound Investments 187
6.4.2.2.6.4 Treatment of Companies Entering the Group 188
6.4.2.2.7 Treatment of Companies Leaving the Group 189
6.4.2.3 Formula Apportionment 190
6.4.2.4 Related Issues 194
6.4.2.4.1 Optional or Mandatory? 194
6.4.2.4.2 Local Profit Taxes, Non-profit Taxes and Social Security Contributions 195
6.4.3 Summary 197

7 Conclusions 201

List of References 207

List of Abbreviations

ACE	Allowance for Corporate Equity
BRD	Bundesrepublik Deutschland
CCCTB	Common Consolidated Corporate Tax Base
CEPR	Centre for Economic Policy Research
CEPS	Center for European Policy Studies
COM	Communication
D.C.	District of Columbia
Ed.	Editor
Eds.	Editors
EG	Europäische Gemeinschaft
EStGB	Einkommensteuer Gesetzbuch
Et al.	Et alii
EU	European Union
FDI	Foreign Direct Investment
GAAP	General Accepted Accounting Standards
GmbH	Gesellschaft mit beschränkter Haftung
HGB	Handelsgesetzbuch
IAS	International Accounting Standards
IBFD	International Bureau of Fical Documentation
ICT	Information and Communication Technology
IFRS	International Fiancial Reporting Standards

MNE	Multinational Enterprise
No.	Number
Nr.	Nummer
OECD	Organisation for Economic Co-operation and Development
SE	Societas Europaea
SEC	Staff of the European Commission
SG	Subgroup
U.S.	United States
USA	United States of America
WG	Working group
ZEW	Zentrum für Europäische Wirtschaftsforschung

List of Figures

Fig. 1.	Nominal Corporation Income Tax Rates Including Surcharges in %	54
Fig. 2.	Comparison of Effective Tax Burdens – Deviation from the EU Average in % (Corporate Level, 10 Periods)	133
Fig. 3.	Impact of Common Rules Regarding Depreciation on the Effective Tax Burden in %	143
Fig. 4.	Impact of Common Rules Regarding a Simplified Valuation of Inventory on the Effective Tax Burden in %	144
Fig. 5.	Impact of Common Rules Regarding the Determination of Production Costs on the Effective Tax Burden in %	145
Fig. 7.	Setting 1	168
Fig. 8.	Setting 2	169
Fig. 9.	Setting 3	170

List of Tables

Table 1.	Organisational Forms of Multinational Enterprises	11
Table 2.	Relationship between Financial and Tax Accounting	55
Table 3.	Recognition of Revenues Arising from the Sale of Goods	56
Table 4.	Recognition of Revenues Arising from Construction Contracts and the Rendering of Services	57
Table 5.	Definition of Asset	58
Table 6.	Capitalisation of Research Costs	58
Table 7.	Capitalisation of Development Costs	59
Table 8.	Determination of Production Costs	59
Table 9.	Simplified Valuation Methods	60
Table 10.	Regular Depreciation of Industrial Buildings	61
Table 11.	Regular Depreciation of Plant and Equipment	62
Table 12.	Regular Amortisation of Rights and Intellectual Property	62
Table 13.	Recognition of Provisions	63
Table 14.	Taxation of Inter-company Dividends (Domestic Investments)	64
Table 15.	Tax Relief of Capital Gains (other than Shares)	66
Table 16.	Intertemporal Loss Relief	68
Table 17.	Group Taxation Regime Available	69
Table 18.	Shareholding Threshold	70
Table 19.	Manner of Election	71
Table 20.	Minimum Period	71
Table 21.	System of Group Taxation	72
Table 22.	Elimination of Intra-group Transfers	73
Table 23.	Corporation Tax Systems	74
Table 24.	Local Taxes	75
Table 25.	Avoidance of Double Taxation with respect to foreign permanent establishments	78
Table 26.	Avoidance of Double Taxation with Respect to Foreign Dividends	79
Table 27.	Deductibility of Refinancing Costs and Thin-Capitalisation Rules	82
Table 28.	Recognition of Losses of Foreign Permanent Establishments	83
Table 29.	Territorial Scope	84

Table 30. Scenarios of a Common Tax Base and their potential to eliminate tax obstacles 107
Table 31. Model Firm's Structure of the Balance Sheet (Period 6) 130
Table 32. Financial Ratios of Companies from Differen Industries 131
Table 33. Comparison of Effective Tax Burdens (Corporate Level, 10 Periods) 132
Table 34. Impact of Particular Tax Categories on the Effective Tax Burden in % 134
Table 35. Industry Specific Effective Tax Burdens – Deviation from the EU-Average 137
Table 36. Assets of the Model firm and their tax depreciation 140
Table 37. Changes in the Effective Tax Burden in Case of a Common Corporate Tax Base (Base Case) 142
Table 38. Changes in the Tax Burden Resulting from a Common Corporate Tax Base for Different Industries in Each Country 149
Table 39. Differences between the Effective Tax Burdens in Case of 151
Table 40. Intra-group income is ignored 176
Table 41. Intra-group income is realized but adjusted in the seller's account 177
Table 42. Intra-group income is realized but adjusted in a combined report 178

1 Introduction

The debate over EU corporate income tax harmonization is not new. The European Commission has already launched several initiatives aimed to improve corporate income taxation in Europe. These initiatives are based on the notion that company taxation is an important element for the establishment and the completion of the Internal Market.

The first formal proposals to harmonize or coordinate corporate tax systems in Europe date as far as from the early 1960s when the committee chaired by Neumark stressed the need to eliminate taxation differences between member states and proposed in July 1962 (see Europäische Wirtschaftsgemeinschaft: 1962) to harmonize the income tax and corporation tax systems, the tax rates and the tax bases and to sign a multinational double-taxation agreement. However, these far reaching proposals were not followed by policy action. A proposal on the harmonization of the corporate tax systems in 1975 (see European Commission, 1982) and a proposal focussed on the national loss relief in 1984 (see European Commission, 1984) were withdrawn. Moreover, a draft proposal on the harmonization of the rules on determining taxable profits (see European Commission, 1988) was never tabled, due to the reluctance of most member states.

Since the efforts of the European Commission to have its far reaching initiatives implemented failed, the European Commission changed its strategy. In its communication on company taxation in 1990 (see European Commission, 1990a) the European Commission stressed the importance of the principle of subsidiarity for its tax policy and decided from now on to restrict its initiatives to targeted measures for cross-border business activities. The necessity for a tax reform would only arise, if cross country differences in corporate taxation lead to distortions of cross border business activities in the EU.

Based on this new orientation of tax policy, following Commission proposals which originated in the late 1960s, two directives and a convention were finally adopted in July 1990:

- The Merger Directive 90/434/EEC,
- Parent-Subsidiary Directive 90/435/EEC and
- Arbitration Convention 90/436/EEC.

At the same time the European Commission asked a Committee of independent experts chaired by Ruding to examine whether differences in corporation tax caused distortions in the Internal Market, particularly as regards investment decisions and competition. The final "Ruding" report (see European Commission, 1992a) was submitted in 1992 and contained comparably far reaching conclusions. The core elements of the recommendations were a harmonized corporation tax rate between 30% and 40%, the harmonization of the tax accounting rules, and the integration of local taxes into income tax and corporation tax. Furthermore, a common corporation tax system, at least in the long run, was recommended. Although the need to eliminate double taxation, to ensure effective taxation and prevent tax evasion was recognized, the Commission was reluctant concerning the more concrete proposals contained in the report (see European Commission, 1992b). This applied in particular with respect to the harmonization of the corporate income tax rate.

About five years later, the political discussion on taxation received a new momentum. In its communication in 1996 the European Commission introduced a new tax policy concept (see European Commission, 1996). The aim was to ensure that taxation policies were better geared towards achieving important Union objectives, such as promoting growth and employment and completing the single market, while at the same time protecting tax bases against harmful tax competition. Following this strategy paper the Council agreed in December 1997 on the outline of a "Tax Package" of measures to tackle harmful tax competition in the EU (see European Commission, 1997a, 1997b). The package consisted of:

- A political code of conduct to eliminate harmful business tax regimes;
- A legislative measure to ensure an effective minimum level of taxation of savings income; and
- A legislative measure to eliminate source taxes on cross-border payments of interest and royalties between associated companies.

EU Finance Ministers formally adopted the package at their meeting of 3 June 2003 (see European Commission, 2003a).

The prospects for more coordination in corporate taxation were revived in 2001 when the European Commission issued a study (see European Commission, 2001a) prepared by the Commission Services and a policy communication (see European Commission, 2001c) from the Commission. The Commission Services study and communication of 2001 were prepared following a specific mandate given to the Commission by the Council of the European Union in 1999. In accordance with this mandate, the study contained a detailed analysis of the level, the dispersion and the determinants of corporate effective tax rates for 15 EU member states, the identification of the remaining tax obstacles hindering cross-border economic activities in the EU, an analysis of targeted solutions to the different tax obstacles that have been identified and an analysis of more comprehensive solutions to tackle the identified tax obstacles.

For domestic and cross-border investment in 1999 and 2001, a large dispersion of effective marginal and average tax rates was found, the average effective tax rate varying from 10.5% in Ireland to 34.9% in Germany. The effective tax rates were mainly influenced by statutory tax rates. As regards the identification of tax obstacles to cross-border business activities, it was highlighted that the co-existence of separate national tax systems within the EU causes additional tax burdens associated with doing business in more than one member state. Each member state has its own set of rules, in particular laws and conventions on financial accounting, rules for determining taxable profits, and arrangements for the collection and administration of tax, and its own network of tax treaties. Furthermore, the need to comply with different national tax rules entails considerable compliance costs which undermine the international competitiveness of European companies and waste resources. This is particularly relevant for cross-border activities of small and medium-sized companies. According to the Commission's European Tax Survey (see European Commission, 2004a), compliance costs in case of multinational enterprises amount to 1.9% of total annual tax payments while they amount to 30.9% in case of medium-sized companies.

Furthermore, the fact that each Member State is a separate tax jurisdiction has a number of further consequences. In particular:

- relief for losses incurred by associated companies located in other Member States is not allowed in many cases, which may lead to double taxation (cross-border loss relief);

- the allocation of profits of multinationals to different jurisdictions on an arm's length basis by transaction based transfer prices causes methodological problems. This gives rise to numerous problems, notably high compliance costs and potential double taxation;
- in many situations cross-border restructuring operations give rise to tax charges with a risk of double taxation;
- double taxation may occur as a result of conflicting taxing rights (e.g. thin capitalisation rules, deduction of headquarters costs).

In terms of policy recommendation, the European Commission considered a two-track strategy to remedy all or most of the identified obstacles: specific measures which are targeted at particular obstacles and comprehensive solutions aimed to systematically remedy all or most of the obstacles. Targeted measures are intended to address the most urgent problems in the short and mid-term. In this context, improved versions of existing company tax directives have been adopted. This is the case of the Parent-Subsidiary Directive and the Merger Directive.

However, in the Commission's view, a comprehensive solution providing multinational companies with a single framework of company taxation is the only means to overcome the tax obstacles identified. Therefore, the Commission decided to steer its company taxation policy towards achieving such a comprehensive solution. Four options or models were identified for achieving this objective:

- Home State Taxation (see Lodin and Gammie, 2001: 21-24): According to this concept, companies doing business in more than one member state would have the option of determining their EU-wide consolidated income according to the company income tax rules of the member state where their headquarters are located.
- Common Consolidated Corporate Tax Base: Under this concept, all or a group of member states would agree on a set of common rules for determining the consolidated tax base of EU corporate groups.
- European Corporate Income Tax: This model provides for a uniform EU tax base and tax rate. Revenues would go to the Community budget and would partly be allocated to the member states according to an agreed formula.
- Harmonized Tax Base: Under this alternative, national rules on company taxation would be harmonized by devising a single EU company tax base and system as a replacement for existing national systems.

At present, the European Commission is mainly pursuing the concept of a Common Consolidated Corporate Tax Base.[1] This strategy was confirmed several times (see European Commission, 2003d, 2005b, 2006a and 2007c). Consequently, the Common Consolidated Corporate Tax Base is one of the issues currently dominating the debate in the EU tax arena. The European Commission has identified three alternative policy options for a Common Consolidated Corporate Tax Base (see European Commission, 2007c). The alternatives include a "no change" scenario, a Common Corporate Tax Base and a Common Consolidated Corporate Tax Base. In contrast to a Common Corporate Tax Base, the Common Consolidated Corporate Tax Base would include some form of consolidation and apportionment. There are a number of issues related to the different structural elements of a common tax base. For instance, common tax accounting rules, a definition of what constitutes a group of companies for consolidation, a technique in computing the income of the group and a mechanism for sharing the base will be required. In 2004, a working group was set up in order to work on these issues. However, the Commission pointed out, that additional expert opinion from beyond the Commission and Member state administrations on these issues can be helpful (see European Commission, 2007a: 4).

Against this background, this thesis analyses the necessity, the concept and potential advantages and effects of a common concolidated corporate tax base. In this context, alternative options for the issues related to the determination of taxable income, the consolidation and formula apportionment are considered. In order to analyse the necessity for a tax reform and to develop alternative options for the design of a Common Consolidated Corporate Tax Base, the presence and economic characteristics of multinational enterprises have to be assessed first. The aim is to explain what multinational enterprises are and why they arise. Based on these findings, the tax systems currently applied by EU member states are compared and evaluated. The evaluation criteria used here are efficiency and neutrality, equity among taxpayers and countries as well as administrative aspects. Furthermore, the effects on tax competition and the influence

1 Home State Taxation is considered to be particularly beneficial for small and medium sized businesses (see European Commission, 2005a). This concept would address precisely the tax issues which hamper small and medium-sized companies most in their cross-border activities, i.e. compliance costs which are often disproportionately high for small and medium-sized companies and difficulties with the cross-border offsetting of losses. Moreover, since Home State Taxation refers to the existing tax rules of the country where the company's headquarter is located there is no need for harmonized tax rules but only for mutual recognition. Thus, Home State Taxation could be introduced before a Common Consolidated Corporate Tax Base is implemented. However, in the Commission's view, the Common Consolidated Corporate Tax Base constitutes the best

of major decisions of the European Court of Justice are considered. The analysis aims to identify the main deficits of the current tax systems that explain the necessity of a common tax base. The focus of this thesis consists in developing and evaluating alternative scenarios and concepts of a common consoliated corporate tax base in the EU. The reform concepts have to be consistent with the economic characteristics of multinational enterprises and must guarantee a taxation that is in line with the aforementioned evaluation criteria.

The thesis is organised as follows: Chapter 2 deals with multinational enterprises. First a definition and some stylized facts are presented. These facts provide the foundation for the theories explaining the presence of multinational enterprises. These theories are developed along two dimensions. One dimension refers to the location issue. The question to be answered here is why companies choose to engage in horizontal and vertical foreign direct investment. The other dimension refers to the decision of firms on the extent of control they want to exert over different stages of the value chain.

After explaining and characterising the presence of multinational enterprises, the focus of this thesis shifts to taxation issues. In chapter 3, guidelines for company taxation are presented. These guidelines are used for the assessment of the tax systems currently applied by the EU member states and for the design of a harmonised tax base. Important criteria commonly agreed on by economists and tax experts considered here are equity with respect to taxpayers and nations, as well as efficiency and neutrality at the national and international level. Moreover, administrative aspects of taxation are taken into account. Before normative criteria for the taxation of corporate income are outlined, the question of why corporate income taxes are imposed is addressed.

Important structural elements of the member states' current national tax systems are described and compared in chapter 4. The analysis is mainly concerned with corporation income tax. However, additional local taxes are also taken into account. After comparing statutory tax rates and tax accounting rules at the national level, the taxation of cross-border investments is outlined. A special focus is on tax rules for corporate groups. At the end of this chapter, effective tax burdens of corporations, resident across the EU are persented. Effective tax burdens combine the elements of the corporate tax rate, the corporate tax base and additional local taxes. They serve as an indica-

means by which companies in the Internal Market can overcome tax obstacles in a systematic way.

tor for the attractiveness of member states from a tax point of view and the impact of tax rules on effective tax burdens.

Chapter 5 highlights the main deficits of the prevailing corporation tax in the EU with respect to multinational enterprises and the necessity of a tax reform. The evaluation focuses on the separate entity approach along with the arm's length principle and the coexistence of source- and residence-based taxation. Furthermore, measures of member states to protect their national tax bases are evaluated. In this context, especially restrictions to the deductibility of expenses and losses are taken into account. Empirical evidence is provided where available.

In chapter 6 the proposals of the European Commission for a Common Consolidated Corporate Tax Base are addresses. At the beginning of this chapter, possible scenarios and their potential to eliminate tax obstacles are outlined. Two scenarios are considered: a Common Corporate Tax Base and a Common Consolidated Corporate Tax Base. Regarding the first scenario, general accounting principles are deducted from the abovementioned tax principles. Against these accounting principles, the appropriateness of IFRS as a starting point for a common tax base is investigated. The analysis is based on a comparison of IFRS and current national tax accounting rules. Furthermore, the work done by Commission Service is considered. A scenario of a common tax base is defined and the consequences this scenario would have on the size of the corporate tax bases of companies resident in one of the member states are analysed using the European Tax Analyzer. Concerning the scenario of a Common Consolidated Corporate Tax Base general attributes are analysed first. Then, issues and concepts of a consolidated tax base as intended by the European Commission are elaborated and evaluated. As regards the conceptual issues, different criteria for defining the consolidated group as well as the personal and territorial scope of the Common Consolidated Corporate Tax Base are discussed first. Second, issues regarding the methodology of consolidation are considered. Special interest is devoted to cross-border loss compensation, adjustments of intra-group transfers, distinctions between apportionable and non-apportionable group income, as well as income arising on cross-border investments involving third countries. Furthermore, rules regarding the treatment of companies entering and leaving the consolidated group are considered. Third, different options for formula apportionment are considered. At the end of chapter eight, questions of whether the Common Consolidated Corporate Tax Base should be optional or mandatory and about consequences of the Common Consolidated Corporate Tax Base regarding local taxes and social security contributions are addressed. The final chapter offers a summary of the main findings.

2 Theory of Multinational Enterprises

This book deals with the taxation of multinational enterprises. Before the taxation issue is addressed, it is important to assess what multinational enterprises are and why and where they arise. This assessment is necessary in order to evaluate how the presence and characteristics of multinational enterprises affect the effectiveness and optimal design of tax systems.

2.1 Definitions

There is no uniform definition of what constitutes a multinational enterprise (see Buckley, 1985: 1-2, Kutschker and Schmid, 2006: 236). Definitions may either rely on structural characteristics, on performance characteristics, or on behavioural characteristics (see Grünärml, 1975: 230). Here, a definition of a multinational enterprise based on its structure is chosen. Accordingly, a multinational enterprise may be defined as an enterprise that controls and operates business establishments located in at least two countries (see Grünärml, 1975: 231). Multinational enterprises and foreign direct investment flows are related objects (see Frebel, 2006: 8). According to the OECD (1996: 7-8) a foreign direct investment reflects the objective of obtaining a lasting interest by an entity resident in one country in an entity resident in another country. A lasting interest implies the existence of a long-term relationship between the two entities and a significant degree of influence of the investing entity on the management of the entity invested in.

The investing company is in general referred to as the parent company. The parent company may be an incorporated or unincorporated public or private enterprise. Similarly, the investment entity may be an incorporated enterprise, i.e. affiliate, or an unincorporated enterprise, i.e. a branch. There are two types of affiliates: (1) subsidiaries are more than 50% owned by the direct investor; (2) associates are owned between 10-

50% by their parent company. Foreign direct investments may be made up of equity capital, reinvested earnings, and other capital associated with an inter-company debt transaction.[2]

There are several theories explaining why multinational enterprises arise. Before turning to these theories, some stylized facts about multinational enterprises and foreign direct investment are presented. These facts provide a foundation for the theories outlined.

2.2 Some Facts about Multinational Enterprises

Foreign direct investments play an increasingly important role. Worldwide foreign direct investment flows have dramatically increased, especially between 1986 and 2000 (see Barba-Navaretti and Venables, 2004: 3). Inflows of foreign direct investment grew much faster than either trade or income as measured by the real gross domestic product. In Europe, inward foreign direct investment flows have increased from 5,226 million US Dollar in 1970 to 4,680,062 million US Dollar in 2005. During the same time period, outward foreign direct investment flows have increased from 5,095 million US Dollar to 6,244,371 million US Dollar (see UNCTAD, 2007).

Foreign direct investment flows arise mainly between developed countries (see Barba-Navaretti and Venables, 2004: 5). Between 1998 and 2001, the European Union as a whole accounted for 69.7% of worldwide foreign direct investment outflows and for 49.9% of worldwide foreign direct investment inflows.

There are two types of foreign direct investment: (1) Greenfield investment and (2) mergers and acquisitions. Greenfield investment is associated with the creation of a new plant. If the investment is associated with the purchase of an existing plant, this is referred to as a merger and acquisition. A large part of foreign direct investment flows is accounted for by mergers and acquisitions, especially between developed countries. Barba-Navaretti and Venables (2004: 9-10) report that between 1998 and 2001, merger and acquisitions accounted for 89% of foreign direct investment into developed countries, and for 35.7% of foreign direct investment inflows into developing countries.

2 For more details on different types of foreign direct investment as well as accounting practices and reporting methods see OECD 1996.

Intra-firm trade is an important component of international goods trade flows. About 60% of the volume of world trade is intra-firm trade (see European Commission, 2001b: 23; Hay, Horner and Owens, 1994: 423).

Industries in which multinational enterprises are prevalent are characterised by large investments in research and development, a large share of professional and technical workers in their workforces and the production of technically complex or differentiated goods (see Caves, 1996: 7-9). Furthermore, multinational enterprises tend to be important in industries which feature high productivity dispersions (see Helpman, Melitz and Yeaple, 2003: 23).

Table 1. Organisational Forms of Multinational Enterprises

	Internalization Issue	
Location Issue	Domestic Integration	Domestic Outsourcing
	Foreign Integration	Foreign Outsourcing

In developing their global strategy, firms principally have to make two decisions. First, they have to decide on where to locate the different stages of the value chain. Second, firms have to decide on the extent of control they want to exert over these processes. Accordingly, there are in general four organizational options in an international context (see Table 1).

2.3 Dunning's OLI Framework

A first comprehensive framework to analyse the location and the internalization choices of multinational enterprises was developed by Dunning (see Dunning, 1981: 9-31; 1993: 183-218). Dunning's theory is based on the notion that doing business abroad entails added costs, such as communications and transport costs or higher costs of stationary personnel abroad. Therefore, there must be some special advantages associated with firms doing business in more than one country (see Hymer, 1976: 34). The OLI Framework groups the advantages to undertake foreign direct investment in three categories: (1) ownership advantages, (2) location advantages and (3) internalisation advantages.

Ownership advantages could be a product, know-how, a reputation or a production process to which other firms do not have access. These are called firm-specific assets. Firm-specific assets can be either tangible, e.g. access to natural resources, or intangible, e.g. specialized know-how, patented products or brand distinctiveness (see Caves, 1996). They are easily transferred across countries and are not-excludable, to a large extent. Thus, the generation of rents associated with the firm-specific assets is not linked to a specific location. Ownership advantages confer some valuable market power or cost advantage of the firm that outweighs the disadvantage of doing business abroad.

In addition to ownership advantages, the foreign country must provide location advantages that make it profitable to produce directly in the foreign country rather than producing at home and exporting to the foreign country. Possible location advantages include the availability of necessary production factors, e.g. well-trained employees or a favourable environment for R&D, cheap factor prices offering cost advantages, tariffs and transportation costs or access to customers. The existence of location-specific advantages is decisive for doing business abroad and enables a company to generate location-specific economic rents.

Finally, a firm must have an internalization advantage. This is the most abstract concept and refers to corporate governance issues, such as the boundaries of the firm. Generally, the internalization advantage is thought to arise from the existence of imperfect markets. When the contracting mechanism breaks down, the market is unable to correctly value and protect firm-specific advantages that are intangible in nature.

Theories on multinational enterprises have basically developed around Dunning's OLI framework. They have first focused on ownership and location advantages to explain foreign direct investment, while leaving aside the internalization issue. A distinction is generally drawn between horizontal and vertical foreign direct investment. Horizontal integration acknowledges that firms have access to two modes for servicing a foreign market. The first mode is the exporting option, which allows for a concentration of production in a single country. The second mode is to duplicate production operations abroad in order to service foreign markets. Vertical integration refers to a situation in which a producing company may decide to fragment the production process and to undertake different parts of the production process in different countries.

2.4 Horizontal Foreign Direct Investment

Theories on horizontal foreign direct investment are concerned with the issue of why some firms choose to engage in foreign direct investment to service a foreign market instead of focusing on simple exporting. If a company chooses the mode of servicing the foreign market, it anticipates the profits it would obtain under each of these choices. Referring to Hymer (1976), setting up a production plant in a foreign country entails fixed costs. These fixed costs do not arise if a company chooses to service the foreign market through exports. On the other hand, relative to horizontal foreign direct investment, exporting is subject to higher transport costs. The theory predicts that foreign direct investment will be more prevalent whenever transport costs are high and fixed costs of setting up a foreign production plant are low (see Brainard, 1997). This seems reasonable, since low transport costs reduce the costs of exporting while high fixed plant costs increase the costs of foreign direct investment.

Besides fixed plant costs and transport costs, firm-level economies of scale are assumed to be a driving force for horizontal foreign direct investment (see Markusen, 1984).[3] These firm-level economies of scale are closely related to Dunning‘s notion of ownership advantages. These advantages rely on firm-specific assets which contribute to a firm's sustained competitiveness. By spreading the costs incurred in producing or acquiring these firm-specific assets over a number of plants producing a good gains known as firm-level economies of scale can be achieved (see Markusen, 1984). To put it in other words, firms with two plants have fixed costs that are less than double the costs of a firm with only one plant. Firm-level economies of scale may be especially important with reference to research and development expenses, brand development, accounting or finance operations, since these costs can be spread over larger numbers of production facilities located in more than one country. The higher these firm-level economies of scale are, the easier it will be to amortize the fixed costs of setting up a production plant in a foreign country. Therefore, all other things being equal, higher firm-level economies of scale are supposed to increase the attractiveness of horizontal foreign direct investment over exporting.

These theories have been empirically tested by Brainard (1997). Her results indicate that transport costs as measured by tariffs and freight costs are negatively correlated to

---

3 Extensions to this model can be found in Horstmann and Markusen (1987, 1992) and Brainard (1993), who referred to this approach as the "proximity-concentration" hypothesis.

exports instead of horizontal foreign direct investment. Furthermore, plant-level economies of scale turned out to be positively correlated to exporting while the reverse is true for firm-level economies.

Helpman, Melitz and Yeaple (2004) analysed the impact of intra-industry heterogeneity on horizontal foreign direct investment. Their model predicts that the ratio of exports to horizontal foreign direct investment should be higher in industries with higher productivity dispersion. Firms with only low productivity would not choose to set up a foreign production plant, because for these firms profits do not cover the fixed plant-specific costs. Assuming that exporting also entails fixed costs, they obtain a sorting by which the most productive firms serve the foreign market via subsidiary sales, the lower productive firms serve the market via exporting and still lower productive firms serve only the domestic market (see Heplman, Melitz and Yeaple, 2004). Evidently, this sorting is consistent with the empirical evidence that multinational corporations are more productive than exporters who are not multinationals, and exporters who are not multinationals are more productive than firms who serve only the domestic market (see Heplman, Melitz and Yeaple, 2004 for evidence from the United States, Girma, Görg and Strobl, 2004 for evidence from Ireland and Girma, Kneller and Pisu, 2005 for evidence from the United Kingdom).

Regarding location specific advantages, cross-country differences in market size and factor prices are supposed to have an impact on the decision whether horizontal foreign direct investment or exporting is more profitable in servicing a foreign market (see Markusen and Venables, 1998, 2000). Theory predicts that countries with a larger market size and thus more demand will tend to attract more inflows of horizontal foreign direct investment because the larger local sales in those countries make it easier for foreign firms to amortize the fixed costs of setting up a production facility in the foreign country. If countries differ in market size, horizontal multinational enterprises are at a disadvantage relative to domestic firms headquartered and producing in the large country. The multinational enterprise would have to install a costly plant in the small market, while the domestic firm would only incur trade costs on a relatively small amount of output exported to the small market. Suppose instead that the countries are of similar size but have very different relative factor prices. If factor prices differ between countries, the costs of production will tend to differ as well. In this situation, a company would choose to locate its production solely in the country with the lowest factor prices and to service foreign markets through exporting. Accordingly, horizontal foreign direct investments are at a disadvantage, because they have to incur a substantial portion of costs in a high-cost country. Domestic firms located in the low-cost country, however, incur all of their costs in the low-cost location. Hence, the larger the relative factor price differences between countries are, the less likely it will be that transport costs are high enough to justify a replication of the production process in the foreign countries.

2.5 Vertical Foreign Direct Investment

The models concerning horizontal foreign direct investment have treated multinational enterprises and trade flows as substitutes. Horizontal multinationals replace exports and thus trade flow. However, as mentioned before, a significant fraction of world trade flows arises within multinational enterprises. These trade flows within multinational enterprises may be seen as an indicator of vertical integration, i.e. vertical foreign direct investment.

According to the theory, vertical foreign direct investment is mainly associated with the ability of enterprises to exploit cross-country differences in factor prices by shifting production processes with different input requirements to the locations where they can be most cheaply produced (see Helpman, 1984). This argument is based on the assumption that firms need two activities in their production. These activities are assumed to have different factor intensities and the ability to be geographically separated. Specifically, vertical multinational enterprises are assumed to occur in the presence of factor price differences across countries, when a firm has an incentive to separate capital-intensive stages of production from labour-intensive stages of production and to locate capital-intensive production in the country where the costs of capital are relatively lower and the labour-intensive production where the labour costs are relatively lower. The prevalence of multinational enterprises is expected to increase in relative factor endowment differences across countries. This means that companies are likely to locate capital-intensive productions in the capital-abundant country while labour-intensive productions are located in the labour-abundant country. This result is based on the notion that prices for a certain production factor are lower in countries with a higher endowment of this factor. The higher the relative factor endowment differs across countries, the higher are factor price differences and thus vertical foreign direct investment should become more prevalent. However, the geographic fragmentation of the production process is unlikely to occur if there are no differences across the different parts of the production process. This model seems to imply that vertical foreign direct investment should shift to the country with the lowest factor prices. However, this reasoning abstracts from productivity differences across countries. Therefore, if productivity is low in a country, this country is not likely to attract multinational firms even if factor prices are low. The arguments explaining vertical foreign direct investment contrast to those explaining horizontal foreign direct investment. With respect to horizontal foreign direct investment, cross-country similarities in factor endowments are assumed to be positively correlated to foreign direct investment, while vertical foreign direct investment is supposed to occur if factor endowments differ across countries.

Another factor assumed to be relevant for vertical foreign direct investment is transport costs. When production is geographically fragmented, intermediate products have to be transported across borders. Similarly to the reasoning regarding horizontal foreign direct investment, theory predicts that vertical foreign direct investment is more likely to occur whenever transport costs are low.

Empirical evidence for vertical foreign direct investment has been provided by Yeaple (2003). He finds that the ratio of exports to foreign direct investment sales is decreasing in the interaction of a measure of human capital abundance and a measure of skilled-labour intensity. Hanson, Mataloni and Slaughter (2003) find that a large and increasing fraction of foreign direct investment flows is related to exports of intermediate inputs to foreign affiliates for further processing. This finding is a clear indication of the empirical relevance of vertical foreign direct investment.

2.6 Knowledge-Capital Model

A further step in the theory explaining foreign direct investment was to combine the approaches to horizontal and vertical integration into a single framework that allows firms to choose between domestic, horizontal and vertical strategies. This approach has been developed by Markusen (1997, 2001) and is called "Knowledge-Capital Model".

Three important assumptions about the technology used by firms are what Markusen refers to as the knowledge-capital model:

– the location of knowledge-based assets may be fragmented from production. Any incremental cost of supplying services of the asset to a single foreign plant versus the cost to a single plant is small.
– Knowledge-based assets are skilled-labour intensive relative to final production.
– The services of knowledge-based assets are joint inputs into multiple production facilities. The added cost of a second plant is small compared to the cost of establishing a firm with a local plant. This assumption is crucial to the existence of firm-specific economies of scale.

Fragmentation and skilled-labour intensity motivate vertical foreign direct investments that locate their single plant and headquarters in different countries depending on factor prices and market sizes. Jointness of inputs gives rise to horizontal foreign direct investment, which have plants producing the final goods in multiple countries.

In the knowledge-capital model, both horizontal and vertical foreign direct investments can arise depending on country characteristics such as size, size differences, relative endowment differences, trade costs, and investment costs. The model predicts that horizontal foreign direct investment is prevalent if countries do not differ in size and in relative factor endowments. On the other hand, if one country is both small and skilled-labour abundant, most or even all of the firms are vertical integrated headquartered in the small country, with a single plant in the large, skilled-labour-scarce country. The location of headquarters is chosen on the basis of factor prices, and the location of the plant is chosen both on the basis of factor prices and on the basis of market sizes. These motives reinforce one another for vertical foreign direct investment when one country is small and skilled-labour abundant.

2.7 Internalization

2.7.1 Theory of the Firm

In the previous chapters, several theories of vertical and horizontal foreign direct investment are presented. According to these theories, the emergence of multinational enterprises is determined by location specific advantages related to the host country, e.g. factor prices, factor endowments or distance as captured by transport costs, and by firm-specific factors, e.g. firm-specific economies, plant related fixed costs and transport costs. These theories could explain why and where horizontal and vertical foreign direct investment occurs. However, these theories do not explain why foreign direct investment occurs within firm boundaries, rather than through arm's length subcontracting. This issue is addressed by several theories of the firm which are outlined in the following.

In the neoclassic theory of the firm, the size of the firm is determined by the extent to which it can exploit economies of scale and scope (see Tirole, 2003: 18). Economies of scale refer to decreasing costs per unit resulting from higher levels of productions. This effect is based on the notion that higher levels of production may permit the use of more efficient technologies and more specialized workers (see Scherer, 1980: 81-84). Economies of scale are generally also associated with the gathering of activities that avoids duplication of fixed costs or at least reduces these costs on average. Examples of activities that permit the realisation of these economies of scale may be auditing, marketing, finance or research and development (see Tirole, 2003: 18). Economies of scope arise from the sharing or joint use of input factors for the production of two or more products. Due to economies of scope, the overall cost of producing several products jointly is less than the sum of the producing them separately (see Bailey and Friedlander, 1982).

This technological view of the firm (see Tirole, 2003: 16) is mainly based on the notion that economies of scale and scope encourage the gathering of activities. However, this view of the firm has some caveats. First, it seems questionable that economies of scale should necessarily be exploited within the firm, as they may also be obtained in market transactions. Second, this theory does not pin down firm boundaries. As pointed out by Coase (1937: 394), the neoclassic theory is perfectly consistent with the existence of one big firm carrying out the entire production in the world. Therefore, it is better thought of as a theory of plant size than as a theory of firm size. This is obviously not consistent with reality. Third, the technological view of the firm treats the firm as a perfectly efficient black box and has nothing to say about the internal organization of firms (see Hart, 1995).

According to Coase (1937) firms emerge when certain transactions can be undertaken with less transaction costs inside the firm than through the market mechanism. Thus, it is assumed that the size of transaction costs varies in market transactions and in intra-firm transactions. Transaction costs of the market may be higher due to costs of discovering the relevant prices, costs of negotiating and concluding a separate contract for each exchange transaction, costs of specifying all possible contingencies in a long-term contract or taxes on market transactions (see Coase, 1937).

Williamson (1985) developed this transaction cost approach further. He introduced three concepts that can explain the source of transaction costs associated with the market mechanism: (1) bounded rationality, (2) opportunism and (3) asset specificity:

1. The assumption of bounded rationality provides a foundation of incomplete contracts (see also Salanié, 1997). Economic agents who are boundedly rational are unable to sign a contract that takes into account all the contingencies that may arise. Thus, due to bounded rationality, the parties of a contract are forced to neglect some key variables whose effect on the relationship they find difficult to evaluate. Furthermore, even when contingencies are foreseen, the cost of writing such contracts, in the sense of time and money, may outweigh the benefits of writing a specific clause for the contingency in the contract. Finally, even if parties can plan and negotiate contingencies, enforcing these contracts may be costly, due to the inability of a third party to verify ex post the values taken by certain variables and eventually settle the disputes that may arise. As a result, contracts will tend to be vague or silent on a number of key features and thus incomplete and will tend to be renewed or renegotiated as the future unfolds.
2. Opportunism means that economic actors are "self-interest seeking with guile" (Williamson, 1985: 47). This assumption is a necessary condition for the incompleteness of contracts to lead to inefficiencies. If economic actors could credibly pledge at the outset to execute the contract efficiently, then although the contract would be incomplete, renegotiation would occur in a joint profit maximizing and thus efficient manner.
3. A final source of transaction costs associated with the market mechanism is based on the concept of asset specificity in that an investment is geared to a particular buyer. Certain assets or investments may be relationship-specific, in the sense that the value of these assets or investments is higher inside a particular relationship than outside of it. This relationship-specificity of certain assets or investments implies that, at the renegotiation stage, parties cannot switch to alternative trading partners and are partially locked in a bilateral relationship. This may be the case due to switching costs or missing outside opportunities. In contrast, if standardized assets are transferred, economic actors could terminate the relationship without any significant disadvantages and search for a new customer.

As a general rule, the firm will replace the market system when transaction costs are minimized by governance inside the firm. Whether this is more likely to occur also depends on the characteristics of the respective transaction. According to Williamson, asset specificity is the most important characteristic of a transaction, explaining why firms replace the market (see Williamson, 1990: 54). He distinguishes between several types of asset specificity. Site specificity is associated with the gain in trading with a nearby supplier or buyer. Specific investments in human capital involve, for example, the learning of processes and team work. Another type of asset specificity refers to idiosyncratic investment. This is the case, for instance, when a supplier designs equipment to meet the special needs of the buyer.

Given incomplete contracts, asset specificity influences the choice between intra-firm and market transactions. This effect may be illustrated as follows. Consider a situation in which a supplier and buyer select each other in a pool of competitive suppliers and buyers. The supplier provides a specialized intermediate input geared to the needs of the buyer who converts it into a final good. The contract may be incomplete because due to bounded rationality the supplier and the buyer fail to write an ex-ante contract in a way that would account for all contingencies and would allow a third party to verify ex post the values taken by certain variables and eventually settle the disputes that may arise. Since the contract is incomplete, the economic actors know that later on there will be gains from trade between them to be exploited ex-post through bargaining. It is important that these gains are exploited correctly and that they are divided properly in order to induce the efficient amount of specific investment ex-ante. Asset specificity implies that outside opportunities are absent for the supplier. Therefore, the bargaining position of the supplier is worse than the bargaining position of the buyer. The buyer realises that the investment incurred by the supplier has a relatively lower value outside the relationship and will thus try to lower the share of the gain from trade allocated to the supplier. This behaviour refers to opportunism. Foreseeing this, the supplier will have lower incentives to ex-ante investment, and this will tend to reduce joint surplus.

Due to these inefficiencies, economic actors may choose to integrate. When a firm integrates another firm, it acquires its assets. This ownership of assets is supposed to be the source of power to fill unspecified contingencies (see Grossman and Hart, 1986; Hart and Moore (1985). In particular, in the presence of unforeseen contingencies not accounted for in a contract, an opportunistic owner of assets will tend to decide on the use of the asset that maximises his payoff in the ex-post bargaining with the other party. Thus, ownership changes the ex-post bargaining process and puts the owner in a better bargaining position. In turn, the ex-post division of the gains from trade will affect ex-ante investments. Via integration, residual rights of control are allocated to one of the parties. According to the theory, the optimal arrangement of ownership is the one that best protects the specific investment of the one that yields the highest gains from trade (see Tirole, 2003: 31).

Empirical studies have focused on the effects of asset specificity on the occurrence of vertical integration. Several studies provide evidence that asset specificity leads to vertical integration (see Klein, Crawford and Alchian, 1978; Monteverde and Teece, 1982; Masten, 1984; Anderson and Schmittlein, 1984).

2.7.2 Boundaries of the Multinational Enterprise

As argued before, the theories of foreign direct investment presented so far have dealt with trade and foreign direct investment flows but share a common failure to adequately explain the crucial issue of internalization. They can explain why firms sort into exclusive domestic producers, exporters or foreign direct investors. However, these models cannot explain why some firms outsource while others integrate. In the following, theories addressing the internalization issue of multinational enterprises are presented. These theories build on a common assumption, namely that some inputs are highly specific to a final product and that their supply is not fully contractible. Thus, these models examine the implications of the theory of incomplete contracts for internalization and off shoring decisions.

Many theories addressing the issue of internalisation in an international context identified the dissipation of knowledge capital as a main determinant of internalization. These theories follow Dunning's intuition of the internalization advantage. Accordingly, the decision whether to integrate or not is usually explained in terms of costs and benefits of using the market regarding firm-specific assets, especially intangible assets. Doing business abroad is associated with costs firms would like to avoid. Firms could avoid these costs by licensing. However, licensing carries costs as well. Several problems of licensing in an international context are used to explain the costs associated with licensing and thus the emergence of integration (see Markusen, 1995).

For instance, problems may relate to reputation concerns (see Horstmann and Markusen, 1987). A licensee may free ride on the reputation for product quality (see Caves and Murphy, 1976). If the licenser attempts to extract all rents from the licensee, the licensee in turn may skimp on quality by producing an inferior substitute product in order to earn rents. In this situation, integration may be more profitable than licensing.

Licensing may also cause problems due to asymmetric information concerning the foreign market to be serviced (see Horstmann and Markusen, 1992). The potential licensee usually has superior information about the demand of the product in the foreign market. If the agents reveals demand to be high, the licenser may decide to produce directly, or a larger share of the rents will be extracted from the foreign licensee in subsequent periods. Since in this situation, the licensee has an incentive to cause sales to be low even when demand is high, the multinational may be better off with direct investment instead of licensing.

Another problem of licensing caused by information asymmetries is addressed by Ethier (1986). The firm owning the knowledge capital may not want to reveal it to a potential licensee. If a contract ensuring full revelation of the knowledge is infeasible, this may lead to inefficiencies in market transactions. This reasoning is closely related to the theory of the firm and incomplete contracts.

Ethier and Markusen (1996) also tackle the issue of internalization focussing on the dissipation of knowledge capital. In their model, licensing may be subject to defections in two forms. On the one hand, the foreign producer can defect by opening a rival firm in the second period. On the other hand, the parent firm can defect by issuing a second license to another foreign firm. However, designing a contract in such a way as to prevent the licensee's defection may be costly, since some rents must be shared with the licensee to make defection unprofitable. The licenser might then prefer to operate with a wholly owned subsidiary. If integration is chosen, the licenser transfers the technology to the foreign subsidiary and an enforceable contract is signed precluding the subsidiary from defecting and exploiting the technology independently.

In the model of Ethier and Markusen, firms choose between exporting, opening a subsidiary or licensing their technology to an independent firm in order to service a foreign market. Exporting is assumed to be costly due to the presence of transport costs, while foreign production entails a potential dissipation of knowledge and consequent loss of rents. Importantly, it is posited that the extent of dissipation under foreign direct investment differs under licensing. According to their model, integration is preferred when technology can be used as a joint input for multiple plants such as knowledge and the technology is of medium or high importance to the final product. Ethier and Marcusen embed their model on firm behaviour in a two-country general equilibrium model and relate the size of the rents to more fundamental parameters, such as factor prices and costs of production. In contrast to the model on vertical foreign direct investment of Helpman (1984), they show that international wage disparities do not necessarily encourage direct investment.

More recent contributions on the internalization issue of multinational enterprises have combined insights from the theory of the firm as developed by Coase, Williamson and Grossman and Hart with international trade theories to study the location and control decisions of multinational enterprises in a unified framework. These theories are able to predict the relative prevalence of the four main organisational forms of multinational enterprises: integration at home, outsourcing at home, integration abroad and outsourcing abroad.

Grossman and Helpman (2002) address the choice between outsourcing and integration in a one-input general equilibrium framework, assuming that all firms of a given type are equally productive. Their firms face the friction of incomplete contracts in arm's length relationships, which they weigh against the less efficient production of inputs in integrated companies. As a result, some sectors have only vertically integrated firms whereas others have only disintegrated firms. Grossmann and Helpman identify sectoral characteristics that lead to one or the other structure. Crucial to the decision on whether to integrate or disintegrate is the quality of the match between a final goods producer and a supplier. According to the model, potential buyers of an intermediate input find it more attractive to outsource, the more sellers of adequate inputs to serve the buyers' needs exist. Similarly, sellers of an intermediate input find it more attractive to operate, the larger the number of potential buyers is.

This approach of Grossman and Helpman has been extended by Antràs (2003) by introducing two new features. First, the friction of incomplete contracts also exists within integrated firms, and integration provides well-defined property rights. However, these property rights may or may not give integration an advantage over outsourcing. These assumptions refer to the theory of the firm developed by Grossman and Hart (1986). Second, there are two inputs: an intermediate input that is under direct control of the final goods producer, and an intermediate input that requires the engagement of suppliers. The relative intensity of these inputs turns out to be an important determinant of the choice between integration and outsourcing. In this context it is important to note that intermediate inputs under the direct control of the final goods producer suffer less from agency problems than intermediate inputs that require the engagement of suppliers.

The model is based on a situation, in which a final goods producer buys a special and distinct input from a supplier. Thus, the input requires a relationship-specific investment in capital and labour. Since contracts are assumed to be incomplete and not enforceable, the buyer and the supplier will engage in ex-post bargaining over the terms of trade. As a variation to the property rights model of Grossman and Hart, the final goods producer contributes to the relationship-specific investment of the supplier. The intuition behind is that if the input supplier's default option is very low, the allocation of residual control rights may not be enough to induce sufficient levels of investment by the input supplier, resulting in a severe hold up problem that may be alleviated if the final goods producer contributes to the supplier relation specific investment. This transferability of investment is a crucial variation, since it causes a two-sided hold up problem. Due to the cost sharing, the capital investment is specific to both, so both parties are locked in the relationship. Another interesting point to note is that in this model there are no organization-specific costs. There are fixed entry costs, but these are independent of whether the firm chooses to outsource or integrate. In this event, the power of incentives dominates the integration decision.

Antrás embodies this structure in a general equilibrium model with two trading countries, each of which specializes in certain intermediate input varieties and exports them worldwide. Capital-abundant countries tend to produce a larger share of capital intensive varieties than labour abundant countries.

Two interesting results are derived from this model. First, capital intensive goods are transacted within the boundaries of multinational firms, while labour intensive products tend to be traded at arm's length. Second, imports from capital abundant countries take place through foreign direct investment, while capital scarce countries are arranged through international outsourcing.

Antràs (2003) provides empirical evidence supporting his predictions. He finds that capital-intensity and research and development intensity seem to be the major determinants of the decision to internalize imports. Moreover, intra-firm imports as a fraction of total imports are positively correlated with capital abundance across 28 exporting countries.

A combination of variation in contractual input intensity across sectors and variation in productivity across firms within industries generates equilibria in which all four organizational forms – domestic integration, domestic outsourcing, foreign integration and foreign outsourcing – coexist in an industry and their relative prevalence varies across industries as a function of sectoral characteristics. This approach was chosen by Antràs and Helpmann (2004), which builds on the model of Antrás (2003).

As a variation of the model of Antràs (2003), the production of the final product requires two specialized inputs – headquarter services and manufacturing components. It is assumed that headquarter services are only provided in country A and only the final goods producer has the know how to contribute headquarter services. This implies that headquarters can be located only in country A. Manufacturing components can be produced in either country with wages in country A exceeding wages in country B. It is further assumed that organizing production is associated with fixed costs which are higher in the foreign country (country B) than in the home country (country A) and higher under vertical integration than through outsourcing. Sectors vary in their intensity of headquarter services and firms differ in productivity. The setting is one of incomplete contracts. Production entails relationship-specific investments by both the final goods producer and their suppliers, and it is assumed that the nature of these investments does not enable the parties to specify them in an enforceable contract. Accordingly, it is assumed that, regardless of the location of intermediate input production, parties have to bargain ex-post in order to divide the surplus of trade. Ex-post bargaining takes place both under outsourcing and under integration, but residual property rights improve the bargaining position of the owner. The improvement of the bargaining position is assumed to be higher in domestic transactions relative to transnational ones.

Under these circumstances, Antràs and Helpman make the following predictions:

- In component intensive sectors, outsourcing dominates integration because outsourcing has lower fixed costs and provides better incentives to suppliers of manufacturing components. Component intensive firms with a low level of productivity exit the industry, while component intensive firms with a high level of productivity import components from unaffiliated producers in country B and component intensive firms with an intermediate level of productivity acquire components from unaffiliated domestic firms. The trade off in the offshoring decision lies between the lower variable cost in country B and the lower fixed costs in country A.
- In headquarter intensive sectors all four organizational forms can coexist. Headquarter intensive firms with low levels of productivity exit the industry as is the case for component intensive firms. High productivity firms integrate to produce intermediate inputs in the country in which variable production costs are lower. In between, the less productive firms outsource into the domestic country, the more productive

firms outsource into the foreign country and firms with intermediate productivity levels integrate into the domestic country.

To summarize, the degree of productivity dispersion and the intensity of headquarter service are shown to be relevant in determining the relative prevalence of alternative organizational forms. The model predicts that multinational enterprises are more prevalent, if the intensity of headquarter services is comparably high and the productivity dispersion is high when the most productive firms integrate foreign suppliers of components.

2.8 Summary

Foreign direct investment has become increasingly important, especially between developed countries like the EU member states. In developing their global strategy, firms principally have to decide on where to locate stages of the value chain and on the extent of control they want to exert over these processes. As a result, there are four possible organizational forms of multinational enterprises: domestic integration, domestic outsourcing, foreign integration and foreign outsourcing.

The theories on multinational enterprises mainly rely on Dunning's OLI framework which explains the presence of multinationals by ownership, location and internalisation advantages. Early theories on foreign direct investment have focussed on ownership and location advantages, leaving the internalisation issue aside. Central to these theories are firm-specific assets and the economies of scale associated with them. Besides firm-specific economies of scale, plant-level economies of scale and transport costs are considered to be decisive in the choice of multinational enterprises as to whether to set up a plant in a foreign country or to export in servicing the foreign market. Moreover, intra-industry heterogeneity is identified to have an impact on foreign direct investment. The higher the productivity, the more likely a firm engages in foreign direct investment.

Besides these firm and industry specific determinants of foreign direct investment, the theory predicts that differences in market size and factor endowment have an impact on foreign direct investment. While cross-country differences in factor endowments are assumed to increase the prevalence of vertical foreign direct investment, they will decrease the prevalence of horizontal foreign direct investment.

The knowledge-capital model combines the approaches to horizontal and vertical integration, focussing on characteristics of knowledge-capital which constitutes a key firm-specific asset. Knowledge-capital may be fragmented from production, is skilled-labour intensive and can be used as a joint input for multiple plants. The model predicts that horizontal foreign direct investment is prevalent if countries do not differ in size and in relative factor endowments. If, instead, one country is both small and skilled-labour abundant, most or even all of the firms are vertical integrated headquartered in the small country, with a single plant in the large, skilled-labour-scarce country.

The theories on the internalization issue mainly rely on the theory of the firm, i.e. transaction costs theory and property-rights theory. These theories are based on the notion of incomplete contracts and hold-up problems that can cause inefficient underinvestment in a relationship between economic agents. In this situation, integration may be seen as a second best approach. The transactions cost approach and the property-rights theory have been combined with theories of international trade in order to explain the four organizational forms for multinational enterprises. Early models concentrated on knowledge capital and the problems associated with licensing that make firms integrate vertically. More recent theories predict that, given the incomplete contracts and factor price differences, the degree of productivity dispersion and the intensity of headquarter services, such as knowledge capital, are relevant in determining the relative prevalence of alternative forms. Multinational enterprises are supposed to be more prevalent if the intensity of headquarter services is comparably high and the productivity dispersion is high with the most productive firms integrating foreign suppliers of components.

In the following, the identified factors explaining the existence of multinational enterprises are used to evaluate, how the current tax rules fit with the economic reality of multinational enterprises. The specific characterstics of multinational enterprises may require specific tax rules. This argument becomes especially important regarding the international allocation of profits (see section 5.1). Furthermore, the characteristics of multinational enterprises may be used to define a taxable group for purposes of the Common Consolidated Corporate Tax Base (see section 6.4.2.1).

3 Guidelines for Income Taxation of Multinational Enterprises

In this section guidelines for company taxation are presented. These guidelines are used for an assessment of the tax systems currently applied by EU member states and for the design of a harmonised system of taxation. Important criteria commonly agreed on by economists and tax experts considered here are equity and neutrality and efficiency. Moreover, administrative aspects of taxation are taken into account. Before normative criteria for the taxation of corporate income are outlined, the question of why corporate income taxes are imposed is addressed. In fact, all member states of the EU levy a corporation income tax.

3.1 Functions of Corporation Income Taxes

The case for imposing a corporation income tax is a controversial one (see Gammie et al., 2005: 10). It is often based on the perception that corporations ought to pay their fair share of tax. While this may be a popular justification in political terms, it is questionable from an economic point of view, since the corporation tax incidence is uncertain (see Bird, 1996: 1-3). According to the theory, the burden of the corporate income tax is borne by individuals in their capacity as owners or employees (see Harberger, 1962: 224-230) of corporations and/or in their role as consumers of the goods and services produced by corporations (see Kryzaniuk and Musgrave, 1963). And since the corporation tax is an impersonal tax, it is not well suited to help policy-makers shape the profile of personal income distribution.

From an economic point of view, three rationales are generally given for the corporation income tax (see Bird, 1996: 3-12; Mintz, 1996: 24-36):

- The corporation income tax is a withholding tax at source for some forms of capital income that serves as a backstop for personal income tax;

- The corporation income tax is a charge for the benefits received from public goods and services provided by the government;
- The corporation income tax is a tax on rents realised from non-reproducible factors of production.

These three rationales for corporation income tax are discussed in the following chapters.

3.1.1 The Corporation Income Tax as a Withholding Tax

The most important rationale for levying corporation income tax is that it serves as a withholding tax for personal income tax (see Mintz, 1996: 25). In this respect, corporation income tax is often thought of as a tax on the owners of capital (see Gammie et al., 2005: 11). If governments impose taxes on comprehensive income, this would also include income derived from capital income, such as dividends and accrued capital gains (see Simons, 1938). However, levying taxes on capital income, especially on accrued capital gains, is difficult. For instance, the market value of assets such as private corporate shares often cannot be assessed periodically (see Mintz, 1996: 26). Moreover, if accrued capital gains are taxed, taxpayers might not be able to finance the payment of tax without liquidating the asset (see Gammie et al., 2005: 16).

As a consequence, capital gains are generally only taxed on a realised basis (see section 4.1.1.2.2). Therefore, taxes on capital income could be deferred or even avoided at the personal level. The owners of capital could defer taxation of capital income using tax-free companies retaining and reinvesting profits rather than paying them out to shareholders as taxable income. The value of corporate shares increases by the amount of accumulated income retained by the corporation. Taxation of this accrued income, however, is postponed until the time chosen by the shareholder, since taxation of any capital gain occurs only on realisation (see Mintz, 1996: 26). A tax at the corporate level on retained corporate income can thus act as a substitute for a personal income tax in order to restrict the ability of shareholders to use corporations as tax shelters. Under the withholding role of the corporation income tax, the corporation pays a tax on income on behalf of the shareholder. Therefore, corporation income tax should generally follow tax principles similar to those applied to personal income tax and there should be some form of integration between corporation and personal income tax (see Mintz, 1996: 28).

In an international context, capital-importing countries may use the withholding role of the corporation income tax to exploit revenue transfers from capital-exporting countries. This is particularly the case, if the country in which the owner of capital is resident operates a tax credit system allowing the corporation income tax levied in the source country to be credited against the income tax of the capital owner in the residence country (see Bond and Samuelson, 1989). Thus corporation income tax in the source country becomes a revenue-sharing device with the residence country (see Mintz, 1996: 27).

3.1.2 The Corporation Income Tax as a Benefit Tax

A second rationale offered is that a corporation income tax may act as a charge for public goods provided by the government and consumed by the company (see Bird, 1996: 4). Thus, corporation income tax would have the function of a price for public goods, thereby ensuring an efficient allocation of resources between the public and the private sector (see Mintz, 1996: 25). According to this rationale, it would be necessary to levy corporation tax on a base that is correlated to the service of good provided by the government that benefits the corporation. For instance, if public education is valuable to a corporation, payroll tax may be an appropriate benefit tax (see Mintz, 1996: 25). However, for practical and political reasons it may be difficult to assess how public services benefit the corporation and to determine special user charges accordingly. A tax on corporate income may then be seen as a practical alternative, since infrastructure and other public services increase the profitability of corporations (see Mintz, 1996: 25). However, the profitability of a corporation generally depends on more than public services. Thus, corporation income tax is an imperfect measure for the benefits associated with public expenditures. As a conclusion, corporation income tax as a benefit tax seems imperfect but attractive from a practical point of view.

3.1.3 The Corporation Income Tax as a Tax on Economic Rents

The third rationale for a corporation income tax relates to the desirability of taxing pure profits or economic rents (see Mintz, 1996: 34). Corporation income tax is regarded as an efficient method of taxing the rents earned from non-reproducible factors of production such as land and natural resources.[4] This rationale is mainly based on

4 This concept is originally discussed by the Meade Committee (1978).

economic efficiency grounds. If corporation income tax is levied on pure profits or economic rents, it is efficient since investment and financing decisions of economic agents are not distorted (for more details see section 3.3.1). Thus, a corporation tax on economic rents would raise revenues for the government and at the same time would minimise the distortions to economic behaviour. However, pure rents are difficult to measure in practice (see section 3.3.1).

At an international level a corporation income tax on economic rents may not be completely neutral, since some economic decisions may be affected. For instance, a high source-based tax on economic rents may induce a company to shift its location to a lower-tax jurisdiction (see Gammie et al., 2005: 21). Furthermore, the vast majority of existing corporation taxes are levied on income instead of economic rents. Therefore, the taxation of economic rents cannot be the one and only rationale for corporation income tax applied in practice (see Devereux and Sørensen, 2006: 23).

An important aspect of the argument for taxing rents relates to foreign direct investment (see Bird, 1996: 6). A source-based corporation tax on economic rents may be seen as a means to effectively tax rents accruing to non-resident investors. As outlined in the previous chapter (see section 2.5), foreign direct investment is motivated by firm-specific economic rents and location-specific rents, the latter being tied to a specific location. Taxation of location-specific rents may be attractive from a national perspective of source countries, because they can impose taxes without affecting investment decisions (see Devereux and Sørensen, 2006: 24). Unfortunately, it is difficult to differentiate between mobile firm-specific economic rents and location-specific rents. At least, corporation income tax in the source country may be seen as an appropriate way for countries to share the rents earned by international investment. This rationale is based on inter-nation equity, a concept described in more detail in section 3.2.2.

3.2 Equity

Equity is widely regarded as an important principle of taxation. Two dimensions of equity may be distinguished: individual equity and inter-nations equity. Individual equity refers to the relationship between the individual liable to tax and the government that levies the taxes. Inter-nation equity is concerned with the relationship between the country in which the taxpayer is resident and the country in which a taxable event is realised. In the following two sections, both dimensions of equity are addressed separately.

3.2.1 Individual equity

Taxes are generally levied in order to finance government expenditure for public needs (see Jachmann, 2000: 9). The tax burden required to fund government expenditure has to be shared among the taxpayers. In this context, there is a general agreement that each taxpayer should contribute his or her fair share to the cost of government (see Musgrave and Musgrave, 1989: 218; Tipke, 1981: 9). In order to legitimate the levying of taxes and to determine a taxpayer's fair tax liability, tax criteria have to be determined. Criteria for a fair distribution of the tax burden may be derived from two different concepts: the benefit principle[5] and the ability to pay principle (see Musgrave and Musgrave, 1989: 219-233).

The benefit principle calls for a distribution of the tax burden among taxpayers in proportion to the benefits they receive from public goods and services. According to this principle, taxation is perceived to be fair if the tax burden depends on the benefits received from public goods and services by each individual taxpayer (see Haller, 1981: 13). Analogous to the charging for private goods and services, taxes would act as a compensation for the provision of public goods and services by the government (see Musgrave and Musgrave, 1989: 219).

If taxation would follow the benefit principle, the equitable distribution of the tax burden depends on the benefits received by each individual taxpayer. The benefits may be defined with reference to the costs associated with the consumption of public goods, the willingness to pay for a public good or the utility associated with the consumption of public goods (see Müller, 2001: 7-8). However, each concept of the benefit principle is difficult to apply to many categories of public expenditure (see Frebel, 2006: 36). These difficulties stem from the general characteristics of public goods and services.[6] Public goods are often not excludable, nor is their exclusion always desirable (see Musgrave and Musgrave, 1989: 220). Moreover, despite being excludable, their provision may be desired free of direct charge. These characteristics differ significantly from those characteristics associated with private goods. If public goods and

5 This principle is very similar to the idea that corporation income tax may serve as a benefit tax (see section 3.1.2).

6 For an analysis of the characteristics of public goods see Frank, 2003: 654.

services are non-excludable or free of charge, individuals have no reason to reveal their preferences and a tax charge in proportion to the costs associated with the consumption of the public goods or services by an individual does not seem feasible. In contrast to the case of private goods, where all consumers pay the same price and those who value the product more buy a larger amount, in the case of public goods, the same level of provision is enjoyed jointly and by all. In this case, each consumer would ideally be charged a tax price in line with his or her evaluation and consumers who value the public goods more highly should therefore pay more. In practice, however, it seems impossible to fit individual tax prices to each customer (see also Kraft, 1991: 8).

The benefit principle may only be applied in those instances, if the nature of the goods or services provided by the government is that of private goods (see Neumark, 1970: 42; Jakob, 1996: 4). In these cases, public goods and services are financed via fees or user charges. However, the range of government expenditures to which taxation according to the benefit principle can be applied is relatively limited and most tax revenues may not be derived on a benefit basis.

An alternative and widely used concept of taxation relies on the ability to pay principle.[7] Taxation according to the ability to pay principle calls for a distribution of the tax burden in line with the economic capacity of the taxpayer rather than in relation to expenditure benefits. The determination of an individual's tax liability, therefore, is more closely related to what society considers an equitable and thus, fair distribution of the tax burden (see Musgrave and Musgrave, 1989: 223-232).

Two aspects of the equity principle based on the ability to pay principle can be distinguished: Horizontal and vertical equity (see Wellisch, 1999: 41-42). To obtain horizontal equity, the taxable units with equal ability to pay should contribute an equal amount of tax. Vertical equity calls for a distribution of the tax burden, where taxpayers with an unequal ability to pay should correspondingly be liable to different amounts of tax.

Defining equals calls for an index by which equality in position or differences therein can be measured and a definition of the appropriate taxable unit.[8] The determination of a taxpayer's ability to pay is by no means without its difficulties (see Nobes,

7 For more details on the ability to pay principle see Musgrave and Musgrave, 1989: 223-232; Tipke and Lang, 2002: 78-83; Vogel, 1994: 367-369; Neumark, 1970: 121-137; Haller, 1981: 14-16.

8 For a discussion of different indicators in determining an individual's ability to pay see Kraft, 1991: 41-48.

2004: 37; Schön, 2005: 129). Ability to pay has to be defined in terms of measurable economic characteristics.

Traditionally, income has been viewed as the most appropriate indictor of the ability to pay.[9] This has led to the concept of a comprehensive income tax, originally developed by Schanz (1896) and later refined and improved by Haig and Simons (see Haig, 1959: 54-77). According to this concept, economic activities of individuals are indented to earn income to be used for consumption and to increase wealth. Thus, income may be described as the increase in consumption power during a particular period and irrespective of whether consumption is carried out during the same period or in future periods (see Schön, 2005: 129). Comprehensive income includes all forms of income, both realised and accrued in the form of an appreciation of assets held by the taxpayer.

Income has to be determined using objective and non-arbitrary rules (see Jacobs, 1971: 24-27). Otherwise taxation may be perceived as unfair. Against this background, the application of the concept of comprehensive income taxation is not without its difficulties. Given uncertainty and imperfect capital markets, there are two problems associated with the concept of a comprehensive income tax (see Schön, 2005: 136-139). First, taxation of accrued capital gains requires the determination of fair values of assets. However, there are situations in which it is impossible to determine the true amount of accrued gains and losses, or of accrued receipts and expenses, until the transactions take place. Thus, a measurement of income that is based on fair values may be subject to estimates and discretion. Under the equity principle, however, there is no room for discretion, as it would entail scope for avoidance and manipulation. Second, in imperfect capital markets accrued income does not coincide with the ability to pay tax. As a consequence, a taxpayer may lack the liquidity to pay the tax and is forced to sell assets only to obtain liquidity to meet his tax liabilities. Due to these two problems, taxation generally relies on the realisation principle (see Homburg and Bolik, 2005: 2335), even though this principle deviates from the ideal of a comprehensive income tax. According to the realisation principle, an inflow of liquid assets has to

9 An alternative tax base is consumption, which may be defined as the difference between income and savings. A consumption-oriented tax would exclude reinvested returns from savings. The idea behind this is that the interest rate would be exempt from taxation leading to a tax that has no inter-temporal distortions (see Bradford, 1986). As the interest rate is the price at which current consumption is exchanged to purchase future consumption goods, taxing interest is equivalent to increasing the price of future consumption relative to current consumption (see Bradford, 1986). However, no country has attempted to impose a direct personal tax on consumption. Countries

be sufficiently assured, before a corresponding profit is recognised for tax purposes. Furthermore, taxation should be based on the net income, taking into account decreases of a taxpayer's assets (see Homburg and Bolik, 2005: 2335). Only the net income indicates whether the taxpayer will be able to satisfy any tax liability.

The ability to pay taxes rests with individuals (see Musgrave and Musgrave, 1989: 371). Income as the indicator for ability to pay has to be traced to the final recipient, who is liable to tax with this income. As a consequence, the ability to pay principle cannot be easily used for corporation income tax. Where income is received via distinct legal entities such as corporations, the ability to pay is assessed at the level of the individual who owns a corporate share, because he or she is the final recipient of income. The legal entity as such has no ability to pay. Ideally, all business income should be imputed to the individual owner and there would be no additional tax on the business unit as a separate taxpayer. In the case of distributions the additional personal tax can follow such principle. However, if earnings are retained and reinvested at the corporate level, the imputation of profits to owners is rather complicated, as it would require a taxation of accrued capital gains. If the taxation of accrued capital gains is not feasible, corporation tax serves as a substitute for personal income tax of the shareholder at source. And since taxation at the corporate level influences the income flowing to the shareholders, the ability-to-pay principle can also be applied at corporate level (see Hey, 1996: 119).

According to the ability to pay principle, income should be assessed on a global basis, including all sources of income. It does not make any difference for the ability to pay of an individual from where income is derived (see Musgrave and Musgrave, 1972: 68-69; Homburg, 2007: 286-289). Therefore, foreign-source income should be taken into account in determining a resident's tax liability. Otherwise, the principle of equity would be violated. If the foreign-source income earned by a resident is also taxable in the foreign source country, the residence country should recognize the foreign tax paid in order to avoid double taxation. Avoidance of double taxation is necessary, since the criterion of taxpayer equity requires that each taxpayer is taxed at exactly his ability to pay. Otherwise, the taxpayer would be taxed as if he disposed of a higher ability to pay (see Flick, 1961: 172; Schaumburg, 1998: 600).[10] Taxation in the source country leaves the residence country with a national loss. Hence, the issue arises

only rely on some form of consumption taxation with respect to retirement savings such as pension plans. Therefore, a consumption based tax is ruled out here.

whether a jurisdiction should be entitled to tax the income that non-residents derive from within its borders. A guiding principle for this issue is inter-nation equity, which is described in the following section.

3.2.2 Inter-nation equity

Jurisdictions are territorially limited. In contrast, economic activities extend across borders. This constellation raises questions of who is entitled to tax income arising from cross-border economic activity and how the potential to extend the jurisdiction's tax authority outside its own borders should be exercised. Each country involved in cross-border economic activity has an interest to levy income taxes in order to fund government expenditure (see Fohr, 2001: 75). However, neither state has an original right to tax the income in question (see Vogel, 1988: 398). Therefore, as in the discussion of individual equity, a legitimate and fair allocation of the international tax base between the different countries involved has to be determined (Fohr, 2001: 75).

There are varying interpretations of what constitutes inter-nation equity. One interpretation refers to the benefit principle that is also seen as a rationale for corporation income tax (see chapter 3.1.2). According to this principle, each jurisdiction would be entitled to levy tax as a charge for public goods and services provided (see Musgrave and Musgrave, 2000: 313; Zuber, 1991: 109). This is based on the assumption that countries rendering public goods and services promote the profitability of economic activities of multinational enterprises within their borders. Company taxation would thus be imposed largely by the country in which a company engages in economic activities. Under the benefit principle both countries involved in cross-border business activities would be entitled to impose taxes on a share of the overall international income.

Another concept of inter-nation equity justifies a country's entitlement to tax as a national rental charge for the use of its investment environment and natural resources (see Musgrave and Musgrave, 2000: 315). This concept is based on the notion that cross-border investments generate benefits above the level which would be obtained from domestic investments. These benefits do not only include profits but also labour and capital income. It is assumed that foreign investment outflows increase capital earnings in the capital-exporting country above the level which would be obtained

10 Avoidance of double taxation is not only required at the international but also at the national level.

from domestic investment. At the same time, labour income in the capital-exporting country is assumed to be lower in the case of an international investment. With respect to the capital-importing country, the opposite effects are assumed to occur. Labour income in the capital-importing country will gain from the capital inflow, while its own capital income will fall. Overall, however, it is assumed that both countries stand to gain from cross-border investments. This concept of inter-nation equity is difficult to implement in practice, since the level of the rental charge is difficult to determine. First, the idea of isolating and measuring the effects of cross-border investments on labour and capital income does not seem feasible (see Zuber, 1991: 110). Second, besides effects on labour and capital income, cross-border investments might also bring intangible gains such as technical and managerial know-how as well as intangible burdens such as foreign control and slowed-down emergence of a native entrepreneurial class (see Musgrave and Musgrave, 2000: 315). Again, these effects are difficult to isolate and to measure. Thus, there is obviously no precise level at which to fix the rental charge.

A third concept of inter-nation equity is based on the rationale that taxation of income arising from cross-border investments should be used as an instrument of international redistribution (see Zuber, 1991: 107-108). The allocation of taxing rights may then be used to adjust an unequal distribution of resource endowments and per capita income among the involved countries. Hence, the tax share in profits earned in cross-border economic activity allocated to the source country may be allowed to rise inversely to the level of per capita income and the resource endowment in the source country. This adjustment could be achieved if the corporate tax rate in the source country is higher in low-income countries than in high-income countries. However, the idea of redistributing income among countries via an allocation of taxing rights is not supported (see Zuber, 1991: 111).

As a conclusion, inter-nation equity is generally aligned to the benefit principle, which calls for an entitlement to tax in accordance with the benefits derived from the provision of public goods and services. This view is also reflected in the OECD Model Double Taxation convention, which allows the source countries to tax the income from foreign direct investment inflows within their country. The concept of inter-nation equity justifying taxation as a rental charge is difficult to implement in practice. Furthermore, the concept according to which the international assignment of taxing rights is used as an instrument of international redistribution is not accepted at the international level.

Under the benefit principle, the country within whose borders the profits are generated contributes to this generation of profits and therefore should be entitled to tax the profits.[11] In order to allocate taxing rights according to the generation of profits, the profits' source has to be identified. Since it is not possible to clearly identify the source of income under economic terms (see Schreiber, 1994: 243; Ault and Bradford, 1990: 30-31), it is defined by conventions the jurisdictions agreed on (see Schreiber, 2005: 46). In general, two approaches for identifying profit-generating factors exist: the supply approach and the supply-demand approach (see Musgrave, 1984: 234; Oestreicher, 2000: 179). Both concepts have in common that the source of income is aligned to the location of profit-generating factors. However, with regard to the question of which profit-generating factors are decisive in this issue, both approaches differ. According to the supply-approach, the geographic location of a company's income generating production factors is supposed to indicate the source of income. Thus, this approach focuses on the supply side. Under the supply-demand approach, not only the supply side but also the demand side is considered. This approach is based on the assumption that profits are generated through the interaction of supply and demand. Relevant attributes which have an impact on the demand of a product are, for instance, the size and infrastructure of the market. Hence, since a country contributes to the generation of a company's profits by providing a consumer market, the demand jurisdiction should also have the entitlement to tax. The issue of whether source country entitlement to tax should be based on the supply-approach or the supply-approach is controversial (see Oestreicher, 2000: 180). It seems questionable whether the existence of a consumer market constitutes an income-generating factor (see Schäfer and Spengel, 2003: 6). Moreover, the supply-demand approach is associated with feasibility concerns. These concerns refer to the difficulties in defining the place of demand, which may arise due to the use of information and communication technology and in the case of intermediate inputs (see Oestreicher, 2000: 184; Schäfer and Spengel, 2003:6-7). As a consequence, the supply approach is currently the prevailing convention (see Schreiber, 2004: 221).

11 For a detailed description see Musgrave, 1972: 399-400; Musgrave and Musgrave, 1989: 219-222; Zuber, 1991: 108-109; Musgrave, 2000: 52; Oestreicher, 200: 154-155, 173-174; European Commission, 2001: 26.

3.3 Efficiency and Neutrality

Efficiency is widely recognized as a fundamental economic principle of optimal taxation (see European Commission, 2001b: 26). This postulate is not only agreed on by economists, tax experts and tax politicians but also inherent to the EC Treaty. According to Articles 2 and 98 of the EC Treaty, the promotion of an efficient allocation of resources is a fundamental economic goal of the Common Market. Generally, an efficient tax system is one that is neutral in the sense of not distorting economic decisions (see European Commission, 2001b: 26). Although accepted as a key concept in the economic analysis of corporation taxation, tax efficiency is a controversial concept and there is more than one possible definition of efficiency. As regards the definition of efficiency, a distinction is generally made between the national perspective and the international perspective.

3.3.1 The National Perspective

The concept of efficiency concerning taxation is based on the notion of production efficiency. Aggregate production efficiency is desired as one part of achieving a Pareto optimum (for more details see Pareto, 1909: 354-379). It holds if the production factors cannot be relocated across projects in such a way as to increase the overall output (see Devereux and Pearson, 1995: 1658). Diamond and Mirrlees (1971) demonstrated that, in a perfectly competitive economy, an optimal tax structure would preserve production efficiency because production efficiency is preferred, despite that a full Pareto optimum is not achieved (see Diamond and Mirrlees, 1971: 8). Thus, even if taxes inevitably distort the choices of consumers, it is optimal to leave the input choices of firms undistorted by taxes, thereby allowing a minimisation of aggregate production costs. Tax induced adjustments of the allocation of resources would result in inefficiencies and welfare losses (Sinn, 1985: 5; Wagner, 1992: 294). In order to avoid this excess burden of taxation, the tax system should not interfere with or affect economic decisions (see Harberger, 1980: 299).

This leads to a concept of neutrality which is derived from a more microeconomic point of view. The microeconomics' approach focuses on taxation effects regarding single companies and its shareholders, rather than on the taxation effects on the national welfare (see Spengel, 2003a: 224). In this context, an optimal tax system would not distort decisions on the allocation of production factors within and between companies (see Spengel, 2003a: 224; Elschen, 1991: 106). Business decisions in a world without taxation should be the same in a world with taxation (see Schreiber, 2002a: 97; Wagner and Dirrigl, 1980: 13-14). If decisions between different business options do not depend on taxation, this would ease the decision process, since the gathering of tax information and tax planning is not necessary (see Schwinger, 1992: 12; Wagner, 1989: 264-265). Depending on the decision to be taken, one can distinguish between different forms of intersectoral neutrality (see König and Wosnitza, 2004: 142). Most important are neutrality considerations concerning decisions on different types of investment, modes of investment finance and organizational forms (see Kiesewetter, 1997: 24-25; Wagner, 1995: 742-746).

Investment decisions are generally based on the net present value of an investment (see Knoll, 2001: 336). Against this background, a tax system is neutral with respect to investment decisions if the ranking of the net present values of different investment projects is not affected by taxation (see Schreiber and Stellpflug, 1999: 190).[12] That is, if the pre-tax net present value of an investment project A is higher than the pre-tax net present value of an alternative investment project B, the same should hold when comparing the post-tax net present values of the investment project A and B (see Homburg, 2007: 240). Taxation has two effects, which may compensate each other. On the one hand, taxation lowers the periodic net cash flows, thus lowering the net present value. On the other hand, the discount rate of the net present value, which provides a benchmark rate of return for an investor, is also lowered by taxation. If both effects exactly compensate each other, taxation does not change the net present value of an investment (see Homburg, 2007: 243).

Both cash flow taxation (see Brown, 1948: 309-310; Schneider, 2002: 103-104; Meade Committee, 1978) and taxation of economic rents (see Samuelson, 1964; Johansson, 1996) will be neutral with respect to investment decisions (see Schön, 2005: 131). Under these tax systems, the cost of capital, or minimum rate of return required from investment projects is left unchanged and net present values are reduced proportionally (see Homburg, 2007: 240).

A cash flow tax means that tax is levied on net cash flows, which is the difference between cash revenues and cash outflows. Under this tax investments are immediately expensed. Taxation reduces net cash flows proportionally and the discount rate is not

---

12 To ensure tax neutrality, it is generally not required that the level of investment is not affected by the presence of tax. Instead, neutrality across different types of investment is supposed to be sufficient (see König, 1997: 45).

affected by taxation. After-tax net present values are a proportional factor of pre-tax net present values, thus maintaining the pre-tax ranking of investment alternatives (see Homburg, 2007: 247). An introduction of a cash flow tax, however, would imply significant changes to the current tax practice, since corporation tax is currently levied on income in most countries (see section 3.2.1). This may be a reason why a cash flow tax hardly gathers any political support within the EU (see Oestreicher and Spengel, 2007: 5). Moreover, if only some countries rely on a cash flow tax, this will result in complications in an international context (see Mintz and Seade, 1991). Therefore, a cash flow tax is ruled out here.[13]

Investment neutrality would also be achieved, if only pure economic rents or pure profits were taxed (see Johansson, 1961: 211-216; Samuelson, 1964: 604-606). Pure profits are defined as net cash flows adjusted by economic depreciation. Economic depreciation is the difference between the net present value of remaining cash flows at the beginning and at the end of a given period. In contrast to the cash flow tax, investments are not immediately expensed but depreciated. Although this concept is to a certain extent similar to the current tax system, it may be difficult to apply in practice for several reasons. First, the concept to determine pure profits refers to the entire enterprise. Therefore, it is difficult to isolate pure profits associated with a specific investment from other investments conducted by the same company (see Wagner, 2005: 101). Second, given uncertainty and imperfect competition on capital markets, the determination of pure profits is complicated (see Mintz, 1996: 35).

A proposal for such a tax on economic profits is the allowance for corporate equity scheme (ACE) (see Wenger, 1983; Boadway and Bruce, 1984). Under this tax system companies are allowed to deduct an imputed normal rate on the equity from the corporate income tax base, parallel to the deduction for interest on debt. Thus, pure profits are determined as the difference between gross profits on the one hand and true economic depreciation and the financing costs of both debt (i.e. interest) and equity financing (i.e. opportunity costs of equity) on the other hand (see Keen and King, 2002 for an evaluation).

Firms may finance investments via debt, new equity issues or retained earnings. Tax neutrality would require taxation of these alternative modes of financing in the same way. The tax system should not distort a firm's financial decisions. This is achieved, if only pure profits are taxed, both at the level of the creditor and the debtor, and all

[13] For merits of a cash flow tax see Homburg, 2007: 247-248.

modes of investment financing are subject to the same tax rate (see Homburg, 2007: 251-252).

Neutrality regarding the organisational form means that the tax burden of a company and its shareholders should be the same, irrespective of the organisational form, i.e. corporation, partnership or sole proprietor (see Jacobs, 1980: 293-297). This postulate is closely aligned to the concept of neutrality regarding the financial structure of an investment. Since different organisational forms can be considered as alternative forms of equity investments neutrality with respect ot the organisational form can be subsumed under the criterion of neutrality concerning financial decisions (see Schreiber, 2002a: 563; Schreiber and Spengel, 2006: 281-282). There are two concepts achieving neutrality regarding the organisational form of an investment: partnership tax (Teilhabersteuer) (see Kiesewetter, 1999: 83-86; Schneider, 1999: 9) and business tax (Betriebssteuer) (see Homburg, 2007: 265; Spengel, 2003a: 226). According to the concept of the partnership tax, corporations and partnerships are treated equally. Corporate profits are taxed at the level of the shareholders when they accrue and thus, irrespective of whether these profits are retained at the level of the corporation or paid out to the shareholder. Under a business tax, corporation income tax would also be applied to partnerships as well as capital income, such as interest. Business profits and capital income would be subject to a flat tax similar to the corporation income tax and dividends as well as capital gains arising from the sale of shares would be tax exempt at the level of the shareholder. The postulate of a neutral treatment of different organisational forms also requires that both permanent establishments and subsidiaries should be taxed in the same way (see Jäger, 2001: 102).

The postulate of neutrality concerning alternative business organisations is also applied to affiliated corporations on the one hand and divisions on the other hand (see Herzig and Wagner, 2005: 1; Scheuchzer, 1994: 33-39). Tax law is generally tied to civil law. According to civil law, a corporation represents a distinct legal entity. Consequently, a corporation is generally subject to corporate income tax. The incorporation of a business activity results in a separate entity both from a legal and a tax point of view. Each corporation has to determine its individual taxable income and is taxed separately. The transfer of goods and the provision of services between affiliated corporations have to be priced at arm's length and any profit or loss arising is recognized for tax purposes in the period the transaction occurs. Losses of a corporation can generally not be offset against profits of an affiliated corporation. They can only be offset against profits in previous or future periods of the same corporation. Furthermore, dividend payments between affiliated companies are generally taxable at the level of the receiving corporation. In order to avoid double taxation, received dividend payments are either tax exempt or a tax credit is granted.

In contrast, divisions are regarded as parts of a single corporation both under civil law and tax law. Transfers of assets and the rendering of services between two divisions are ignored for tax purposes, because they are merely internal asset realignments within the same corporation without involving contractual relationships with third parties. Moreover, losses of a division are automatically offset against profits of other divisions or the headquarters.

Tax neutrality between affiliated corporations and divisions is based on the notion that a corporate group forms an economically integrated entity. Tax neutrality towards the decision on the organisational business structure would require a similar tax treatment of integrated groups of companies. Affiliated corporations should be taxed like divisions of a single taxable entity (see Bauer, 1987: 60; Kessel, 1974: 10; Oestreicher, 2005: 14; Rupp, 1983: 20-41; Salzberger, 1994: 230; Scheuchzer, 1994: 32; Schön, 2007: 416-417; Jacobs and Spengel: 1994: 100-101). Otherwise, an incorporated business activity would be placed at a disadvantage when compared with an unincorporated business activity. The disadvantage mainly stems from a timing effect. Loss relief obtained in the same period results in a lower net present value of tax payments than a loss carry forward. Only if a loss carry back is provided is there no time lag compared to an immediate loss relief. Deferred taxation of profits arising from intra-group transactions also results in a comparably lower net present value of tax payments. Another advantage of an immediate loss relief is that it prevents situations in which losses cannot be offset at all. This might be the case if there is a time limit on the loss carry forward.

Based on the principle of tax neutrality, it is therefore claimed that taxation of profits and losses arising from intra-group transfers of assets and provisions of services should be deferred until they have been realised in a market transaction with an unrelated party. Furthermore, losses of one group member should be relieved against profits of other group members. Finally, double taxation of dividend payments among affiliated corporations should be avoided (see Scheuchzer, 1994: 39).

However, it has to be recognised that the two organisational forms do not represent exactly the same economic situation. An individual or corporate shareholder of a corporation benefits from limited liability protection against debtholders. Her economic risk to bear a loss is generally restricted to her share capital. In contrast, there is no limitation of the liability to a loss within a single corporation consisting out of several divisions. Therefore, intra-group loss relief should be restricted to the liability to economically bear a loss.

The two concepts underlying neutral taxation cannot be equated with one another, since one concept is based on production efficiency from a national perspective and the other concept is based on neutrality regarding decision making at the microeconomic level. However, at the very least, if taxation distorts investment decisions of companies, this would presumably result in an inefficient allocation of resources at the level of the whole national economy. Under a neutral tax system, the arbitrage behaviour of investors will ensure that the (risk-adjusted) marginal pre-tax rates of return to investment are equalized across all investment projects. In this way capital will be allocated so as to maximize the value of total output, and production efficiency will prevail (see Devereux: 2006: 25). Thus, neutral taxation at the firm level serves to achieve efficiency at the national level (see Spengel, 2003a: 226; Homburg, 2007: 240).

3.3.2 The International Perspective

In an international context, the neutrality principle calls for the neutral treatment of cross-border transactions within the framework of national tax systems (see Spengel, 2003a: 230). Basically, there are three different concepts of neutrality: capital import neutrality, capital export neutrality and capital ownership neutrality.

Capital import neutrality is obtained when foreign and domestic investors supplying capital to a given country are faced with the same effective tax rate on investment undertaken in that country (see Spengel, 2003a: 231). Thus, all income originating within a given jurisdiction is subject to the same tax burden, regardless of whether that income accrues to residents or non-residents. In order to implement capital import neutrality, taxation has to be based on the source or territoriality principle. According to this principle, income from investment abroad is ultimately taxed in the source country – the country in which the income is generated, i.e. the capital is invested – and is exempt from taxation in the country of residence – the country in which the investor resides (see Jacobs, 2007: 18-19; Schreiber, 1992: 833-834). Capital import neutrality ensures that foreign investors are not placed at a competitive disadvantage compared to domestic investors doing business in the same market in the source country (see Jacobs, 2007: 21).

With capital import neutrality, international capital mobility tends to equate after-tax rates of return across countries. In contrast, cross-country differences in pre-tax rates of return will occur if tax rates differ across countries. Therefore, capital import neutrality violates international production efficiency (see Homburg, 2007: 305-306). Moreover, if foreign income is tax exempt in the country of residence, domestic companies and investors would have an incentive to invest in low-tax countries, thereby taking full advantage of tax incentives for investment provided by the capital importing country, and of lower taxation in that country (see Jacobs, 2007: 23). Therefore, capital import neutrality causes distortions of companies' decisions on where to locate their business activity, thereby violating the postulate of decision neutrality.

An alternative concept of international neutrality is that of capital export neutrality. This form of international neutrality is achieved if income is taxed only in the investor's country of residence, and if there is no discrimination between domestic and foreign-source income in the capital exporting country. Such a basis for taxing international income is known as the residence or worldwide principle. According to this principle, the worldwide income accruing to residents, regardless of whether that income is from domestic or from foreign sources, would have to be determined and taxed according to the tax rules of the residence country. If the source country levies a tax on income generated within its jurisdiction, capital export neutrality would also be achieved if foreign taxes could be fully offset against domestic taxes on foreign source income. As a consequence, net domestic tax is payable only to the extent that domestic tax liabilities on the same income, had it been earned at home, would have exceeded the foreign taxes actually paid. In this case, total foreign and domestic taxes on income from foreign investment would equal domestic taxes payable on income from capital used at home. Such a situation would arise if firms and individual investors were taxed on the basis of their residence, with relief for international double taxation being granted by means of a full credit (refundable if necessary) for foreign taxes without any deferral.

Under taxation according to the principle of capital export neutrality, international mobility of capital would tend to drive pre-tax rates of return on investment across countries into equality. In this manner production efficiency is achieved (see Homburg, 2007: 304-305). If pre-tax rates of return are equalized across countries, no gain in output could be accomplished by reallocating capital from one country to another. However, the application of the production efficiency theorem has had to face criticism. It has been shown that the production efficiency theorem is relevant in an international context only if national government budgets are linked through a system of international transfers (see Kean and Wildasin: 2004). As mentioned in the previous section, the optimality of production efficiency also rests on the assumption that governments can tax pure profits, which in practice seems unrealistic. If they cannot, global optimality does not require capital export neutrality but rather a compromise between capital export and capital import neutrality (see Keen and Piekkola: 1997).

Since capital export neutrality implies that investors face the same tax burden regardless of the geographical location of their investment, it promotes decision neutrality. Thus, capital export neutrality reflects the goal that the tax system ought not to affect the decisions of businesses as to where they should invest. However, if national tax rules differ, distortions of business decisions remain even under the concept of capital export neutrality. These distortions concern a multinational company's decision as to where it should locate its headquarters. Multinational companies could escape a high tax burden on their worldwide income by moving their residence to a low-tax country. However, although headquarters may be quite mobile internationally, in practice the mobility of corporate headquarters may be limited by the fact that shareholders often have to pay a toll charge on capital gains since share-for-share exchanges and other options may not be available for corporate reorganizations (for an analysis of the effects see Schreiber and Führich, 2007: 12-17). Nevertheless, capital export neutrality may distort business decisions.

In practice, there are two important reasons why countries relieving international double taxation through a foreign tax credit do not achieve capital export neutrality. The first reason is that residence countries limit the foreign tax credit to the amount of domestic tax payable on the foreign-source income. Credits are either limited on a country-by-country basis or on a worldwide basis. The reason for the limitation on credits is that governments are not willing to allow taxes levied abroad to erode the revenue from tax on domestic source income. Due to the limitation on credits, investors are subject to the higher of the foreign and the domestic tax rate, whereas capital export neutrality would require that they should always face the same tax rate whether they invest at home or abroad.

The second reason for the failure of capital export neutrality in current countries' practice is that residence countries usually defer domestic tax on the active business income of foreign subsidiaries until this income is repatriated in the form of a dividend to the domestic parent company. Profits retained abroad are thus only subject to the foreign corporation tax, so for retained earnings, existing credit systems tend to work like an exemption system. This foreign tax credit with deferral may distort the investment and distribution policies of multinationals.[14]

A third concept of international neutrality is that of capital ownership neutrality. This neutrality concept is achieved, if tax systems do not distort cross-country ownership patterns (see Desai and Hines: 2003: 24). If the productivity of capital depends on the identities of its owners, then the efficient allocation of capital is one that maximizes output given the stocks of capital in each country. It follows that tax systems promote efficiency if they encourage the most productive ownership of assets within the set of feasible investors.

This result is attained if all countries practice residence-based taxation with unlimited foreign tax credits or if they all exempt foreign income from domestic tax. Considering the case in which all countries exempt foreign income from taxation, the tax treatment of foreign investment income is the same for all investors, and competition between potential buyers allocates assets to their most productive owners. Instead, if all countries tax foreign income whilst permitting taxpayers to claim foreign tax credits, then ownership would also be determined by productivity differences and not tax differences. In this case, the total tax burden on foreign and domestic investment varies between taxpayers with different home countries, but every investor has an incentive to allocate investments in a way that maximizes pre-tax returns. Under worldwide income taxation this acquisition policy will also maximise after-tax returns. Hence, assets will be held by those companies that would be willing to pay the highest reservation prices in the absence of tax. To conclude, international capital ownership neutrality can be achieved either by source based taxation or by residence based taxation with foreign tax credits. In this context it has to be recognised that foreign direct investment between developed countries mostly occurs in the form of mergers and acquisitions. In this respect, capital ownership neutrality is important. This may be also a reason, why most member states' tax systems are based on the source principle.

In conclusion, neither residence-based taxation achieving capital export neutrality, nor source-based taxation achieving capital import neutrality is fully optimal.

14 Based on US data, Desai, Foley and Hines (2001, 2002) estimate that one percent lower tax rates on dividends are associated with one percent higher dividends from foreign subsidiaries. Grubert (1998) also reports estimates indicating that repatriations are quite sensitive to their tax prices.

3.4 Administrative Aspects of Taxation

From an administrative point of view, the tax system should be simple and easily applicable. This implies the minimisation of operating costs associated with the tax system. Operating costs comprise compliance costs for the taxpayer and administrative costs for the public authorities. Compliance costs of taxpayers arise from fulfilling tax-reporting requirements and from the efforts made to evaluate the tax consequences of different business decisions (see Slemrod, 1996; Slemrod and Sorum, 1984). Administrative costs of public authorities include costs incurred to enforce the tax law, for example monitoring costs. It is evident that the simpler the tax laws, the less compliance and administrative costs there will be.

The requirement of simplicity is linked to cost effectiveness. In general, the effectiveness of a tax system refers to its capacity to achieve its basic objectives (see European Commission, 2001: 27). Accordingly, the operating costs of a tax system should be in reasonable proportion to the tax revenues, since the generation of the desired level of revenues is the main objective of taxation (see Koop, 1993: 103; Nobes, 2004: 40). Simple tax systems can improve cost effectiveness, because they imply low compliance and administrative costs and at the same time they can assure a sufficient level of tax revenues. A simple and cost effective tax system would promote the competitiveness of EU-companies as they can direct resources from administrative tasks to productive activities that promote growth.

Simplicity is promoted by tax rules that are transparent and certain to the taxpayer (see European Commission, 2001b: 28). Tax laws, regulations and administrative procedures have to be defined in a clear and coherent manner. Transparency will thus minimise the costs associated with the evaluation of tax rules and tax consequences by taxpayers. Certainty requires tax rules to be defined in such a way that the taxpayer can reliably calculate his tax liability. Tax rules should not allow for various interpretations and leeway in describing the taxable event. Furthermore, the tax system and tax practices should be stable over time, since frequent changes in tax legislation and its interpretation make it difficult for a taxpayer to foresee and estimate his tax burden, which may have a negative effect on investment decisions.

Another aspect associated with the criterion of simplicity is enforceability. The tax system has to be enforceable in practice and opportunities for tax evasion and for tax avoidance have to be avoided (see Utescher, 1999: 335; Schaumburg, 1998: 79;

Theisen, 1990: 22). In order to ensure equal enforcement of tax law, a sufficient degree of simplicity is required. In contrast, complex rules are difficult to enforce and thus can easily be avoided or evaded.

The administrative aspects of taxation outlined above are related to the principles of equity and neutrality. On the one hand, there is often a trade-off between improvements in equity and neutrality and administrative simplicity (see Gammie et al., 2005: 15). Improvements to equity and neutrality may imply more detailed tax laws and tax procedures, thereby causing additional administrative and compliance costs. On the other hand, a neutral tax system may lead to lower compliance and administration costs. Under a neutral tax system, there is no incentive for tax planning. Therefore, compliance costs of taxpayers are reduced. At the same time, complex rules intended to prevent tax evasion and avoidance can be abolished. As a result, neutrality promotes the minimisation of compliance and administration costs associated with operating a tax system (see Sachverständigenrat, 2006: Tz. 398; Wagner, 2005). Enforceability of a tax system promotes taxpayer equity. A tax system that cannot be enforced is unlikely to be equitable or neutral, as taxpayers will face different tax burdens depending on their possibilities for tax avoidance and evasion.

3.5 Summary

Levying corporation income tax is a controversial issue. Three different rationales are generally used to justify their existence. The role of corporation income tax as a withholding tax on retained profits and profits earned by foreign-owned companies is of utmost importance. Furthermore, it may serve as a charge for benefits obtained from consuming public services and there is also a role of corporation income tax as a tax on pure rents.

Since corporation income tax is seen as a substitute for personal income tax on retained profits, it also has to adhere to the principle of individual equity calling for the distribution of the tax burden according to each taxpayer's ability to pay. Comprehensive income is the widely agreed on indicator for the ability to pay taxes. Accordingly, the accrued global net income, irrespective of its source should be taxed. However, the taxation of accrued capital gains raises several concerns. As a consequence, income taxation relies on the principle of realisation. Thus, income may not be recognised until the relevant inflow of economic benefits is realised.

While the principle of individual equity is concerned with the relationship between different taxpayers, the principle of inter-nation equity addresses the relationship between different countries in an international setting. Inter-nation equity is achieved, if taxing rights concerning cross-border investments are allocated according to the source of profits. This is based on the benefit principle, which implies that tax is levied as a charge for the benefits received from the provision of public services. It is, however, difficult to determine the source of profits on economic grounds. Instead, the source of profits relies on conventions. Currently, the supply-approach is prevalent. According to this approach, the source of profits is located in the country in which the profit generating production factors are located.

Neutrality and efficiency are regarded as important properties of corporation income tax. The taxation of pure profits would ensure neutrality and efficiency. In practice, however, the measurement of pure profits is difficult. With reference to the ability to pay principle, the realisation principle has to be followed. If the taxation of pure profits is not feasible, neutrality should ensure that different modes of financing, organizational forms and different investments should bear the same tax burden.

At the international level, a neutral tax system would not distort a company's decision on where to invest. The concepts of capital import neutrality, capital export neutrality and capital ownership neutrality can be distinguished. These concepts of neutrality can be achieved either by residence or source taxation. Unfortunately, neither residence taxation achieving capital export neutrality nor source-based taxation achieving capital import neutrality is fully optimal. While capital export neutrality avoids distortions of a company's decision on where to locate a subsidiary or permanent establishment, it affects the choice of the location of the parent company. In contrast, capital import neutrality would leave the location decision regarding the headquarters unchanged but would distort the location decisions concerning the subsidiary or permanent establishment. From an international perspective, the avoidance of double taxation seems to be an important property of optimal taxation.

Administrative ease is associated with simplicity, certainty and transparency. The aim is to minimise compliance costs for taxpayers and administrative costs for the tax authorities, thereby ensuring a cost efficient tax system. Feasibility concerns are promoted by a neutral tax system, since it reduces incentives for costly tax planning and the necessity to introduce rules restricting tax avoidance and evasion. However, there is also a trade-off between administrative objectives and neutrality and equity. As mentioned above, administrative constraints impede a fully optimal tax system in the light of equity and neutrality.

To conclude, taxation in the EU should be based on realised net income, determined on a global basis and irrespective of its source. Moreover, it should be neutral with respect to different organizational forms and modes of investment financing. Furthermore distortions to cross-border investments, particularly cases of double taxation should be avoided. Finally, the tax system should be as simple, certain and transparent as possible.

4 Company Taxation in the European Union – a Stocktaking

In this chapter, important structural elements of the member states' current national tax systems effective on 1 January 2006 are compared. 25 member states are taken into account. Bulgaria and Romania are not considered. First, tax rules concerning national investments are addressed. These include the nominal corporate income tax rates as well as rules governing the determination of the corporate income tax base. As regards the tax base, the comparison deals with the relationship between financial and tax accounting, the method to calculate the taxable income, the recognition of assets and liabilities and the determination of cost values. Furthermore, specific tax areas such as the tax treatment of dividends paid to affiliated companies and individuals, losses and group taxation are dealt with. Besides corporation income tax, this chapter also provides a brief overview on additional local taxes. Second, member states' tax rules with respect to cross-border investments are compared. They include concepts of taxing foreign income, the tax treatment of interest expenses and foreign losses, group taxation, business regorganisations and methods used to determine arm's length prices. Finally, national effective tax rates of corporations combining the elements of the corporation income tax rate, the corporation income tax base and additional local taxes are presented using the methodology developed by Devereux and Griffith.

Most of the information for this analysis was derived from a study the author of this thesis was involved. The study was conducted with support from Pricewaterhouse-Coopers (see Endres et el., 2007). Additional information has been extracted from databases of the International Bureau of Fiscal Documentation.[15]

---

15 Two databases have been used: "Corporate Taxation in the EU" and "Individual Taxation in the EU".

4.1 National Investments

4.1.1 Corporate Income Tax

4.1.1.1 Nominal Tax Rates

The overview on the different elements of the corporation income tax regimes in the member states begins with a comparison of the nominal tax rates. Figure 1 sets out the nominal tax rates as at 1st January 2006.

Fig. 1. Nominal Corporation Income Tax Rates Including Surcharges in %

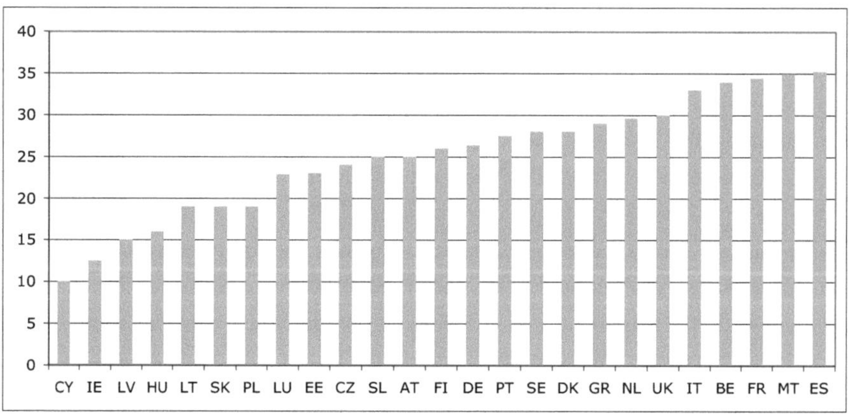

It becomes evident that there is a large variation in corporation tax rates across the European Union. The spread between the nominal corporation tax rates amounts to 25 percentage points. Cyprus has the lowest tax rate (10%) and Malta and Spain the highest (35.26% (35% corporation income tax rate and 0.75% commerce surcharge)).

Corporation tax rates are usually linear. Occasionally, countries apply different levels of flat rates, depending on the size of a corporation and its profits, to differentiate the tax burdens of small, medium and large companies. This is the case in Belgium, Cyprus, France, Hungary, Luxembourg, the Netherlands, Spain, and the United Kingdom. A special tax system exists in Estonia. At the time of distribution, the distributed profits are taxed at a rate of 23%, whereas retained earnings are exempt from taxation. Corporations in Slovenia are subject to a reduced tax rate of 10% if they perform activities in a free economic zone. In some member states (Belgium, France, Germany, Luxembourg, Portugal and Spain) the standard tax rates are increased by surcharges.

4.1.1.2 Tax Accounting Rules

4.1.1.2.1 Relationship between Financial and Tax Accounting

Financial accounting profits or losses form the starting point for the tax base in all member states (see Table 2).

Table 2. Relationship between Financial and Tax Accounting

Reference / Adjustments to IFRS	Reference / Adjustments to national GAAP
Cyprus, Estonia, France, Ireland, Malta, Slovakia, Slovenia, United Kingdom	Austria, Belgium, Cyprus, Czech Republic, Denmark, Finland, France, Germany, Greece, Hungary, Ireland, Italy, Latvia, Lithuania, Luxembourg, Malta, Netherlands, Poland, Portugal, Slovakia, Slovenia, Spain, Sweden, United Kingdom

However, the level of uniformity between tax and financial accounting varies across member states. Adjustments for corporate income tax purposes are required to a different extent in order to derive the taxable income from profits or losses registered in the financial accounts. Some member states have achieved substantial uniformity while in others tax and financial accounting are substantially independent. The accounting profit or loss is adjusted to reflect the differences between tax and financial accounting rules. These adjustments encompass differences in calculation, and therefore in the point in time at which revenue is taxed or expense recognised. Moreover, expenses recognised in accounting, but not deductible for corporate income tax purposes, have to be added back and revenues not recognised in the accounting, but taxable for tax purposes have to be included. Specific tax rules are also necessary when corresponding financial accounting rules are not available. For instance, this applies to rules governing loss relief or dividend taxation. In the following, existing differences between member states' tax accounting rules concerning different elements of the tax base are examined.

4.1.1.2.2 Taxable Income

Corporation income tax is levied on an annual basis. It is determined on a net basis, which may broadly be defined as the difference between revenues and expenses. Principally, all member states determine the net taxable income according to the accrual principle. Thus, income is described as the change in value of all assets and liabilities of the tax-paying corporation (see Spengel and Oestreicher, 2007: 3).

Revenues are generally defined as the gross inflow of economic benefits of an entity. With respect to the timing of revenue recognition, the realisation principle is of significant importance in all member states. However, the timing of revenue recognition may differ.

With regard to the sale of goods, there is no significant variation between the member states' tax practice (see Table 3). The majority of member states define realisation as the transfer of the significant risks of a transaction to the buyer. In contrast, seven member states link the realisation to the date of delivery.

Table 3. Recognition of Revenues Arising from the Sale of Goods

Transfer of Significant Risks and Rewards of Ownership	Delivery
Austria, Belgium, Cyprus, Estonia, Germany, Ireland, Latvia, Lithuania, Luxembourg, Malta, Netherlands, Poland, Portugal, Slovakia, Slovenia, Spain, Sweden, United Kingdom	Czech Republic, Denmark, Finland, France, Greece, Hungary, Italy

However, as far as construction contracts and the rendering of services are concerned, member states are divided (see Table 4). The completed-contract method must be applied in nine member states. According to this approach, revenues are not taxed until all relevant obligations are fulfilled. In contrast, revenue may be recognised in proportion to the stage of completion of contract activity if the outcome of a construction contract can be estimated reliably. This approach is called percentage-of-completion method and is applied in nine member states. The remaining seven member states allow the taxpayer to choose one of the two methods.

Table 4. Recognition of Revenues Arising from Construction Contracts and the Rendering of Services

Percentage-of-Completion Method	Completed-Contract Method	Option between these two Alternatives
Cyprus, Estonia, France, Ireland, Italy, Lithuania, Malta, Slovakia, United Kingdom	Austria, Czech Republic, Germany, Greece, Hungary, Luxembourg, Poland, Slovenia, Sweden	Belgium, Denmark, Finland, Latvia, Netherlands, Portugal, Spain

Revaluation gains are not generally considered taxable, since funds do not accrue to the entity. Only France and Greece tax revaluation gains on tangible assets. Most member states follow the principle of nominal value, according to which revaluation beyond acquisition cost is not allowed. Other member states neutralise the gain by assigning it to a capital reserve, at least insofar as it exceeds recovery of a previous write-down.

Decreases in economic benefits which are incurred for business purposes during the taxable period constitute deductible expenses for their justified amount, to the exclusion of expenses explicitly listed. Expenses representing acquisition or production cost of an asset are generally not tax deductible. Since these expenses are associated with future benefits, they are deferred and matched with revenue of later periods. Thus, the costs of assets with a useful lifetime of more than one period are capitalized and depreciated of amortized over the expected period of usage in order to allocate the respective costs of stocks and work in progress. Whether expenses are tax deductible in the period they are incurred or have to be capitalised depends on the definition of an asset. This issue is dealt with in the following section.

4.1.1.2.3 Recognition of Assets

In the majority of member states the definition of an asset relies on future economic benefits (see Table 5). In this sense, an asset is defined as being the source of probable future economic benefits obtained and controlled by a particular entity as a result of past transactions or events. Ten member states follow a different approach. Their definition refers to civil law and other test criteria of a distinct value and being potentially saleable proving the existence of an economic value.

Table 5. Definition of Asset

Continental Approach Referring to Civil Law and other Test Criteria	Definition According to International Standards Focused on Future Economic Benefits
Austria, Belgium, Czech Republic, Finland, Germany, Greece, Hungary, Luxembourg, Spain, United Kingdom	Cyprus, Denmark, Estonia, France, Ireland, Italy, Latvia, Lithuania, Malta, Netherlands, Poland, Portugal, Slovakia, Slovenia, Sweden

This distinction is of particular relevance when it comes to intangibles. While accounting for purchased intangibles is generally not problematic, internally generated intangibles are often difficult to measure and thus hard to recognise in the balance sheet. Research costs are expensed immediately in most member states (see Table 6). The reason for this may be that in the research phase, it can not reliably be demonstrated that an intangible asset exists that will generate future economic benefits. Ten countries, however, grant taxpayers the option of capitalising these assets. Only Cyprus and Ireland require research costs to be capitalised for tax purposes.

Table 6. Capitalisation of Research Costs

Mandatory	Optional	Prohibited
Cyprus, Ireland	Belgium, Denmark, Finland, Greece, Hungary, Italy, Luxembourg, Portugal, Spain, Sweden	Austria, Czech Republic, Estonia, France, Germany, Latvia, Lithuania, Malta, Netherlands, Poland, Slovakia, Slovenia, United Kingdom

Research costs are not easily distinguished from development costs. However, a significant number of member states treat them differently (see Table 7). In about half of the member states, the capitalization of development costs is optional. Ten countries require capitalization. It appears that development leads to a product, rendering its future benefits more immediately apparent. Capitalization in Ireland, Malta, Poland, Slovakia, Spain and the United Kingdom depends on a benefit test, which demonstrates a serious intention of completing the development phase and leads to expectations of future economic benefits. Four countries prohibit the capitalization of development expenses.

Table 7. Capitalisation of Development Costs

Mandatory	Optional	Prohibited
Cyprus, Czech Republic, Estonia, Ireland, Malta, Netherlands, Poland, Portugal, Slovakia, Slovenia	Belgium, Denmark, Finland, France, Greece, Hungary, Italy, Luxembourg, Spain, Sweden, United Kingdom	Austria, Germany, Latvia, Lithuania

4.1.1.2.4 Determination of cost values

In all member states the acquisition cost is the purchase price less discount and rebates. Generally, directly attributable costs of purchase and installation must also be included, though in Belgium this is only an option. As regards indirect costs, such as interest costs and general overhead costs, the member states' tax practices differ. The majority of member states, however, either prohibit their inclusion or allow their inclusion as an option.

Production costs are generally determined following the full cost approach. Almost all member states follow this approach or, at least allow it as an option (see Table 8). The Czech Republic and Finland are the only countries that allow capitalization of the direct costs.

Table 8. Determination of Production Costs

Full Cost Approach	Direct Cost Approach	Option Between the Two Alternatives
Austria, Cyprus, Estonia, France, Germany, Greece, Hungary, Ireland, Italy, Latvia, Lithuania, Luxembourg, Malta, Netherlands, Poland, Spain, Sweden, United Kingdom	Czech Republic, Finland	Belgium, Denmark, Portugal, Slovenia, Slovakia

Although the full cost approach is predominant within the European Union, differences in the determination of production costs remain. While material overhead cost, production overhead cost and depreciation are included throughout, interest costs and general administration costs are treated differently. The inclusion of interest cost is optional or prohibited in most member states; it is only mandatory in four member states. Administration costs are generally only required to be taken up if they relate to the production process. Accordingly, the vast majority of member states do not permit the inclusion of general administration costs.

Table 9. Simplified Valuation Methods

FIFO	LIFO	Weighted Average Cost Method	Other Methods
Austria, Belgium, Cyprus, Czech Republic, Denmark, Estonia, Finland, France, Greece, Hungary, Italy, Ireland, Latvia, Lithuania, Luxembourg, Malta, Netherlands, Poland, Portugal, Slovenia, Slovakia, Spain, Sweden, United Kingdom	Austria, Belgium, Germany, Italy, Luxembourg, Netherlands, Poland, Portugal, Slovenia, Spain	Austria, Belgium, Cyprus, Czech Republic, Estonia, France, Germany, Greece, Hungary, Italy, Ireland, Latvia, Luxembourg, Malta, Netherlands, Poland, Portugal, Slovakia, Slovenia, Spain, Sweden, United Kingdom	Austria, Germany, Netherlands, Portugal, Spain, United Kingdom

All member states allow the use of simplified valuation methods for inventories for tax purposes (see Table 9). The first-in, first-out method (FIFO) and the weighted-average method are widely used. The FIFO method is available in all 25 member states. It assumes that the costs of goods sold are those of the earliest purchases of the item still in stock. The value of the goods on hand at the end of a period is therefore the cost of the most recent purchases. The weighted-average method is available in all member states except Denmark and Finland. This method takes the weighted average of all items available for sale during the accounting period und uses this average cost to determine the value of the inventory. Ten member states provide for the last-in, first-out method (LIFO), which assumes that the items sold were those most recently purchased. LIFO thus tends to undervalue inventories to the detriment of the profit and loss account if prices are rising. And finally, some member states also allow other simplified valuation methods such as base-stock or resale-price-minus.

4.1.1.2.5 Amortization

The initial depreciable base for capital assets is uniform across the European Union in that it essentially equates to the acquisition or production cost. Despite this fact, depreciation methods and rates differ to a large extent across the EU. The most common methods in use are the reducing balance and straight line or a combination of the two. A great diversity can be observed with respect to the depreciation rates. Most member states provide a number of rates depending on the type of asset involved. In the following, the different national depreciation methods and rates applied to buildings, plant and equipment as well as to intangible assets are compared.

With regard to buildings, most member states only permit the straight-line method at specified rates. The declining and accelerated methods are common in some eastern member states. These methods allow higher first-year amortization charges than the straight-line method, resulting in a tax incentive to encourage investment. Depreciation rates for buildings in Europe vary from 12% in Greece to 1.47% in Spain. In Ireland and the United Kingdom, tax law disallows depreciation of capital assets and instead grants capital allowances for certain buildings.

Table 10. Regular Depreciation of Industrial Buildings

Straight-line over the Useful Life	Straight-line with Specified Rates	Straight-line or Declining Balance with Specified Rates	Straight-line or Accelerated with Specified Rates	Declining Balance with Specified Rates	Other Methods
Netherlands	Austria, Cyprus, Denmark, France, Germany, Greece, Hungary, Italy, Luxembourg, Malta, Portugal, Slovenia, Spain, Sweden	Beglium, Lithuania	Czech Republic, Poland, Slovakia	Finland, Latvia	Estonia, Ireland, United Kingdom

In the majority of member states, plant and equipment can be depreciated according to the straight-line method (see Table 11). However, more than half of all member states either require or allow for the declining-balance method. Four member states also apply the declining-balance method on a pool basis. Furthermore, there is a considerable variation between the depreciation rates. For machinery, depreciation rates range from three to 30% in case of the straight-line method and from nine to 48% in case of the declining balance method.

Table 11. Regular Depreciation of Plant and Equipment

Straight-line over the Useful Life	Straight-line with Specified Rates	Straight-line/Declining Balance with Specified Rates	Straight-line/Accelerated with Specified Rates	Declining Balance (Pool) with Specified Rates
Estonia, Netherlands	Austria, Cyprus, Ireland, Italy, Malta, Slovenia	Belgium, France, Germany, Greece, Lithuania, Luxembourg, Portugal, Spain, Sweden	Czech Republic, Poland, Slovakia	Denmark, Finland, Latvia, United Kingdom

Tax rules governing the regular amortization of intangible assets vary widely across the European Union (see table 12), both with respect to the method and to the rate. Depreciation rates are generally specified depending on the type of intangible asset. With regard to patents for instance, the applicable rates range from two to twenty years. Only seven countries do not fix the depreciation rate. These findings also hold true for the tax depreciation of research and development costs.

Table 12. Regular Amortisation of Rights and Intellectual Property

Systematic over Useful Life	Straight-line over Useful Life	Straight-line with Specified Rates	Straight-line/Declining Balance with Specified Rates	Straight-line/Declining Balance/by Usage	Straight-line/Declining Balance/Sum of the Digits over Useful Life	Straight-line/Declining Balance/Sum of the Digits with Specified Rates
Cyprus, Estonia, Malta	Austria, Portugal	Czech Republic, Denmark, Finland, France, Germany, Greece, Ireland, Italy, Latvia, Poland, Slovakia, Slovenia, United Kingdom	Belgium, Lithuania, Luxembourg, Sweden	Netherlands	Hungary	Spain

Provisions for an extraordinary write-down of assets exist in about half of the member states. In general, only apparently permanent decreases in value justify an extraordinary write down of an asset to the lower fair value. With respect to buildings, plant and equipment, eight member states require an extraordinary write-down. Three member states grant an option, at least if the fall in value is permanent. If the reasons for the decrease in value cease to apply, a write-back to historical value less accumulated regular depreciation is generally mandatory.

4.1.1.2.6 Recognition of Liabilities and Provisions

Under the accrual basis of accounting, not only past transactions involving the payment and receipt of cash but also obligations to pay cash in the future and of resources that represent cash to be received in the future are recorded in the accounting records and reported in the financial statements of the periods to which they relate.

Most member states do not have a legal definition for liabilities. However, even without a legal definition practice shows that all member states require a present obligation towards a third party arising from past events as a basic principle. The probability of occurrence has to exceed 50% in most member states.

Only eight member states permit the recognition of provisions for tax purposes (see Table 13). The majority of member states do not allow provisions apart from – and only in some countries – exceptional cases. In the new member states in particular, accounting for provisions is not widely accepted.

Table 13. Recognition of Provisions

Permitted with Certain Exceptions	Disallowed (General Rule) with Certain Exceptions	Disallowed or Not Tax-effective
Austria, Belgium, Estonia, France, Germany, Ireland, Luxembourg, Netherlands	Denmark, Czech Republic, Finland, Greece, Hungary, Italy, Lithuania, Portugal, Slovakia, Spain, Sweden, United Kingdom	Cyprus, Latvia, Malta, Poland, Slovenia

Apart from current obligations towards third parties, some member states allow provisions for future expenses. Ten member states allow an accounting of provisions for future expenses such as restructuring or deferred repair and maintenance, if certain requirements are fulfilled. Thus, more than half of the member states disallow deferred maintenance provisions.

As far as pensions are concerned, unfunded retirement benefits are found in ten member states. However, only four grant a tax deduction in the form of a provision. In the others, the deduction is not available until the pension payments fall due. While in twelve member states, unfunded retirement plans are not common, in Belgium, Denmark and Spain they are explicitly prohibited. In almost all member states funded retirement plans are estabilished and contributions are tax deductible.

Provisions for future operating losses are confined to specific cases in the Netherlands only. Moreover, most member states do not accept provisions for anticipated losses on onerous contracts. Austria, Belgium, the Czech Republic, Estonia, France and the Netherlands permit such provisions.

4.1.1.2.7 Inter-Company Dividends

As a common rule, corporations are taxed separately from their shareholders in the European Union. In this respect, tax law follows civil law, which treats corporations as separate legal entities. Accordingly, profits are taxed by the corporation when earned and the taxation on the shareholder is deferred. Shareholders are only subject to taxation if the profits are distributed. This system of corporate taxation may result in the double taxation of distributed profits by imposing both corporation tax on the company and corporation tax on the shareholder.

There are two different methods of avoiding double taxation of dividends distributed to corporations: (1) exemption and (2) credit. Most member states follow the exemption method (see Table 14).

Table 14. Taxation of Inter-company Dividends (Domestic Investments)

Exemption Method (100%)	Exemption Method (95%)	Credit Method
Austria, Cyprus, Czech Republic, Denmark, Estonia, Finland, Greece, Hungary, Ireland, Latvia, Lithuania, Luxembourg, Netherlands, Poland, Portugal, Slovakia, Slovenia, Sweden, United Kingdom	Belgium, France, Germany, Italy	Malta, Spain

This method exempts inter-company dividends in the hand of the shareholder. Profits are only subject to corporation tax when earned by the distributing company. Consequently, retained and distributed profits are burdened with an equal charge. Belgium, France, Germany and Italy also apply the exemption method, but with the variation of charging 5% of the dividends received to tax. In some member states a certain minimum shareholding, a minimum period of ownership or other qualifications are required for the exemption method to apply.

Ireland, Malta, Spain and the United Kingdom are the only countries that apply the tax credit method to avoid double taxation of dividends. Dividends received by the shareholder are grossed-up by the underlying corporation tax and taxed. At the same time, the corporation tax paid by the distributing company is credited against the corporation tax of the dividend receiving parent company. In Spain, full imputation is only granted if the receiving company has had a direct or indirect participation of a least 5% in the capital of the subsidiary for a continuous period of a least one year. Otherwise only 50% of the corporation tax attributable to the gross dividend is credited.

4.1.1.2.8 Capital Gains

In general, capital gains comprise gains realised from the sale of capital assets. In some member states capital gains also include gains on revaluation. The actual gain is the difference between the sales price and the book value of the asset.

Within the European Union, capital gains are generally taxed with ordinary income. In Cyprus and Ireland capital gains are subject to a tax rate which is higher than the corporation tax. However, the vast majority of member states including Cyprus and Ireland provide tax relief if certain conditions are fulfilled. Features of the preferential treatment vary in many ways. With regard to the scope of the capital gains subject to relief, a distinction can be made between capital gains realised from the sale of shares and capital gains realised from the sale of other business assets.

Capital gains realised on the disposal of shares are either partially or fully exempt from tax, subject to a reduced tax rate, or can be deferred.

Full exemption is granted in almost half of the jurisdictions under review. However, this preferential treatment is often only available on shares above a minimum shareholding level that have been held for a minimum period. In this respect, the taxation of inter-company dividends as outlined in the previous section and the taxation of capital gains arising on the sale of shares show many similarities. As a result, the two forms of profit realisation, profit distribution on the one hand, and profit retention with a subsequent sale of the shares on the other, are taxed similarly in many member states. Germany, Hungary, Italy, Malta and Portugal partially exempt capital gains realised on the disposal of shares. While in Germany (95%) and Italy (91%) there is almost full exemption, Hungary and Portugal exempt only 50%. The partial exemption in Germany, Italy and Portugal is subject to certain conditions. In France, the net long-term capital gains resulting from the sale of shares are subject to a reduced tax rate (8%). For financial years beginning on or after January 1, 2007, long-term capital gains arising from the disposal of participations and certain licences will be subject to taxation at a rate of 0%. 5% of the net capital gain, deemed to correspond to the expenses incurred by the vendor, will be excluded from the exemption and will remain subject to corporate tax. Estonia does not tax capital gains when earned, as only distributed profits are subject to corporation income tax. In Greece, the taxation of capital gains arising from the disposal of shares, either listed in the Athens Stock Exchange or in foreign stock markets, is deferred until distribution if the gains are transferred to a special reserve. Moreover, a special transfer tax is imposed at a rate of 0.15% if the shares are listed on the stock exchange and 5% if they are not. Upon the taxation of the tax-free reserve, a credit is given for that part of the transfer tax paid which corresponds to the gain.

There are various different forms of relief for capital gains arising on the sale of business assets other than shares (see Table 15). The application of a specific preferential tax treatment often depends on the type of asset and on the fulfilment of certain conditions.

Table 15. Tax Relief of Capital Gains (other than Shares)

Exemption, Indexation, Roll-over Relief	Indexation, Roll-over Relief	Partial Exemption, Indexation	Roll-over Relief	Special Tax Rates	Deferment of Taxation
Cyprus	Portugal	Malta, Spain, United Kingdom	Belgium, Denmark, Germany, Luxembourg, Netherlands	France, Greece	Estonia, Italy

Cyprus, Malta, Portugal, Spain and the United Kingdom apply an indexation allowance in order to relieve gains of inflation. The indexation allowance is generally calculated by multiplying the cost of acquisition by a price index. In eight countries, provisions for roll-over relief exist for capital gains realised on the sale of certain fixed business assets. In order to receive roll-over relief, the taxpayer has to reinvest the capital gain within a certain period of time. Moreover, some member states require the taxpayer to own the asset for a certain period of time prior to the sale. Roll-over relief generally defers the tax charge on reinvested gains by deducting the gain from the base cost of the replacement asset. Therefore, the gain is not taxed at the time the sale occurred, but decreases the depreciable amount and thus, increases the tax base in subsequent years. A reduced tax rate for capital gains arising on the sale of certain types of business assets is applied in France and Greece. In Estonia, tax is only levied on distributed profits, which results in a tax deferment. In Italy, tax deferment of capital gains is achieved through the approach of charging a gain to tax in equal portions over the next five years. However, the asset must have been owned for no less than three years. Finally, Cyprus and Portugal exempt certain capital gains from taxation. While in Cyprus realised capital gains other than gains on immovable property and on shares in a company which owns immovable property are fully tax exempt, Portugal provides only a 50% exemption for fixed assets and only if the sales proceeds are reinvested within a qualifying period.

4.1.1.2.9 Loss Relief

The offset of losses against profits is a key feature of every corporate tax system within the European Union (see Table 16). As a general rule, there are no restrictions on the offset of profit and losses within the same period, at least where the losses were incurred in the ordinary course of business.

Apart from Estonia, all member states allow the carry-forward of losses. However, various limitations exist. In eleven countries losses can be carried forward only for a certain period varying between five and fifteen years. Among those member states which allow for an unlimited loss carry-forward, some have introduced a kind of minimum taxation which limits the amount of the loss offset in any given subsequent period to a certain percentage of the profits of that period (e.g. Austria, Germany and Poland).

In contrast to the loss carry-forward, a loss carry-back is only available in France, Germany, Ireland, the Netherlands and the United Kingdom. Moreover, losses can be carried back only for a period of one or three years. In Germany, the amount of losses that can be set off against the profits of the preceding period is limited to EUR 511,500.

Table 16. Intertemporal Loss Relief

Loss Carry Forward	Loss Carry Back
Unlimited: Austria, Belgium, Cyprus, Denmark, France, Germany, Hungary, Ireland, Luxembourg, Malta, Netherlands, Sweden, United Kingdom	3 years: France, Netherlands
15 years: Spain	1 year: Germany, Ireland, United Kingdom
10 years: Finland	
6 years: Portugal	
5 years: Czech Republic, Greece, Italy, Latvia, Lithuania, Poland, Slovakia, Slovenia	

As a general rule, capital losses are treated as ordinary business losses. Exceptions to this rule apply to capital losses arising from the disposal of assets that qualify for specific capital gain taxation. This is apparent in Cyprus and Ireland. As described in section 4.1.1.2.8, capital gains are taxed separately from other sources of income at a special rate. Accordingly, capital losses can only be set off against future capital gains. In France and Latvia comparable rules exist for certain types of capital gain which are subject to a reduced tax rate.

Most member states, however, exempt wholly or largely capital gains on the sale of investments in other companies from taxation in the hands of the corporate shareholders. In consequence, corresponding losses are not deductible.

All member states allow loss carry-forwards, but nearly all protect their tax revenue with anti-avoidance provisions designed to prevent the transfer of loss relief to other companies except in instances seen as justified. These rules impact corporate reconstructions as well as the sale of "tax-loss" companies. The triggering event in Belgium, Denmark, Finland, Sweden and Slovenia is a change of ownership. France and Portugal put restrictions on the use of losses after a major change in the nature or conduct of the business. In nine countries loss relief is forfeited if both the ownership structure and the business change. Under Maltese law, rules apply to thwart any scheme which has a transfer of loss relief as its sole or main purpose. French law disallows the loss carry-forward if the company changes its tax regime or disappears as a consequence of reorganisation. Reorganisations and reconstructions also have tax consequences in Greece, Luxembourg and Poland. Finally, in Hungary past losses may only be carried forward after a corporate reconstruction with the permission of the tax office. No restrictions exist in Slovakia and, by definition, in Estonia.

4.1.1.3 Group Taxation

Tax law is generally tied to civil law. Since corporations are distinct legal entities, they are taxed accordingly. Thus, corporations are generally taxed separately from their affiliated corporations according to separate accounting under the arm's length principle. However, the majority of member states recognise that affiliated corporation form an economic entity and provide a special taxation regime for groups of affiliated companies. Eighteen member states have such a special group taxation regime (see Table 17).

Table 17. Group Taxation Regime Available

Group Taxation Regime Available	No Group Taxation Regime Available
Austria, Cyprus, Denmark, Finland, France, Germany, Ireland, Italy, Latvia, Luxembourg, Malta, Netherlands, Poland, Portugal, Slovenia, Spain, Sweden, United Kingdom	Belgium, Czech Republic, Estonia, Greece, Hungary, Lithuania, Slovakia

In general, these regimes entitle qualifying groups of companies to compute the tax liability on a combined or consolidated basis. However, the details differ widely across Europe, both with reference to the scope and availability as well as to the techniques and functions.

In most countries surveyed, only corporation tax payers are eligible for group taxation. In France this also includes partnerships that have opted for corporation tax. Several member states restrict the application of the regime further to certain kinds of corporation. Luxembourg and Portugal allow group taxation only if the relevant entities are fully subject to corporation tax. Germany and Latvia show themselves to be more generous in that they accept sole traders and partnerships as group parents – though not as subsidiaries.

The main requirement for a group of companies to qualify for consolidated taxation is common control by way of shareholdings. The qualifying threshold ranges from 50% to 100% (see Table 18). Six countries require an ownership of over 50% whilst in nine countries the threshold is set at 90% or more. These high shareholding thresholds are sometimes felt to be necessary for the protection of minority shareholders.

Table 18. Shareholding Threshold

100%	> 95%	> 90%	> 75%	> 50%
Slovenia	France (national regime), Luxembourg, Netherlands, Poland	Finland, Latvia, Portugal, Sweden	Cyprus, Ireland, Spain, United Kingdom	Austria, Denmark, France (international regime), Germany, Italy, Malta

In general, the shareholding requirement must be met with respect to voting rights, share capital and/or participation rights in profits and capital repayment on winding up. Nine member states define ownership solely by reference to share capital. In Austria, France, Latvia, Malta and Portugal the qualifying ownership is linked to voting rights and share capital. Participation in profits and capital repayments on winding up is only relevant in Cyprus, Ireland and the United Kingdom. This profits and assets test is intended to ensure that companies forming a group for tax purposes are substantially a single economic entity. In the vast majority of member states, the required shareholding can be direct or indirect. Direct and indirect shareholdings are generally accumulated when testing the threshold. A minimum period of shareholding is never required beyond the stipulation that the threshold be met throughout the period in question.

Denmark, Germany and Slovenia are the only countries that require additional tests to determine whether a group of companies qualifies for group taxation. In Germany and Slovenia, a profit pooling agreement has to be concluded between the parent company and its subsidiaries. The definition of a corporate group for tax purposes in Denmark follows the definition of the financial accounting rules. Accordingly, the focus is on control. This definition encompasses not only the majority of voting rights but also other entitlements to exercise control, e.g. the right to appoint or dismiss a majority of the members of the subsidiary's management.

When the requirements for group taxation are met, its application is generally elective (see Table 19). Only in Denmark qualifying resident entities are obliged to apply the rules of group taxation. Fourteen jurisdictions allow "cherry-picking" from the qualifying group companies. This contrasts with the "all-in or all-out" approach.

Table 19. Manner of Election

Cherry Picking Allowed	All-in or All-out Approach
Austria, Cyprus, Finland, France (national regime), Germany, Ireland, Italy (national regime), Latvia, Luxembourg, Malta, Netherlands, Poland, Sweden, United Kingdom	Denmark, Portugal, Slovenia, Spain

In nine member states the option for the group taxation regime is binding for a minimum period of time (see Table 20). The periods vary between three and ten years. Interestingly, all countries that provide for international group taxation set a minimum period. In Denmark the minimum period only applies to the international group members. At home, group taxation is binding as long as the requirements continue to be met. A comparable distinction exists in Italy. While the national regime is subject to a minimum period of only three years, the international regime has to be followed for five years. If group taxation is terminated before the minimum period has elapsed, the entire tax consequences are generally reversed.

Table 20. Minimum Period

10 Years	5 Years	3 Years	No Minimum Period
Denmark	France, Germany, Italy, Luxembourg, Portugal	Austria, Italy, Poland	Cyprus, Denmark, Finland, Ireland, Latvia, Malta, Netherlands, Slovenia, Spain, Sweden, United Kingdom

Among the member states of the European Union, there are many differences between systems and consequences of group taxation regimes. With respect to the technique of combining the individual results of group members, three groups can be identified (see Table 21):

- Full consolidation: The mechanism of full consolidation can only be found in the Netherlands.
- Pooling of profits and losses: The majority of countries pool profits and losses. Each group member computes taxable income separately and the total is accumulated (pooled) by the parent. Some countries require adjustments.

– Group relief and loss subvention: Five member states operate a system of "group relief", i.e. a group member may transfer its loss to a profitable member of the group for immediate offset. Sweden and Finland transfer loss relief through subvention payments. These consitute taxable income for the recipient and are tax deductible for the payer, so the loss offset follows the flow of cash.

Table 21. System of Group Taxation

Consolidation	Pooling Onto Parent	Subvention Payments	Group Relief
Netherlands	Austria, Denmark, France, Germany, Italy, Luxembourg, Poland, Portugal, Slovenia, Spain	Finland, Sweden	Cyprus, Ireland, Latvia, Malta, United Kingdom

The system of group taxation does not necessarily determine the tax consequences. There are always different ways of achieving the same object. The two main objectives are the offset of profits and losses between group members and a defer tax treatment of gains realised from intra-group transfers.

A starting point in every group taxation regime is the separate accounting by each group member. In all member states, group members have to apply the same accounting rules when computing their income. Most countries also require identical business years for all members of the group.

All forms of group taxation provide rules to offset losses and profits between entities forming a tax group. This can be achieved either by accumulating profits and losses on a parent (full consolidation, pooling), by transferring losses incurred by one group member to be offset against profits by another group member (group relief) or by assuming a loss through a subvention payment. Generally, losses and profits can be offset irrespective of the level of ownership.

It is common practice across the European Union to exclude or restrict the offset of losses incurred prior to the start of a tax group. Generally, such losses remain with the company that has incurred them. Exceptions apply in Germany and in Austria which allow a parent company to offset current profits from group members with its own losses brought forward. Other limitations exist for the offset of losses if a member leaves the group. However, this is only relevant where losses have been allocated to the parent. Some countries prescribe that losses incurred during the period of the tax group remain with the parent, while others allow leaving companies to take their own losses with them. In Portugal such losses are cancelled altogether.

The vast majority of jurisdictions within the European Union treat sales and purchases within a group of companies the same way as corresponding transactions between unrelated parties. They are accepted in principle, as long as they meet the arm's length test, and their profits are taken up in the profit and loss account. Only seven countries provide for deferral of the gains (or losses) realised at the time the intra-group transfer occurred (see Table 22). Deferred gains or losses are generally subject to recapture. Typical triggering events are the sale of the assets outside the group or the withdrawal of a group member involved in the transfer.

Table 22. Elimination of Intra-group Transfers

Consolidation	Tax Deferral of Intra-group Transfers	No Special Treatment of Intra-group Transfers
Netherlands	France, Ireland, Italy, Malta, Spain, United Kingdom	Austria, Cyprus, Denmark, Finland, Germany, Latvia, Luxembourg, Poland, Portugal, Slovenia, Sweden

Other forms of consolidation are uncommon. A full consolidation system can be found only in the Netherlands. As a consequence of this system, all assets and liabilities of the entities forming the fiscal unit are attributed to the group's parent company. After the constitution of the fiscal unit, the parent company presents one consolidated balance sheet which includes all the entities' assets. In Austria, France, Luxembourg and Spain certain adjustments to the combined income are required, if the application of the group taxation would result in a double relief of losses. For example, such a double deduction would occur, if a parent company writes down its investment in a qualifying, loss-making subsidiary whilst offsetting the same losses through the pooling mechanism. Therefore, all four member states stipulate that any write-down of an investment in a group member must be reversed. France extends the scope of these adjustments to reserves, subsidies and waivers of debt, and Luxembourg requires adjustment whenever the group taxation regime gives rise to double taxation or double deduction.

4.1.2 Corporation Tax System

There are various systems governing the taxation of profits distributed to personal income tax payers. With regard to the extent of integration of the corporation tax into the personal income tax of the shareholder, three main categories can be distinguished:

- The classical system;
- Double taxation reducing systems; and
- Double taxation avoiding systems.

Within the EU, the classical system is currently only applied in Ireland (see Table 23). This corporation tax system results in an unrelieved double taxation of dividends. Profits are first taxed by the corporation and then, on distribution, by the shareholder.

Table 23. Corporation Tax Systems

Classical System	Shareholder Relief System	Partial Imputation System	Full Imputation System	Exemption System
Ireland	Austria, Belgium, Cyprus, Czech Republic, Denmark, Finland, France, Germany, Hungary, Italy, Lithuania, Luxembourg, Netherlands, Poland, Portugal, Slovenia, Sweden	Spain, United Kingdom	Malta	Estonia, Greece, Latvia, Slovakia

In contrast, systems to avoid double taxation ensure that distributed profits are only taxed once. In Malta, double taxation is avoided by applying a full imputation system. Corporation tax paid is credited against the personal income tax of the shareholder as an "imputation credit". The ultimate tax burden thus depends on the personal income tax of the shareholder only. Greece, Latvia and Slovakia eliminate double taxation through a system of dividend exemption for shareholders. Thus, the tax burden of distributed profits is only determined by the corporation tax. Estonia has its own, unique system of taxing profits only once – on the corporation at the time of distribution. This clearly places a burden on the distribution of the profits as opposed to profit retention. Shareholders have the advantage of exemption of dividends from personal income tax, as is the case in Greece and Latvia.

However, the vast majority of member states grant only partial relief from double taxation of distributed profits. Apart from Spain, a preferential treatment for dividend income at the shareholder level is provided, either by a reduced tax base or a reduced rate on dividends. A partial imputation system applies in Spain and the United Kingdom. In contrast to the full imputation system, the tax credit amounts to less than the tax paid by the corporation on distributed profits.

4.1.3 Local Taxes

Corporations may be subject to additional taxes on business profits or on business assets other than corporate income tax (see Table 28).

Table 24. Local Taxes

Real Property Tax	Net Wealth Tax	Payroll Tax	Business Tax on Income	Business Tax on Capital
Austria, Belgium, Cyprus, Czech Republic, Denmark, Finland, France, Germany, Greece, Hungary, Ireland, Italy, Latvia, Lithuania, Luxembourg, Netherlands, Poland, Portugal, Sweden, Slovakia, United Kingdom	Luxembourg	Austria, Cyprus, France, Slovenia	Germany, Hungary, Italy, Luxembourg	Spain, France

All member states except Estonia, Greece, Malta and Slovenia levy real estate tax on business buildings. The tax base generally covers land and buildings. The taxable value is derived from either market prices, lower standard tax values or the area of land (square meters). Hence, the taxable value may vary considerably in different countries even though the tax base covers the same items.

A net wealth tax on business assets of corporations is only imposed by Luxembourg. However, the company can reduce this tax if it creates a corresponding reserve and if it does not distribute this reserve during the following five years.

Additional local business taxes are only levied in a few member states. They are either levied on a profit basis (Germany, Hungary, Italy, Luxembourg) or on a capital basis independent of the profits (France, Spain). Local business taxes on a profit base are not always imposed directly on corporate profits as assessed for purposes of the corporate income tax. In some countries, such as Germany, the base of the local business tax differs considerably from the corporate income tax base. Non-profit business taxes do usually only include tangible fixed assets. Payroll taxes are levied in Austria, Cyprus, France and Slovenia.

4.2 Foreign Direct Investments

4.2.1 Taxation of Foreign Income

As a general rule, corporate income tax is based on the residence principle (see Scheffler, 2002: 11). According to the residence principle, the jurisdiction in which the company is resident has a right to tax the income of the company. Residence taxation is based on the personal status of a taxable entity (see Schreiber, 2005: 353; Jacobs, 2007: 6). A company's residence country can be determined according to legal or economic criteria. With respect to legal criteria, most member states determine the fiscal residence of a company by referring to the place of incorporation or the place of a company's legal seat (see European Commission, 2005c: 16-17).[16] The place of effective management serves as an economic criterion to identify a company's residence in most member states (see European Commission, 2005c: 16-17). However, this concept may differ across the European Union. Under Anglo-Saxon law, the central management and control concept is applicable (see Jacobs, 2007: 485). Compared to the place of effective management, the identification of the place of central management and control requires higher levels of management (see Griemla, 2003: 41).

Since different countries apply different approaches to identify a company's residence, cases in which a company is deemed to be domiciled in several countries may occur with more frequency. These conflicts are resolved by the tie-breaker rule, which is codified in paragraph 3 of article 4 of the OECD Model Convention. According to this rule, the place of effective management is decisive in determining a company's residence if this company may be resident in two countries according to their respec-

[16] For further details on these concepts see Schaumburg, 1998: 302-304; Meilicke, 2003: 794-804.

tive national laws (see Doernberg et al., 2001: 301-302). For its identification, all major facts and circumstances must be examined.

In most member states, resident companies are subject to unlimited fiscal liability. Residence taxation is imposed on the worldwide income regardless of whether it was generated at home or abroad (see European Commission, 2005c: 16-17). In contrast to the principle of worldwide income taxation, the principle of territoriality restricts the tax liability of a company to the income generated within the residence country. Thus, foreign source income is not taken into account in the residence country. The principle of territoriality is only applied in France and in Denmark (see European Commission, 2005c: 16-17).[17]

A company doing business abroad may also become liable to tax in the foreign source country. According to the principle of source country entitlement, the source country should have a fair claim to tax profits generated by business activities carried out within its jurisdiction if the taxable entity participates actively in economic life (see Frebel, 2006: 19). As already mentioned, it is difficult to determine the source of income on economic grounds. Instead, the source of income is generally defined in line with international conventions. In this context, member states generally follow the rules provided by the OECD Model Convention. A distinction is generally drawn between active business income, including business profits and income from services, and passive investment income, such as dividends, interest and royalties (see Li, 2003: 86). The source of passive investment is principally attributed to the country in which the payer is resident. With reference to active business income, the OECD Model Convention follows the permanent establishment rule. The permanent establishment indicates the threshold that must be met by the business activity in the source country in order to entitle the source country to tax. In paragraph 1 of article 5 of the OECD Model Convention, a permanent establishment is defined as a fixed place of business through which the business of an enterprise is wholly or partly carried out.[18]

Since a company's income may be liable to tax in the residence and in the source country, a double taxation of profits may arise. In order to avoid double taxation, either the taxing right of the source country or the residence country is restricted. If the source country is entitled to tax the income arising within its borders, it is up to the residence country to prevent or mitigate double taxation of profits. Double taxation

17 However, it has to be recognised that an exception to this rule applies to international groups of companies (see section 4.2.5).

18 For more details on the concept of permanent establishment see Jacobs, 2007: 323-370.

may be avoided either by the exemption method or the credit method (for more details see Jacobs, 2007: 10-18).[19] Under the exemption method, foreign income is excluded from the domestic tax base. If the tax rate structure is progressive, the income of the source country may be taken into account to determine the tax rate applicable in the residence country. According to the credit method, the residence country grants a tax credit for the taxes paid in the source country. The foreign tax is offset against the tax due in the residence country. In practice, the credit may be capped at the amount of tax payable in the residence jurisdiction without a refund being granted if a higher amount of taxes is payable in the source country. Consequently, the final tax rate applicable is whichever rate is higher between the residence and the source jurisdiction.

The restriction of the source country's taxing right and the obligation of the residence country to avoid double taxation depend on the category of income. If foreign direct investment is carried out through a permanent establishment, the source country is entitled to tax those business profits attributable to the permanent establishment. In addition, the headquarters are subject to tax for the income generated through the foreign permanent establishment according to its unlimited tax liability in the country of its residence. 13 member states avoid the resulting double taxation by applying the exemption method (see Table 25). Thus, those profits attributable to the foreign permanent establishment are tax-exempt in the residence country. The other 12 member states apply the credit method.

Table 25. Avoidance of Double Taxation with respect to foreign permanent establishments

Exemption Method	Credit Method
Austria, Belgium, Cyprus, Denmark, Estonia, France, Germany, Greece, Hungary, Luxembourg, Netherlands, Poland, Spain	Czech Republic, Finland, Ireland, Italy, Lithuania, Latvia, Malta, Portugal, Sweden, Slovenia, Slovakia, United Kingdom

If instead, foreign direct investment is carried out through a subsidiary, this separate legal entity is subject to unlimited tax liability in the country where it is resident. The income of the subsidiary is taxable in the source country regardless of whether the profits are retained or distributed. If the income of the subsidiary is retained, a tax shelter effect results, since no further taxation takes place in the country where the investing parent company is resident. If profits are distributed via dividend payments,

19 The OECD Model does not stipulate which of the two methods to avoid double taxation should be preferred.

the receiving parent company may be subject to a withholding tax on the dividend in the source country. However, according to Directive 90/435/EWG, withholding taxes are abolished if certain requirements regarding the shareholding are fulfilled. In addition, the parent company is subject to tax on these dividends according to its unlimited tax liability in the residence country. In order to avoid double taxation, nearly all member states exempt dividends received from a foreign subsidiary from tax (see table 26). Only five member states tax foreign dividends and grant a limited tax credit for the underlying foreign corporation tax.

Table 26. Avoidance of Double Taxation with Respect to Foreign Dividends

Exemption Method	Credit Method
Austria, Belgium, Cyprus, Czech Republic, Denmark, Estonia, Finland, France, Germany, Hungary, Italy, Latvia, Lithuania, Luxembourg, Netherlands, Portugal, Slovakia, Slovenia, Spain, Sweden	Greece, Ireland, Malta, Poland, United Kingdom

Besides dividend income, an overlapping of residence and source taxation may also arise regarding other categories of passive income. Important income categories to be considered in this context are interest and royalty payments. According to the Directive 2003/49/EC on a common system of taxation applicable to interest and royalty payments made between associated companies of different member states, withholding taxes levied in the source country, i.e. the country where the payer is resident, are abolished.[20] As a result, interest and royalty income are taxed according to the residence principle in all member states (for more details see Jacobs, 2007: 169-172).

4.2.2 Allocation of profits – the arm's length principle

Once taxing rights on the income of a multinational enterprise have been assigned to the residence and/or the source country, the second fundamental issue of international taxation to be addressed is the allocation of the taxable income between the entities of the multinational enterprise and the involved countries. This issue is crucial for both the taxable entities and the tax authorities in order to levy taxes. In general, the allocation of profits is based on the principle of economic allegiance, which requires the di-

20 Council Directive 2004/76/EC of 29 April 2004 allows certain new member states the possibility of transitional periods as regards the application of the provisions of Directive 2003/49/EC.

vision of income according to the origin of the profits, i.e. the place where the profits are generated (see Jacobs, 2007: 579; Scheffler, 2002: 279-281).

The issue of profit allocation among different entities of a multinational enterprise arises for subsidiaries as well as for permanent establishments (see Frebel, 2006: 20). With respect to subsidiaries, separate accounting under the arm's length principle constitutes the international norm (see Li, 2003: 108, 109).[21] This approach is currently codified in paragraph 1 of Article 9 of the OECD Model Convention. Under separate accounting, each separable entity belonging to a multinational enterprise has to calculate its individual income separately on an entity by entity approach. Intra-group transactions, such as the internal transfer of goods and the provision of services, have to be recognised at arm's length. The underlying intention is to treat affiliated companies as if they operate as independent entities (see OECD, 2001: section 1.7; Jacobs, 2007: 584). The benchmark for the determination of transfer prices under the arm's length principle is the price that would have been negotiated for a comparable transaction between unrelated parties (see paragraph 1 of Article 9 of the OECD Model Convention). Thus, the application of the arm's length principle requires the definition of comparables. Factors determining comparability include the characteristics of the goods or services transferred, the functions performed, the assets used and risks assumed by the respective parties, the contractual terms, the economic circumstances of the parties and the business strategy (see Musgrave, 1972: 403; OECD, 2001: section 1.17-1.35). The OECD transfer pricing guidelines (see OECD, 1995) provide guidance for determining comparability between transactions and several transfer pricing methods. These guidelines are followed by all member states (see European Commission, 2001b: 265). There are different methods to determine whether transfer prices are at arm's length. The so-called "traditional transaction methods" are the comparable uncontrolled price method (CUPM), the resale price method (RPM) and the cost plus method (CPM) (see Jacobs, 2007: 750-759; Vögele et al.: 2004: chapter D, sections 1-236). The CUPM is closely related to the idea of the arm's length principle and thus preferred over the other methods (see Baumhoff, 1998: 411). This method compares the price for goods or services transferred in a transaction between affiliated entities to the price charged for the same goods or services transferred in a comparable transaction between independent parties (see OECD, 2001: section 2.6). According to the resale price method (RPM) the arm's length price is based on the price at which a product purchased from an associated enterprise is resold to an independent enterprise. This resale price is reduced by the appropriate gross resale price margin calculated by comparing it with the gross margin of an uncontrolled transaction. The remainder constitutes the arm's length price for the transaction between the associated enterprises (see OECD, 2001: section 2.14; European Commission, 2001b: 258). The CPM starts with the costs incurred by the supplier in a transaction between affiliated companies for products transferred or services provided to a related purchaser (see OECD, 2001: section 2.32). A cost plus mark up that is consistent with mark ups in uncontrolled transactions is then added to raise the price to the level that would have been agreed upon between unrelated parties (see European Commission, 2001b: 258).

In addition to the traditional transaction methods, transactional profit methods may exceptionally be used to determine arm's length prices (see OECD, 2001: section 3.2). These methods are deemed to be consistent with the arm's length principle, but only applicable as a last resort if the traditional transaction methods cannot reliably be applied (see OECD, 2001: section 3.49-3.50). Two transactional profit methods exist: the transactional profit split method (TPSM) and the transactional net margin method (TNMM) (see Jacobs, 2007: 759-773). According to the TPSM, two steps are necessary to determine the arm's length price (OECD, 2001: section 3.5; European Commission, 2001b: 258): In a first step, the combined profit that arises from a controlled transaction between associated enterprises is identified. In a second step, the profit is split among the relevant parties on a basis reflecting the division that would have been concluded between uncontrolled parties. The TNMM examines the net profit margin relative to an appropriate base (for example costs, sales or assets) that a taxpayer realises from a controlled transaction and compares this figure to the net profit margin between uncontrolled parties (OECD, 2001, section 3.26). The appropriate transfer price is then calculated by either subtracting the net profit margin or by adding it to the total costs. Thus, the TNMM operates in a manner similar to the CPM and the RPM (see OECD, 2001: section 3.26; European Commission, 2001: 258). As the case may be, appropriate adjustments might be necessary to ensure the data is truly comparable and to obtain reliable results.[22]

According to paragraph 2 of article 7 of the OECD Model Convention, separate accounting under the arm's length principle is also the preferred method for profit alloca-

21 The method of formula apportionment is clearly rejected by the OECD, since it is not deemed to be consistent with the arm's length principle (see OECD, 2001, sections 3.63-3.74).

22 For further information on transaction methods see Jacobs, 2007: 746-795.

tion with respect to permanent establishments. The application of the arm's length principle here is based on the fiction of the permanent establishment being a separate entity. Alternatively, a consolidation and apportionment approach can be applied, if it has as a matter of history been customary and implicates that the result is in accordance with the result achieved under the arm's length principle (see paragraph 4 of article 7 of the OECD Model; Jacobs, 2007: 582). According to the consolidation approach, the multinational enterprise is regarded as an economic entity (see Jacobs, 2007: 584). The consolidated net income is allocated among affiliated companies using a formula. The factors included in the formula may be payroll and sales. Recently the OECD has advanced the rules governing the profit allocation regarding permanent establishments (see Jacobs, 2007: 583). The aim is to assimilate the rules applicable to subsidiaries and permanent establishments. Accordingly, the profits attributable to a permanent establishment are the profits that it would have earned at arm's length as if it were a distinct and separate enterprise performing the same or similar functions under the same or similar conditions ("functionally separate entity approach"). The indirect method codified in paragraph 4 of article 7 of the OECD Model may only be applied to enterprises carrying on an insurance business.

4.2.3 Deductibility of interest

As a general rule, interest payments on loans are tax deductible. There are exceptions to this general rule (see table 27). Some member states deny the deductibility of interest expenses associated with foreign shareholdings. Often, these restrictions also apply to domestic shareholdings.

Table 27. Deductibility of Refinancing Costs and Thin-Capitalisation Rules

Restriction to the Deductibility of Refinancing Costs	Thin-Capitalisation Rules
Belgium, Czech Republic, Luxembourg, Malta, Netherlands, Slovakia	Austria, Belgium, Czech Republic, Denmark, France, Germany, Hungary, Italy, Luxembourg, Latvia, Lithuania, Netherlands, Poland, Portugal, Slovenia, Spain, United Kingdom

Thin-capitalisation rules are wide-spread in the EU. However, several member states do not have formal rules on thin capitalisation. These are Cyprus, Estonia, Finland, Greece, Ireland, Luxembourg, Malta, Slovakia and Sweden. Thin-capitalisation rules generally restrict the decutibility of interest payments on loans granted by an affiliated company if the debt-equity ratio or interest payments exceed a certain threshold. Austria, Belgium, Luxembourg and the United Kingdom do not have formal rules. Instead, administrative guidelines are used to determine whether thin-capitalisation rules apply.

4.2.4 Loss Relief

Many member states grant, subject to certain conditions, relief for losses from foreign permanent establishments (see Table 28). Only Denmark and France apply a strict territorial principle excluding all profits and losses of foreign permanent establishments from domestic taxation. More than half of the countries under review allow foreign permanent establishment losses incurred to be deducted from domestic, head office income. However, many of these countries relieve double taxation by the credit, rather than by the exemption method. So called "double dips" of foreign losses are generally prevented by making the domestic deduction dependent upon the exclusion of foreign relief. Austria, Belgium, Cyprus, Hungary, the Netherlands and Spain are the only states that grant relief for foreign losses even if foreign profits are exempt from tax. Recapture provisions prevent the deduction of the same loss in both countries.

Table 28. Recognition of Losses of Foreign Permanent Establishments

Non Deductible	Only Under the Credit Method	Also Under the Exemption Method (Recapture of Losses)
Denmark, France	Czech Republic, Germany, Finland, Greece, Hungary, Ireland, Italy, Latvia, Lithuania, Luxembourg, Malta, Poland, Portugal, Slovakia, Slovenia, Sweden, United Kingdom	Austria, Belgium, Cyprus, Netherlands, Spain

4.2.5 Group Taxation

International group taxation within the European Union is still in its infancy. Table 29 shows that in most countries, the regime stops at the border. Non-resident subsidiaries can be part of a tax group only in Austria, Denmark, France and Italy. Six countries allow the local subsidiaries of a foreign parent to form a national group. This is possibly a reaction to European legal developments given that some states exclude non-resident parents from outside the EU or the EEA. About half of the member states allow their tax groups to be controlled by a foreign parent through a domestic permanent establishment.

Table 29. Territorial Scope

Foreign Parent Company (Group Consists of Resident Subsidiaries)	Resident Permanent Establishment of Non-Resident Parent Company	Non-Resident Subsidiaries
Cyprus, Ireland, Italy, Latvia, Malta, Sweden, United Kingdom	Austria, Denmark, Finland, France, Germany, Ireland, Italy, Luxembourg, Netherlands, Sweden, Spain, United Kingdom	Austria, Denmark, France, Italy, United Kingdom

Austria, Denmark, France and Italy and are the only member states allowing cross-border group taxation. However, special provisions can be found in this context. In Austria, France and Italy, the effect is limited to profits and losses in proportion to the share ownership. Austrian tax law only admits foreign losses that cannot be offset in the foreign country. Foreign profits are generally tax exempt in Austria. In order to prevent the offset of the same loss in more than one country, Austrian loss relief is recaptured if the foreign subsidiary claims its own loss relief locally later. In Denmark, France and Italy not only losses but also profits of foreign group members are included in the group's taxable income. Double taxation of foreign profits is avoided by credit for the foreign tax paid.

4.2.6 Business Reorganisations

Taxation of business reorganisations generally follows the rules provided by the Merger Directive 90/434/EEC, which has recently been amended by Directive 2005/19/EC. Most member states have transformed the Directive into national law (see Jacobs, 2007: 164). The Directive covers mergers, divisions of companies, transfer of assets, exchanges of shares, split-offs and the conversion of branches to subsidiaries. According to the Directive taxation of hidden reserves of the transferor company should be deferred until those reserves are actually realized (Art. 4). The historical value of assets transferred has to remain unmodified despite the reorganisation. However, the Directive is silent on those assets, which do not remain connected to a permanent establishment in the member state from which the assets are transferred (see

Jacobs, 2007: 168). Thus, whenever a country looses its taxing nexus, the transfer of assets is subject to an exit charge. This also applies to situations, in which the residence of a company is transferred to another country. Member states also apply different valuation methods in respect of the cross-border transfer of assets. As a result, transfers of assets may be either subject to double taxation or double non-taxation (see European Commission, 2006: 7). Taxation of business reorganisations is a complex issue and it is not possible to provide a detailed comparison of member states' practice here.

4.3 Summary

The comparative analysis of the tax systems in the EU has revealed that corporate taxation is far from being uniform. Differences occur with respect to all elements of the tax system:

- Statutory corporate income tax rates are generally linear. They range from 10% in Cyprus to 35.26% in Spain.
- Accounting rules determining the corporate income tax base generally refer to financial accounting rules. However, adjustments are made to a different extent in order to derive the taxable income from the profits or losses shown in the financial accounts. Within each field of tax accounting, clusters of member states with similar approaches can be identified. However, these clusters are not constant over all elements of the tax base. With regard to certain structural elements of the tax base, such as the recognition of revenues and the determination of production costs, the differences seem to be only marginal. In contrast, with respect to tax depreciation, the capitalisation of research and development expenses and the recognition of liabilities, the differences seem to be substantial. A great disparity concerning tax rules has also been identified with respect to those elements of the tax base that are not covered by financial accounting rules. These elements particularly include loss relief and taxation of capital gains.
- There are various systems governing the integration of the corporation tax into the personal income tax of the shareholder. Most member states apply a shareholder relief system, which provides only partial relief for double taxation.

- In addition to corporate income tax, all member states levy additional local taxes. Real estate tax is the most common local tax in the EU. Additional local taxes are only levied in eight countries. These taxes are either based on profits or on payroll or property.
- As regards the taxation of foreign income the source principle and the residence principle coexist. Depending on the category of income, either source based taxation or residence based taxation prevails. While foreign dividends are tax-exempt in almost all member states, profits and losses of foreign permanent establishments are treated differently across the EU. The allocation of profits between the residence and the source country generally follows common guidelines, which have been established by the OECD.
- A group taxation regime is available in 18 member states. These regimes are generally restricted to national corporations and provide only for an intra-group loss relief. Only Austria, Denmark, France and Italy extend their group taxation regime across the border. However, the rules regarding foreign companies differ from those applied to national group members. Furthermore, the details of the group taxation regimes differ widely across Europe, both with reference to the scope and availability, as well as the techniques and function.

5 An Evaluation of the Prevailing Corporation Tax in the European Union

From the comparative analysis in the previous chapter it has become obvious that member states' current tax systems are far from being uniform. Corporate tax rates, tax accounting rules as well as additional kinds of local taxes differ significantly. Multinational enterprises have to comply with 25 (currently 27) different national tax systems. This causes substantial compliance costs. In the following, conceptual deficits of the current tax systems in the EU are analysed. The analysis focuses on those rules addressing cross-border investments.

5.1 Separate Accounting Under the Arm's Length Principle

As mentioned in chapter 2, trade between affiliated companies is an important component of international trade flows. 60% of the volume of world trade is intra-firm trade. Therefore, the issues of international profit allocation between affiliated companies and equitable allocation of cross-border income between jurisdictions can be seen as crucial international tax issues (see Owens, 1997: 1836). The issue of international profit allocation emerges especially in the context of multinational enterprises. Since different legal entities are under common control and form an economic entity, there is no divergence of interests between two affiliates engaged in an intra-firm transaction and transfer prices may deviate from market prices negotiated between unrelated parties (see McLure, 1984: 105; Jacobs, Spengel und Schäfer, 2004: 271-272).

Separate accounting under the arm's length principle is the prevailing method to allocate profits between affiliated companies. According to this approach, intra-firm transfers of goods and provisions of services have to be accounted for and priced in the same manner as independent companies would do on the market. Thus, market prices constitute the benchmark for profit allocation (see McLure, 1984: 93; Theisen, 1990:

24). The intention behind this approach is to treat affiliated companies as if they operate as independent entities.

If transactions between controlled parties take place under market conditions and are thus comparable to market transactions, profit allocation on the basis of the arm's length principle is in accordance with the profit-generation activities of the members of a multinational group (see McLure, 1984: 93; Oestreicher, 2000: 24, 124). Concerning economically integrated multinational enterprises, however, this transactional approach seems theoretically questionable (see McLure, 1984: 93).

The presence of multinational enterprises can be traced back to several firm-specific characteristics (see chapter 2). According to the theory of the firm, incomplete contracts and hold-up problems can cause inefficient underinvestment in a market transaction. By setting up an integrated group of companies, coordination of transactions via markets is abandoned in favour of coordination using intra-organisational hierarchies based on ownership. Integration changes the relationship between the economic parties engaged in a transaction leading to more efficiency and thus, higher profits of trade. As a result, the profits associated with transactions within an integrated group of companies are greater than the aggregate profits earned by unrelated entities. Therefore, the comparison of controlled transactions with uncontrolled transactions – as the arm's length principle implies – seems conceptually questionable and systematically inapplicable (see Jacobs, 2002: 857; Oestreicher, 2000: 20; Herzig, 1998: 285; McLure, 1984: 94, 105).

Furthermore, headquarter services, especially firm-specific knowledge capital, has been identified to be an important determinant of the presence of multinational enterprises. Firm-specific knowledge-based assets may be fragmented from production and can be used as a joint input for multiple production plants. By spreading the costs incurred in developing and acquiring these firm-specific assets economies of scale can be achieved. Licensing of knowledge-capital entails a potential dissipation of knowledge and consequent loss of rents. As a result, integrated multinational enterprises are supposed to be more prevalent, if the intensity of knowledge capital is high. Via ownership the risk of knowledge dissipation can be reduced or avoided. Empirical analysis also shows that multinational enterprises are characterised by large investments in the fields of research and development. The importance and attributes of knowledge capital has consequences for the appropriateness of the arm's length principle if applied to multinational enterprises. First, firm-specific knowledge is often unique to the firm owning it and other firms do not have access to these assets. In this context, the arm's length principle, which is based on the comparability of transactions between controlled and uncontrolled parties, is difficult to be implemented, because the firm-specific asset transferred or service rendered is not comparable. Secondly, the dissipation of knowledge among different entities belonging to an integrated multinational enterprise makes it difficult to identify transactions. Furthermore, the entities engaged in a transaction involving knowledge-capital are not always easy to identify.

Finally, productivity is an important attribute of multinational enterprises. The theory predicts that multinationals are more prevalent in industries with a high productivity dispersion with the most productive firms integrating. In contrast, firms that service a foreign market through exporting are supposed to have lower levels of productivity. These predictions are also supported by empirical results. Therefore, if transactions between different entities of a multinational group are compared to transactions of exporters this may lead to a misallocation of profits, since the levels of productivity may not be the same.

Taken together, the arm's length principle ignores the fundamental differences between controlled and uncontrolled transactions. Thus, in all those cases in which the aforementioned differences between controlled and uncontrolled transactions exist, the arm's length principle is not a suitable method for profit allocation.

The method of separate accounting under the arm's length principle is conceptually inconsistent with the economic reality of integrated multinational firms. As a consequence, the arm's length principle shows deficits with respect to the criteria of equity and neutrality and to administrative aspects.

To be consistent with the principle of inter-nation equity, the arm's length principle should allocate the profits according to their source, which is defined as the location where the profit-generating activities of a company take place. However, since the arm's length principle cannot cope with firm-specific economies of scale, the importance and nature of knowledge-capital and differing levels of productivity it is not appropriate to allocate profits in line with the profit-generating activities. Hence, separate accounting under the arm's length principle does not seem capable to ensure inter-nation equity (see McLure, 1984: 95-96; Schreiber, 1992: 846-847; Hellerstein, 1993: 1136; Higinbotham and Levey, 1998: 237).

As outlined above, the scope for finding and identifying comparable uncontrolled transactions is strongly diminishing (Commission of the European Communities, 2001b: 264; Doernberg et al., 2001: 312; McLure, 2001: 336; Portner, 2001: 93). Due to the lack of comparables, the determination of arm's length prices is difficult in practice. Although all member states follow the OECD transfer pricing guidelines, the different approaches may result in a range of arm's length prices depending on their use. Furthermore, the guidelines leave considerable room for different interpretations by the member states. As a consequence, international profit allocation under the arm's length principle entails the risk of double taxation. One tax jurisdiction may adjust a given transfer price because it is deemed not to be at arm's length according to their national regulations. If the other jurisdiction does not make a corresponding adjustment, there is a risk of double taxation (see Newlon, 2000: 220-221; Herzig, 1998: 282-293). It is obvious that double taxation of income is problematic with respect to both, taxpayer equity and investment neutrality. According to the equity principle, the global income serves as the indicator of the ability to pay taxes. If income is recognized more than once for tax purposes and thus, subject to double taxation, this would not be in line with the ability to pay principle. Furthermore, double taxation associated with the arm's length principle at the international level would put cross-border investments at a disadvantage and firms might then favour domestic investments.[23] In other words, double taxation might change the ranking of the net present values of a domestic and an alternative foreign investment, thereby distorting a company's investment decision.

Since controlled intra-group transactions and uncontrolled transactions are often not comparable, it is increasingly difficult for businesses to find comparables and challenging for governments to prove the appropriateness of transfer prices. As a consequence, companies are required to demonstrate that they established their transfer prices on an arm's length basis by supplying documentary evidence. In this case, transfer pricing obligations are costly both for companies to comply with and for tax administrations to monitor (see European Commission, 2001b: 263-283).

There are mechanisms to resolve double taxation caused by transfer pricing. A special EU dispute settlement mechanism to avoid double taxation is the EU Tax Arbitration Convention[24]. According to this convention, companies have the right to initiate a procedure and a negotiation process between the competent authorities in order to dissolve the double taxation. The dispute has to be resolved within two years. If the involved authorities cannot agree how to solve the dispute, an arbitration procedure be-

23 Although member states' legislation may also oblige domestic intra-group transactions to take place at arm's length, double taxation in case of transfer pricing is mainly a cross-border issue.

24 Convention on the elimination of double taxation in connection with the adjustment of profits of associated enterprises 90/436/EEC.

gins.[25] However, the EU Tax Arbitration Convention suffers from some shortcomings (see European Commission, 2001b: 279-283). According to a study conducted by the European Commission, nearly 20% of those 107 procedures, which have not been terminated at the end of 2004, were initiated before 2000. Thus, the procedures to resolve cases of double taxation are very time consuming and during this time, companies bear the cost of temporarily having to finance additional taxes caused by double taxation.

5.2 Residence and Source Based Taxation

From the comparative analysis in the previous chapter it has become obvious that the tax rules concerning cross-border investments are far from being uniform. The tax rules depend on the legal form of direct investment as well as the mode of investment financing. As a result, profits arising from foreign direct investment are either taxed according to the source principle or the residence principle. Taxation according to the source principle generally means that foreign income generated in the source country is taxed according to the rules applicable in the source country and tax exempt in the country where the investor is resident. Taxation under the residence principle implies that the worldwide income of a resident investor is taxed according to the rules provided by the residence country. Taxes paid in the source country are credited against the tax due in the residence country, in order to avoid double taxation. The source principle generally ensures capital import neutrality while the residence principle is associated with capital export neutrality.

With respect to the legal form of foreign direct investment subsidiaries and permanent establishment can be distinguished. For both legal forms the source country is entitled to tax business income attributable to these entities within its borders. As a consequence, the tax burden of a foreign direct investment is first determined by the tax rules applicable in the source country (source principle). In case of a foreign permanent establishment, about half of the member states exclude the profits of the foreign permanent establishment from the domestic tax base. The other half of the member states include profits of a foreign permanent establishment in the domestic taxable base and grant a credit for the taxes paid in the source country. Thus, the tax burden on

[25] For more details on the procedure see Rousselle (2005) and Markham (2005).

profits of a foreign direct investment depends on the location of the permanent establishment and the residence of the headquarters.

If foreign direct investment is conducted through a foreign subsidiary, the source principle is always maintained, if the subsidiary retains its profits. Due to the deferral principle retained profits of the subsidiary are not taxed at the shareholder level until they are distributed. If profits of a foreign subsidiary are paid out to the shareholder, the vast majority of member states apply the exemption method, thereby ensuring the source principle. Only five member states tax foreign dividends and grant a tax credit for the underlying foreign corporation tax, which results in a taxation according to the residence principle. In the said member states, the tax burden depends on the decision whether profits are distributed to the shareholder or retained at the level of the subsidiary. Retained profits are finally taxed in the source country while distributed profits are subject to taxation in the residence country.

The tax burden of foreign direct investment does not only depend on the choice between new equity and retained earnings. It also depends on the choice between debt and equity financing. As mentioned above, in the case of equity financing, the tax burden on foreign direct investment is determined by the tax rules in the source country, since dividends are exempt at the level of the shareholder in most member states. If foreign direct investment is financed via debt, the interest paid by a foreign subsidiary is generally deductible from the profits of the subsidiary and only subject to tax in the hands of the creditor. Consequently, profits of a foreign subsidiary are shifted via debt financing to the shareholder and bear a tax burden determined by the tax rules of the residence country. In contrast, if dividends are taxed according to the residence principle, debt and equity financing in case of a distribution of profits are both taxed according to the residence principle.

To conclude, the tax burden of foreign direct investment depends on the legal form as well as on the mode of investment financing. If the source principle can be applied, domestic investments and foreign direct investment are generally subject to different tax burdens. Moreover, if profits of a foreign permanent establishment are taxed according to the residence principle while profits of a foreign subsidiary are taxed in line with the source principle, the two legal forms also suffer different tax burden. A similar reasoning applies to the different modes of finance, i.e. new equity, retained profits or debt. Given the large dispersion of tax rates and differences of tax accounting rules across the EU, these differences may influence the decision of companies on the location, the legal form and the mode of financing of an investment. Therefore, the coexistence of the source and the residence principle is inconsistent with the principle of neutrality.

5.3 Measures to Protect the Tax Base

Measures aimed to restrict profit shifting of multinationals via different modes of investment financing include thin capitalisation rules and limitations to the deductibility of expenses associated with tax-exempt dividends and capital gains. Thin capitalisation rules are widespread in the EU. These rules generally restrict the deductibility of interest payments on loans granted by an affiliated foreign company if the debt-equity ratio or interest expenses exceed a certain threshold. Furthermore, in case of equity financing of a foreign subsidiary, the deduction of costs for refinancing is denied if distributed profits of the foreign entity are tax exempt in the country where the parent company is resident. These resrictions of the deductibility of expenses are clearly inconsistent with the principle of equity, i.e. the principle of net taxation. Furthermore, these limitations may affect a multinational enterprises decision on the financial structure and an optimal debt-equity ratio may not be chosen.

Business reorganisations aimed to relocate real investment often causes considerable exit taxes. If a company transfers assets to an entity in a foreign country, the member state where the transferring company is resident may tax the difference between the market value of assets and liabilities at the time of transfer and their value for tax purposes. At the national level, this difference is usually only taxed upon realisation, and not on an accrual basis. Taxing reorganisations at the national level on a realisation basis and comparable reorganisations at an international level on an accrual basis is a difference in treatment that distorts company's decisions on where to locate real investment. Furthermore, is raises concerns with respect to the principle of taxpayer equity, i.e. the realisation principle. These exit taxes, however, may prevent companies from the relocation of business units and their head offices to low tax countries, since future tax benefits might be compensated by these exit taxes making the restructuring not viable from a tax point of view.

Moreover, many member states restrict the deductibility of foreign losses in order to protect the national tax base. Although the majority of member states recognise that a group of affiliated companies forms an economic entity and should therefore be treated as a taxable unit, the same reasoning is generally not applied to multinational enterprises. Only Austria, Denmark, France and Italy extend their group taxation regime to foreign subsidiaries. The other member states follow civil law and treat corporations as separate legal entities, which cannot claim relief for losses incurred by their subsidiaries. Permanent establishments are unincorporated units of a single entity. At the national level, they are not taxed separately from their headquarters and thus there are no restrictions to immediate loss relief. At the international level, some member states deny relief for losses attributable to a foreign permanent establishment. These countries tax foreign permanent establishments according to the source principle. However, if loss relief depends on whether these losses have been incurred by a foreign affiliate or permanent establishment or by a domestic affiliate or branch, this constitutes an unequal treatment of comparable economic situations. Therefore, these restrictions to cross-border loss relief are inconsistent with both the requirement of equity and international neutrality.

5.4 Effects of Corporate Income Taxes on Business Behaviour

From the analysis in the previous section it has become obvious that the current corporation tax structure available in the European Union may influence business decisions. This is especially relevant for decisions concerning the location of an investment and the way of financing an investment. Moreover, the deficits of the arm's length principle may be used by multinational companies in order to shift income in low-tax countries, if the source principle applies. In the following, these effects of corporate income taxes on business behaviour are analysed and empirical evidence is provided.

5.4.1 International Capital Allocation

There seems to be a general consensus that the current differences of tax systems across the EU have an influence on the investment behaviour of multinational enterprises. An important questions, which may be affected by taxation is, where the investment should take place. The investor is prone to decide in favour of the location with the higher expected after-tax yield. This may imply, though, that large tax differentials promote the company to choose a low tax location although the before-tax yield is lower.

From a tax point of view, the effective average tax rate is the relevant measure for the choice of location for foreign direct investments of multinational enterprises (see Spengel, 2003a: 64-66). Multinationals engaging in foreign direct investments are generally highly productive (see chapter 2). Thus, foreign direct investments are generally more profitable then marginal investments. The effective average tax rate is commonly defined as the effective tax burden held by an infra-marginal investment. The effective average tax rate captures the tax burden on the subsidiary as a whole. For increasing profitability of an investment, the statutory tax rate becomes the dominant factor in determining the effective average tax rate (see Spengel and Lammersen, 2001; Schreiber, Spengel and Lammersen, 2002; Devereux and Griffith, 2003). As a result, both differences in effective average tax rates and statutory tax rates associated with different locations may influence an investor's choice on where to invest.

A number of empirical studies have explored the impact of taxes on the location of foreign direct investment.[26] Devereux and Freeman (1995) use a panel of bilateral foreign direct investment flows between five member states as well as the United States and Japan during 1985 and 1989. Two decisions are addressed. Firstly, the company decides on whether to invest domestically of in a foreign country. Concerning this decision, Devereux and Freeman find that taxes are rather unimportant. Secondly, the company decides how foreign direct investment should be allocated across different countries. In this context, they find that taxes have an influence on the decision. These results are confirmed by a study of Devereux and Griffith (1998) exploring the decision of US firms that choose to locate in France, Germany or the United Kingdom. According to this study, there is a significant impact of the average effective tax rate on the location decision.

Büttner and Ruf (2006) follow the path of Devereux and Griffith. They use micro-data on location choices of German multinationals in other EU countries obtained from the Bundesbank between 1996 and 2001. Alternative measures of the tax burden including statutory tax rates and effective average tax rates are considered regarding their impact on the location decision. However, only the statutory tax rate exerts a significant impact on the company's location choice. This result seems counterintuitive, since theory declares the effective average tax rate to be decisive for the location decision. Büttner and Ruf identify possible accounting profits through profit shifting as a major reason for investment in countries with low tax rates. With access to such locations, profits made in high tax countries could easily be shifted to a low tax country. Overall, however, effective tax rates seem to be more significant than statutory tax rates with the highest elasticity produced by effective average tax rates (see de Mooij and Everdeen, 2006: 20).

5.4.2 International Profit Allocation

In the previous chapter the influence of taxation on a company's decision on the optimal level and location of investment was addressed. Another way companies may react to taxation is described as profit shifting. Profit shifting may be defined as a special form of tax avoidance that is not necessarily linked to economic behaviour (see Slemrod, 2001: 119-128). However, profit shifting may also have real effects as firms may take a joint decision about real investment and income allocation. In particular, profit shifting can partly offset the distorting impact of taxes on real investment decisions because high taxes are less of a distinctive to the extent that income can be shifted out of a country. Profit shifting may also create distortions in real investments. For instance, multinational firms may set up a financing, insurance or service entity in a low-tax country, just to enable the corporation to route income through affiliates in those countries. Moreover, profit shifting may frustrate the benefit principle of taxation. In fact, firms can benefit from a high supply of public goods in countries that levy high tax rates, but at the same time escape this tax burden by means of profit shifting to low-tax countries.

The intention behind this is to shift profits from a high tax country to a low tax country and to benefit from tax rate differences. The most important measures of profit shifting are thin capitalization and transfer pricing. Two tax parameters generally determine the incentive for multinational enterprises to engage in profit shifting. The first parameter denotes the difference between the statutory tax rates, which generally apply to marginal changes in profits. The second parameter refers to the method applied in order to avoid international double taxation. If the residence country uses the exemption method, foreign direct investment is taxed according to the source principle and thus there is always an incentive for income shifting as long as tax rates differ. If the credit method and thus the residence principle prevails, the tax benefits associated with profit shifting depend on the possibilities for deferring home-country tax and limita-

[26] For an overview on the empirical literature on foreign direct investment see de Mooij and Everdeen (2006).

tions on the foreign tax credit. In case profits can be retained at the level of the foreign subsidiary the source principle is held up and profit shifting is still beneficial from a tax point of view.

5.4.2.1 Thin Capitalization

Multinational firms have different options how to finance their foreign affiliates. They can principally choose between debt financing and equity financing.[27] If the parent company grants a loan to a subsidiary, the interest is deductible at the level of the subsidiary in the foreign country. Correspondingly, the interest payment from the subsidiary to the parent company is taxed in the country where the parent resides. If the parent company chooses to finance its subsidiary via equity, the return on capital in the subsidiary is taxed by the corporate income tax in the country where the subsidiary is resident. If the country where the parent company is resident adopts the exemption system, the tax in the source country is final. Therefore, firms will prefer equity financing over debt financing, if the subsidiary is located in a country with a lower tax rate compared to the tax rate in the residence country. On the other hand, debt financing is preferred if the parent company is resident in a country with a comparably lower tax burden. If the parent company resides in a country that applies the credit method, repatriated dividends are subject to the tax system in the residence country of the parent company, while the foreign tax paid is credited. Thus, parent companies in tax credit countries will be indifferent to debt finance and equity finance. However, limitations of foreign tax credits may also pose an advantage to debt financing of investments in high-tax countries.

Several studies provide evidence that financial structures are used as profit shifting tools. For the United States, Desai, Foley and Hines (2004) state that both the internal and external financing of outward United States foreign direct investment is influenced by foreign tax rates. Mills and Newberry (2004) analogously claim that parent companies resident outside the United States with relatively low tax rates use relatively intensive debt finance of their foreign controlled corporations in the United States.

Similar results are also found using data for the EU. Mintz and Weichenrieder (2005) analyse the impact of taxation on the financial structure using a large panel set on German outbound foreign direct investment. They found out, that the host country's

[27] For a detailed analysis including more complex financing strategies see Spengel, 2003a: 140-149, 164-172.

corporate tax rate is positively related to the relation between debt and total assets. According to their study, a 10% increase in the host country's corporate tax rate would result in a 5.6 percentage point increase in the debt ratio. Büttner et al. (2006) also use panel data on German outbound investments. Their analysis predicts that a ten percentage point increase in the statutory tax rate would be associated approximately with a 1.5 percentage point increase in the internal debt ratio. An empirical study using a large sample of EU firms has been conducted by Huizinga, Laeven and Nicodème (2006). The said analysis shows that a multinational enterprise's indebtedness in a country depends on national tax rates and differences between national and foreign tax rates. Debt shifting may not only occur between a foreign subsidiary and the parent country, but also among the various foreign subsidiaries. Hence, multilateral rather than bilateral differences in tax rates determine the financial structure of multinational firms.

5.4.2.2 Transfer Pricing

The transfer of goods and the provision of services among affiliated companies have to be accounted for at arm's length prices. As explained above, the determination of arm's length prices is difficult in practice. Those approaches to determine arm's length prices provided by the OECD result in a range of possible transfer prices. This introduces the issue of profit shifting. Affiliated companies may use the leeway in determining transfer prices in order to shift profits from countries with a high tax burden to those with a comparably low tax burden. Indeed, it is attractive for multinationals to charge an artificially low price for goods that are transferred from high tax countries to low tax countries or an artificially high price for goods that are transferred from low tax countries to high tax countries. The low price would increase profitability of the affiliate in the low tax country while it decreases the profitability of the affiliate in the high tax country. Accordingly, the high price would increase profitability of the affiliate in the low tax country and decrease the profitability of the affiliate in the high tax country. Thus, the multinational would reduce its overall tax liabilities. The incentive to shift profits accrues mainly in case of taxation according to the source principle, because profits shifted to the source country are ultimately taxed according to the rules of the source country.

Several empirical studies for the US find evidence for profit shifting activities (see for example Grubert and Mutti, 1991; Hines and Rice, 1994; Rousslang, 1997). Empirical studies on transfer pricing rely primarily on indirect methods to estimate the extent to which profit shifting occurs. For instance Grubert and Mutti (1991) estimate the correlation between profitability rates and statutory tax rates. For the EU, Weichenrieder (2006) and Huizinga and Laeven (2007) provide evidence. Weichenrieder analyses the reaction of profit distribution with regard to differences in corporate taxation using the data of the German Bundesbank. The results of his regression analysis are as follows: an increase in taxes in the location of the parent company by 10 percentage points is followed by an increase in the profitability of investments in subsidiaries in Germany by 0.5 percentage points. Unfortunately, in this case, the results were not robust to changes in specification, and a replication of the same regression analysis for German subsidiaries abroad was not successful.

Huizinga and Laeven analyse the effects of taxation on profit shifting. Their results are based on data from the Amadeus database, which includes data on European multinational companies. The authors estimate a semi-elasticity of declared profits with regard to tax rate differences in different locations of -1.4. This means that a company with production sites in Germany and Ireland and an actual profit of 15% of the capital stock would then increase its declared profits in Germany by 2.1% if corporate taxation in Germany decreases by 10%. Huizinga and Laeven's estimation clearly shows that especially in high-tax countries such as Germany the distribution of the profits of multinational firms is strongly affected by profit shifting activities.

5.5 An Aside – Influence of Decisions of the European Court of Justice

Principally, the EC Treaty is silent on the subject of direct taxes. Thus, member states are sovereign in designing their corporate income tax. The directives concerning corporate taxation have taken effect under the EC Treaty provisions for the approximation of laws affecting the establishment or functioning of the common market (see Article 94 EC Treaty). As an unanimous agreement is required in the Council of Ministers to carry any EU tax measures, each member state retains an effective right to veto on the adoption of income tax measures that would apply across the EU.

However, member states may only exercise their competence over direct taxation in accordance with the Community law. Both national courts and the European Commission can refer cases to the European Court of Justice to test the conformity of national rules with Community law. With no progress made by the Council of Ministers to resolve the direct tax issues of a common market, the last decade has seen a proliferation of legal challenges by taxpayers to important elements of national corporate income taxes. This period of judicial activism has identified the need for major changes in national direct tax systems, both in the way they treat non-resident taxpayers and in the taxation of resident taxpayers in respect to their cross-border transactions.

Substantial elements of the provisions aimed to protect the national tax base are deemed as discriminatory and as violating the fundamental freedoms laid down in the EC Treaty.[28] In this context, the freedom of establishment (Article 43 EC Treaty) and the free movement of capital (Article 56 EC Treaty) are particularly relevant.

In the Lankhorst-Hohorst[29] case, the European Court of Justice had to decide whether the German thin-capitalization rules were in line with the fundamental freedoms laid down in the EC Treaty. In this case, the European Court of Justice judged a restriction on the deductibility of interest to violate the freedom of establishment, since the rule puts foreign lenders at a disadvantage to domestic lenders.

CFC rules were subject to a revision by the European Court of Justice in the Cadbury Schweppes[30] case. In this case, the Court classified the British CFC regulations as incompatible with the freedom of establishment.

Restrictions on the deductibility of costs for refinancing were dealt with in the Bosal[31] case and the Keller Holding[32] case. In these cases, the European Court of Justice rejected general restrictions on the deductibility of interest expenditure relating to the acquisition of holdings in incorporated companies that are resident in other member states. Such restrictions were judged to be a violation of the freedom of establishment.

In two decisions, the European Court of Justice ruled that a denial of cross-border loss relief is against EU law, if a member state refuses to allow deducting losses of a subsidiary only because it is resident in another member state (Marks & Spencer[33]) or if the deduction of individual losses is refused simply because the source of income is abroad (Rewe Zentralfinanz[34]).

Judgements by the European Court of justice make it increasingly difficult for member states to apply rules aimed to restrict the transfer of real investment or mobile prof-

28 For a detailed analysis see Spengel and Braunagel, 2006.
29 See ECJ of 12.12.2002, C-324/00 (Lankhorst-Hohorst), ECR 2002, I-11779.
30 See ECJ of 12.9.2006, C-196/04 (Cadbury Schweppes), ECR 2006, I-7995.
31 See ECJ of 18.9.2003, C-168/01 (Bosal), ECR 2003, I-9409.
32 See ECJ of 23.2.2006, C-471/04 (Keller Holding), ECR 2006, I-2107.
33 See ECJ of 13.12.2005, C-446/03 (Marks & Spencer), ECR 2005, I-10837.
34 See ECJ of 29.3.2007, C-347/04 (Rewe Zentralfinanz), not published yet.

its to low tax countries. In order to conform to the EC Treaty, member states can either extend the application of these rules to comparable domestic situations or they have to abolish them. The latter option would give multinational enterprises more room for strategic tax planning. The first option, however, may put domestic companies at a disadvantage and may result in conflicts with the national tax system. Without further tax coordination it seems questionable whether member states are able to reform their tax systems so that they respect the fundamental freedoms of the EC Treaty for cross-border activities and at the same time ensure the coherence of domestic company taxation (see Spengel, 2007).

5.6 Summary

Separate accounting using arm's length pricing is the prevailing approach to allocate profits within a multinational enterprises. The intention behind is to treat affiliated companies as if they operate as independent entities. Concerning multinational groups, however, this transactional approach seems theoretically questionable, since it ignores specific characteristics of multinational enterprises.

As the method of separate accounting under the arm's length principle is conceptually inconsistent with the economic reality of integrated groups of companies, its application in practice is difficult and complicated. Applicable transfer pricing methods result in a range of arm's length prices and affiliated companies may use this leeway in determining transfer prices in order to shift profits from countries with a high tax burden to those with a comparably low tax burden. The incentive to shift profits accrues mainly in case of taxation according to the source principle, because profits shifted to the source country are ultimately taxed according to the rules of the source country. Since controlled intra-group transactions and uncontrolled transactions are often not comparable, it is increasingly challenging for governments to prove the appropriateness of transfer prices in order to detect profit shifting. As a consequence, companies are required to demonstrate that they established their transfer prices on an arm's length basis by supplying documentary evidence. These transfer pricing obligations are costly both for companies to comply with and for tax administrations to monitor. Another problem arising in the context of the arm's length principle is that of double taxation. One tax jurisdiction may adjust a given transfer price because it is deemed not to be at arm's length. If the other jurisdiction does not make a corresponding adjustment, there is a risk of double taxation. There are mechanisms to resolve double taxation caused by transfer pricing. These procedures, however, are perceived to take too long and to take up too many resources.

The separate entity approach and the coexistence of source-based and residence-based taxation facilitate additional tax planning strategies aimed to make use of the international differences of tax burdens. Multinational groups of companies may strategically choose the location of an investment or relocate functions and risks in order to benefit from comparably favourable tax rules in a certain country. These tax advantages can be achieved if profits are retained and reinvested in the source country or if distributed profits are tax exempt in the residence jurisdiction. In both cases, companies can generally benefit from a lower tax burden in the source country and avoid taxation in the residence country. Debt financing is favoured over equity financing for investments in a high tax jurisdiction, since accruing interest is tax deductible in the source country and generally subject to residence taxation. The influence of taxation on the behaviour of businesses is generally confirmed by empirical studies.

Against this background, the current international tax system is inadequate with reference to the principles of taxpayer and inter-nation equity. The coexistence of source and residence taxation and the separate entity approach cause distortions to the choice between debt and equity financing, the organizational form as well as the location of investments. These distortions violate the principle of neutrality and thus, fundamental economic goals of the EC Treaty (Art. 2 EC).

Governments react on the relationship between taxation and business behaviour. To protect their tax bases against these means of profit shifting, member states introduced provisions such as the denial of cross-border loss relief, exit taxes and thin-capitalization rules. However, these tax provisions distort business decisions and are not in line with the principle of equity. Moreover, they may violate the fundamental freedoms of the EC Treaty.

6 A Common Tax Base for Multinational Enterprises in the European Union

In the previous chapter deficits of the current tax system applicable to multinational enterprises in the European Union have been highlighted. The coexistence of different national tax systems has been identified as a source for significant compliance costs, which may prevent enterprises from doing business abroad. The method of separate accounting under the arm's length principle has been judged to be inconsistent with the economic characteristics of multinational enterprises. As a consequence, transfer pricing is burdensome and entails the risk of double taxation and scope for profit shifting. Further deficits are associated with the coexistence of the source and residence principle. Given different national tax burdens, the coexistence of the source and residence principle distorts business decisions in various respects. In order to protect their tax bases against strategic tax planning of multinational enterprises member states restrict the deductibility of losses and interest expenses and levy exit taxes on business restructuring operations. These measures are not consistent with the principles of equity and neutrality. Furthermore, they are difficult to enforce in a way consistent with the requirements of the EC Treaty.

6.1 Harmonisation of the Tax Rate

Incentives to allocate capital or shift profits are driven by the existing differences between the national tax systems. In this context, nominal tax rates are most important (see section 5.4). Thus, a harmonisation of corporate income tax rates could be an effective measure to improve tax neutrality and efficiency. Indeed, the European Commission has proposed a minimum corporate income tax rate in the EU twice: in 1975 it proposed a range between 45% and 55%; in 1992 it suggested a minimum corporate income tax rate of 30% and 40% (see chapter 1). However, member states were reluctant to give up their sovereignty to set their tax rates independently. Consequently, the European Commission changed its strategy and stressed the importance of the principle of subsidiarity. At present, a harmonisation of corporation tax rates is no indended.

Although a harmonisation of tax rates would reduce the dispersion of effective tax rates across the EU, it would not resolve all deficits of the current tax system. Different tax accounting rules would continue to exert an influence on the effective tax burdens. Thus, incentives for strategic tax planning would not be totally eliminated. Moreover, compliance costs would not be reduced, since multinational enterprises would still have to comply with different national tax rules. An isolated harmonisation of the tax rate would also not tackle those deficits associated with the international allocation of profits and taxing rights. Incentives to shift profits to low tax countries would be reduced. However, transfer pricing issues would remain important for member states when claiming their fair share of the international tax base. Other measures aimed to protect the national tax base such as restrictions to cross-border loss relief and the deductibility of interest expenses as well as exit taxes imposed on business restructuring operations might also continue to exist. These obstacles to cross-border investments would not be addressed by an isolated harmonisation of the tax rate. Here, a harmonisation of the tax base would be necessary.

6.2 Harmonisation of the Tax Base

The initiatives of the European Commission focus on harmonising the tax base. In order to minimise or even remove the existing tax obstacles to cross-border economic activities the European Commission launched a proposal providing multinational enterprises with a Common Consolidated Corporate Tax Base for their EU-wide activities. In the Commission's view, the Common Consolidated Corporate Tax Base constitutes the best means by which companies in the Internal Market can overcome tax obstacles in a systematic way. This strategy was confirmed several times (see European Commission, 2003d, 2005b, 2006a and 2007c).

In its last communication on the Common Consolidated Corporate Tax Base the Commission described three possible scenarios (see European Commission, 2007c: 5). First, a "no-change" scenario is considered. In the following, this scenario is left on one side, as it would imply that the Common Consolidated Corporate Tax Base is condemned. The second reform option would consist of providing companies with the possibility to opt for a Common Corporate Tax Base for the determination of the taxable income resulting from their EU-wide activities. This scenario would not include a consolidation mechanism. The third scenario would be the Common Consolidated Corporate Tax Base as originally intended by the Commission. In contrast to the Common Corporate Tax Base policy option, this option would also include some form of consolidation. According to this concept three distinct steps are necessary to arrive at the tax base for each jurisdiction:

1. Each group member calculates its taxable profits separately but according to the same set of rules;
2. The individual tax bases are aggregated to the consolidated tax base;
3. The consolidated tax base is allocated to the different member states by applying specific factors (formula apportionment).

Finally, each member state preserves its right to tax the allocated portion of the consolidated tax base applying its own tax rate. According to the Commission's idea, therefore, a group of companies forming an economic entity is not treated as a single taxpayer. The collection of taxes on a group member's income will continue to be assessed on an individual basis; in particular each group member preserves its own and distinct legal capacity. Since the income attributed to a jurisdiction is ultimately taxed according to this country's rules, the Common Consolidated Corporate Tax Base is conceptually aligned to the source principle.

An alternative concept for a Common Consolidated Corporate Tax Base is to combine the residence principle with the world-wide principle (see Wissenschaftlicher Beirat beim Bundesministerium der Finanzen, 2007; Sauerland, 2007). According to this concept profits and losses of all group companies would be attributed to the controlling parent company and taxed in its residence country. However, the source country may still be entitled to tax profits attributable to a group member resident within its territory. In order to avoid double taxation, these tax payments would have to be credited against the parent company's tax payment. Similar to the concept proposed by the European Commission, residence-based taxation can provide a consolidation mechanism. The individual tax bases of all group members are aggregated to the consolidated tax base at the level of the parent company. If the source country maintains its taxing right, a method for international profit allocation is required. Basically separate accounting under the arm's length principle as well as formula apportionment can be combined with the residence principle and the world-wide principle.

In the following, the concept based on the residence principle and the world-wide principle is not considered. Instead, the analysis focuses on the scenarios of a Common Consolidated Corporate Tax Base as proposed by the European Commission. Each of the two proposed alternative scenarios – the Common Corporate Tax Base and the Common Consolidated Corporate Tax Base – involves a different degree of harmonization and each of which will eliminate the tax obstacles to cross-border business activities in the Internal Market to a different extent. In the following sections the two scenarios and their potential to remedy the remaining tax obstacles in the EU are evaluated.

6.2.1 A Common Corporate Tax Base

A Common Corporate Tax Base would replace the current 27 different tax codes for the calculation of taxable income across member states by a single and common set of tax rules. This common set of tax accounting rules would also include rules for a carry-back or carry-forward of losses. Essentially, the inter-temporal loss relief is an important element of the tax base since it links the tax bases of different periods (see Gammie et al., 2005: 49). Concerning multinational enterprises doing business in more than one member state, common tax accounting rules would clearly reduce compliance costs associated with having to deal with different tax codes in each country (see table 30).

Moreover, this scenario has the potential to reduce tax charges arising in the context of cross-border business restructuring, if the tax rules are harmonized accordingly.[35] Despite these potential benefits, however, most tax obstacles on cross-border business activities identified above would remain.

Unified tax accounting rules are also a prerequisite for cross-border loss relief, which may become necessary in order to avoid a violation of the fundamental freedoms of the EC Treaty. Without harmonization of tax accounting rules, foreign losses would have to be recalculated according to the domestic tax accounting rules. This approach may lead to difficulties concerning the recapture of losses in subsequent years if the foreign subsidiary claims its own loss relief. Some mechanism for recapture of foreign losses is necessary, in order to prevent the offset of the same loss in more than

---

35 It seems to be feasible that double taxation on cross-border restructuring operations could also be avoided by amendments of the Mergers Directive if a harmonized tax base is established.

one country, as was emphasised in an earlier proposal for foreign loss relief by the European Commission (see European Commission, 1990b).

Table 30. Scenarios of a Common Tax Base and their potential to eliminate tax obstacles

Tax Obstacles to Be Reduced/Eliminated	Scenarios of a Common Tax Base	
	Common Corporate Tax Base Harmonized Tax Accounting Rules	Common Consolidated Corporate Tax Base Harmonized Tax Accounting Rules + Formula Apportionment
Compliance Costs	Achieved	Achieved
Cross-Border Loss Relief	Not achieved Except to the extent that member states already provide cross-border loss relief	Achieved
Transfer Pricing Issues	Not achieved Transfer prices are still required for the division of the tax base.	Achieved Transfer prices are only relevant if they affect the allocation formula (e.g. if based on sales)
Double Taxation	Not achieved	Achieved
Tax Charges of Restructuring Operations	Achieved But only if the tax treatment of reorganisations is harmonised	Achieved But only if the tax treatment of reorganisations is harmonised

Furthermore, in case of cross-border loss relief, member states may restrict the carrying of losses, since this limitation would cause an allocation of losses to the foreign parent company. In order to avoid this form of loss exportation between member states, unified rules for the inter-temporal loss relief are a necessary prerequisite.

Although, a removal of the limits on cross-border loss relief currently faced by multinational companies doing business in the EU is supposed to be a key advantage of a common tax base, some of the identified tax obstacles would still remain.

6.2.2 A Common Consolidated Corporate Tax Base

A Common Consolidated Corporate Tax Base using formula apportionment would address all of the obstacles to cross-border business activity identified by the European Commission:

- Under a Common Consolidated Corporate Tax Base, cross-border loss compensation among group members can be ensured. The consolidation of domestic and foreign profits and losses would result in a net taxable income, thus making specific domestic and international rules for the recognition of foreign losses superfluous. Furthermore, in contrast to unilateral cross-border loss relief under separate accounting, there is no need for some recapture mechanism under a Common Consolidated Corporate Tax Base, since losses cannot be offset against profits at the level of an individual group member (see Herzig and Wagner, 2005: 9).
- According to the concept of the Common Consolidated Corporate Tax Base, gains or losses realised on intra-group transfers of assets are deferred until they are confirmed in a market transaction and expenses and corresponding income on intra-group transactions are netted out. The consolidated tax base is then apportioned between member states using a formula. As a consequence, transfer pricing issues arising from separate accounting should be eliminated or practically disappear.
- Just as the Common Consolidated Corporate Tax Base would ignore intra-group transactions for tax purposes it may also prevent tax charges on cross-border restructuring operations or the cross-border relocation of functions and risks. In general, these activities would no longer constitute taxable events, but rather transfers of assets within a taxable entity, which are eliminated under a consolidation approach.
- Double taxation of income as a result of conflicting taxing rights could also be avoided under a Common Consolidated Corporate Tax Base. A consolidation approach would disregard intra-group payments, e.g. dividends, interest or royalties, as a taxable event. Therefore, restrictions of the deductibility of business expenses, such as interest or headquarter costs, do not apply under a consolidated tax base. Furthermore, double taxation as a result of deviating transfer prices is avoided, since transfer pricing will vanish.

Finally, a Common Consolidated Corporate Tax Base in principle reduces compliance costs. Multinational enterprises doing business in more than one member state would only have to deal with one tax code, and burdensome transfer pricing is resolved between participants. However, the consolidation and apportionment approach may create additional compliance costs.

6.3 A Common Corporate Tax Base

6.3.1 Elements of a Common Corporate Tax Base

6.3.1.1 Guidelines for the Design of the Tax Base

In designing a Common Corporate Tax Base, the principles of individual equity and neutrality should be followed. Moreover, administrative aspects should be taken into account.[36]

Tax neutrality would be achieved if only pure profits were taxed (see section 3.3.1). Taxation of pure profits would also be consistent with the principle of taxpayer equity (see Schneider, 2000: 1243-1244; Schreiber, 1992: 830). With respect to the administration of taxation, the determination of taxable income should be objective and provide legal certainty (see Spengel, 2003a: 307-308). Tax accounting rules should be clearly defined and minimise the scope for estimations and individual judgements. Moreover, tax incentives, such as accelerated depreciation allowances, should be abandoned from the tax base (see Scheffler, 2001: 153). Instead, if these fiscal incentives should remain, they should rather take the form of tax credits, leaving the tax base unaffected. This approach would improve transparency. Tax accounting rules should be stable over time. If they change frequently, it will become difficult for the taxpayer to foresee and reliably estimate the tax burden associated with an investment, which may have a negative effect on investment decisions.

The theoretical concepts for the determination of the tax base which ensure equity and neutrality are by no means without its difficulties (see chapter 3). Therefore, a pragmatic approach has to be used in order to determine the tax base in such a way as to ensure neutrality and equity (see also Spengel, 2003a: 306).

The starting point should be the general notion that the income derived during one period should be the common tax base for corporate income taxation. Revenues should be only recognised upon realisation, even though this may come along with other deficiencies. The realisation principle is an important tax accounting principle that governs the recognition of revenues (see Spengel, 2003a: 308). It promotes an objective and legally compliant determination of taxable income. In general, revenues are considered to be realised when all contractual obligations are complied with, significant risks are transferred and revenues from the transaction and the related costs can be measured reliably (see Sutton, 2004: 91). Thus, an inflow of liquid assets has to be sufficiently assured, before a corresponding profit is recognised for tax purposes.

Designing the tax base should aim to measure the capacity to pay tax. A taxpayer should become subject to tax when she has the ability to pay the tax. Given imperfect capital markets, it is difficult to pay taxes without sufficient liquidity. Against this background, realisation should be ideally aligned to the cash flows rather than to the stage of completion of a transaction. This would be consistent with the idea of imposing taxes when liquid assets are available (see Spengel, 2003a: 308; Schreiber, 2002b: 108; Kahle, 2002: 186; Schneider, 1997: 273-285, 334-338). This interpretation of the realisation principle would also be beneficial with respect to both simplicity and legal certainty.

Whether or not realisation depends on cash flows or compliance with contractual agreements and the transfer of risks, an increase in the carrying amount of an asset should not be regarded as a taxable event. Capital gains should only be taken into account, if they have been affirmed in a market transaction.

Income is measured by reference to the net increase in value of a taxpayer's assets (see Homburg and Bolik, 2005: 2335). This implies that taxation should permit companies to deduct depreciation, interest expense, and other costs incurred during the production process. With respect to the equity principle, revenues and expenses should be treated symmetrically. A guiding accounting principle in this context is the matching principle. This principle is generally considered to be embodied in the accrual principle (see Sutton, 2004: 91). The matching principle requires expenses to be matched with the associated revenues. Therefore, costs incurred in the acquisition or production of an asset cannot be expensed immediately since assets are associated with future economic benefits. Instead, the costs of assets with a useful life of more than one period are capitalised and amortised on a regular basis over the expected period of usage in order to allocate the respective costs to the periods in which the use of the as-

[36] For more details on these principles see chapter 3.

set generates revenues. If an asset is sold, the carrying amount of the asset is recognised as an expense in the period in which the related capital gain is realised.

The difficulties of determining whether future economic benefits are probable and whether a cost value can be measured reliably become particularly evident in the case of internally developed intangible assets. These assets are often unique to the company and future economic benefits are difficult to estimate, particularly during the research and development phase. Furthermore, it is often difficult to distinguish between internally generated intangible assets such as customer lists and the costs of developing the business as a whole. To ensure an objective determination of income, research and development costs should be expensed in the period they occur. However, this would imply a dinstiction made between internally developed and acquired assets, which is obviously inconsistent with the equity and neutrality principle (see Oestreicher and Spengel, 2007: 6). Here, a decision has to be made as to whether a clear-cut solution distinguishing between different categories of assets or rather subjective rules treating all categories of assets alike are preferred.

A different treatment of internal generated assets on the one hand and acquired assets on the other hand is not in line with the principle of tax neutrality (see Oestreicher and Spengel, 2007: 6). Therefore, matching expenses with revenues requires that the amount of acquisition costs or of production costs that is to be recognized as an asset includes all relevant expenses (see Spengel, 2003: 33). If this is not the case, relevant expenses are charged against taxable income on occurrence, whereas profit is not realised until the goods are sold. The resulting tax deferral is not in line with the equity principle. Options as to whether to include certain categories of costs would also harm the principle of equity since this would give leeway to manipulate the profit of an enterprise. If some parts of the production costs such as interest or overhead expense were not included in cost values, this would also distort business decisions. The internal construction of assets would be more tax benefitial than the acquisition of the respective assets.

The full cost approach would require an attribution of indirect costs, such as the cost of administration or use of property and equipment, to a final asset. However, there is no objective clear-cut approach guiding whether and to what extent indirect costs can be attributed to final assets (see Oestreicher and Spengel, 2007: 14-15). In order to avoid discretionary results, general overhead costs may be excluded from the cost base (see Schneider, 1997: 295). Again, a decision on the extent of objectification has to be made.

With respect to tax neutrality, tax depreciation should follow the true economic depreciation of an asset (see Schneider, 1997: 264-268). The economic depreciation can be defined as the difference between the net present value of cash flows at the beginning and at the end of a tax period. Thus, the structure of economic depreciation depends on the structure of cash flows. Two projects with the same net present value but different cash flows imply different depreciation rules. Applying the same depreciation pattern to both would not be neutral. Therefore, it is difficult to determine economic depreciation in practice. Concerns about objectivication and simplification would favour the straight-line method (see Oestreicher and Spengel, 2003: 933-934; Schneider, 1997: 277, 131-135).

Under the accrual principle, an obligation resulting in an outflow of cash or cash equivalents in future periods should be recognised in the period in which the obligation arises. Liabilities and provisions are relevant in this context. The obligation to be taken into account may be either legally enforceable as a consequence of a binding contract or statutory requirement or it may arise from a normal business practice, a custom and a desire to maintain good business relations or to act in an equitable manner. The settlement of a present obligation usually involves the enterprise giving up resources embodying economic benefits. It results in a decrease in value of the taxpayer's assets and thus in a lower ability to pay tax.

Prudence reflected in the recognition and valuation of assets and liabilities is not essential for the determination of taxable income. Moreover, consideration of foreseeable liabilities and potential losses entails scope for discretion. With respect to the principle of equity, there should be a symmetric treatment of profits and losses. Similar to the recognition of revenues, only realised losses should be taken into account for tax purposes. Losses should not be recognised unless evidenced by a completed transaction. This would rule out the application of the prudence principle for tax purposes (see Jacobs, 2007: 284). A symmetric treatment of profits and losses would also require that the government grants a refund of any loss incurred by the taxpayer. A tax system with full refundability would be neutral with respect to risk. The choice between high-risk and low-risk investments would not be distorted (see Mintz, 1982; Gordon, 1985; Gordon and Wilson, 1991).

6.3.1.2 IFRS as a Starting Point for a Common Corporate Tax Base

Discussions on the definition of a Common Corporate Tax Base have largely focused on the question whether and to what extent IFRS could serve as a starting point. The idea of linking IFRS and tax accounting became particularly attractive from a pragmatic point of view, since according to Regulation (EC) No. 1606/2002 (OJ L 243, 11 September 2002) publicly traded EU parent companies are obliged to present their consolidated accounts in accordance with IFRS as of the year 2005. Member states are granted an option to postpone the requirement to adopt IFRS to 2007 for companies that present their accounts in accordance with US-GAAP. The regulation also provides an option for member states to permit or require the application of IFRS not only for consolidated accounts of listed EU parent companies but also for consolidated accounts of non-listed parent companies and for individual financial accounts. The European Commission recommends member states to use this option. According to a survey of the European Commission, about half of the member states (e.g. Denmark, Finland, Greece, Ireland, Italy, Luxembourg, Netherlands, Slovakia, Slovenia, Sweden, Malta, the United Kingdom) plan to extend the option to individual statements.[37] Several regulations enacted since 2003 transformed most standards into genuine European law. Finally, Directive 2003/51/EC enacted by the European Parliament and the Council of 18.6.2003 amended several accounting directives (78/660/EEC, 83/349/EEC, 86/635/EEC and 91/674/EEC), including the Fourth and Seventh Directive, in order to remove inconsistencies between the accounting directives and the IFRS. If IFRS affect individual financial accounts, this will also have an impact on the taxable income of companies since there is a linkage between tax accounting and financial accounting in most member states (see chapter 4.1.1.2.1).

There are several possibilities of linking international accounting standards and the common tax base. One possibility would be a formal dependency of tax accounting on IFRS. Such an alignment between taxable and accounting profits would reduce compliance costs, as companies would only have to use one set of accounts for both tax and financial accounting purposes (see Gammie et al., 2005: 53). However, there seems to be no legislative support for this approach. According to a public consultation on the application of IFRS regarding the introduction of a consolidated tax base, which was launched in 2003 by the European Commission, member states' opinions were di-

[37] http://ec.europa.eu/internal_market/accounting/docs/ias/ias-use-of-options_en.pdf, 15.5.2006.

vided as to how useful IFRS could be as a starting point (see European Commission, 2003b).

A formal link between tax accounting and corresponding international accounting standards also seems questionable, as many member states currently do not permit the use of IFRS in their official accounts (see European Commission, 2007b: 5).[38] In this respect, the Commission has pointed out that given the importance of the Common Corporate Tax Base for the Lisbon Programme, work on common tax accounting rules cannot be delayed pending on future harmonisation of financial accounting rules (see European Commission, 2006a: 7). Furthermore, if companies had to prepare their tax accounts in accordance with IFRS while at the same time financial accounts had to be determined using national accounting standards, this might result in increasing compliance costs.

Moreover, an alignment of the tax base with IFRS would give rise to difficulties with respect to the future coordination between the Common Corporate Tax Base and these accounting standards (see Gammie et al., 2005: 54). As both systems will require ongoing improvements and updates, there is an issue of how to maintain the alignment. It seems therefore questionable whether the tax base should be directly linked to constantly changing international accounting standards, since this would be inconsistent with the objective of legal certainty.

Even if the Common Corporate Tax Base would be based on IFRS supplementary rules are necessary to take into account special fiscal aspects, which are not covered by financial accounting. Areas for which special tax rules are required comprise the intertemporal loss relief, the taxation of dividend income and the taxation of capital gains.

Reservations against a formal linkage between IFRS and tax accounting also stem from the fact that IFRS are determined by an international private standard setter, i.e. the International Accounting Standards Board (IASB). Critics doubt that accounting standards set by the IASB meet the legal requirements for taxation. However, IFRS are adopted into European law via the endorsement procedure[39]. The endorsement procedure has a regulatory level (Accounting Regulatory Committee), which includes representatives of all member states. Thus, member states can give their opinions as to whether or not an IAS standard is adopted by the EU (see Schön, 2005: 141). The adopted standards are directly applicable legal norms on which taxation could be based

[38] For example, Germany permits IFRS-based individual accounts only for informal purposes. Financial statements that are in line with national accounting law will continue to be required for purposes of profit distribution, taxation and financial services supervision.

(see Schön, 2005: 142; Wissenschaftlicher Beirat beim Bundesministerium der Finanzen, 2007: 39).

Besides these technical and legal concerns, controversial discussions have focussed on the question whether IFRS are suitable for tax accounting purposes. Opinions are divided on this question. On the one hand, it is believed that IFRS and the tax base cannot be aligned, because the aims of taxation and financial accounting conflict (see for example Herzig, 2005: 213-214, Kahle, 2002: 186-188; Hahn, 2001: 1270). The main task of IFRS is to provide decision-useful information about the financial position, performance and changes in the financial position of the enterprise (IAS, Framework 12). The standards are formally intended to provide information to a variety of users of financial statements (IAS, Framework 9). However, the focus is on investors as their needs are believed to meet most of the other users' needs (IAS, Framework 10). In contrast, tax accounting seeks to compute a reliable and fair base for income taxation. Especially the IFRS principles of materiality and substance over form are considered to be not in line with existing tax principles (see European Commission, 2003d: 18). On the other hand, it is stressed that there is common ground between tax accounting and IFRS financial accounting (see Schön, 2005: 129). IFRS aim to measure the performance of a company. This is achieved by assessing the value of net assets as well as the changes in these assets within an accounting period. Principally, this idea is consistent with the idea of comprehensive income taxation. Moreover, there is a broad basis of objective rules, which can be adopted for tax accounting (see Schön, 2004; Spengel, 2003b; Oestreicher and Spengel, 2001).

However, even if the Common Corporate Tax Base uses IFRS as a strating point, common standards for loss relief, the taxation of dividend income and the taxation of capital gains are necessary, since these elements are not covered by financial accounting.

To conclude, a direct formal link between international financial accounting and tax accounting does not appear to be appropriate (see European Commission, 2006a: 10). Instead, IFRS could be seen as a tool in designing common tax accounting rules. Whether and to what extent IFRS can be used for tax purposes is a controversial issue. In the following, general tax accounting principles, their conformity with IFRS financial accounting and their implementation in member states' current tax practice are analysed and compared. The aim is to identify common principles of tax accounting in

39 For more details on the endorsement procedure see Becker (2005: 287-289).

the member states and to observe which IFRS are in line with these principles and could therefore serve as a tool in designing a Common Corporate Tax Base.

6.3.1.3 Comparison of Selective Member States' Tax Accounting Rules and IFRS[40]

The accrual basis of accounting is immanent in tax accounting of member states as well as IFRS financial statements (IAS 1, 25 and Framework 23). According to IFRS (Framework 83, 93) revenues are generally recognised when it is reasonable assured that future economic benefits will flow to the entity and these benefits can be measured reliably (Framework 83, 93). The circumstances under which these criteria are met for different categories of revenues are specified in IAS 18.[41] Concerning the sale of goods, the recognition of revenues is aligned to the transfer of significant risks and rewards of ownership from the seller to the buyer (IAS 18.14). Revenues associated with construction contracts and the rendering of services are recognised by reference to the stage of completion of the transaction (IAS 18.20, IAS 11.22). Thus, recognition of revenues is not postponed until all relevant obligations are fulfilled. However, it has to be possible to reliably estimate the total contract revenue, the stage of completion, and the costs to complete the contract. As regards revenues from the sale of goods, a definition of realisation similar to IFRS can be found in most member states (see section 4.1.1.2.2, table 3). These countries recognise revenues from the sale of goods at the point of time at which contractual obligations are fulfilled and thus, significant risks of the sale are transferred to the buyer. Only seven member states rely on the date of delivery instead. However, it has to be recognised that the civil law in each country may determine the point in time at which the significant risks and rewards of ownership are transferred. Therefore, the recognition criteria may be met at different times in different countries. Nine member states follow IFRS and recognise revenues arising from construction contracts and the rendering of services according to the percentage of completion method (see section 4.1.1.2.2, table 4). Nine member states deviate from IFRS and require the contract to be completed before the associated revenues are taxed. In the remaining seven member states the taxpayer is granted an option between the two methods. The difference between the percentage of completion method and the

40 This analysis is based on a comprehensive study the author was involved. The study was conducted on behalf of PricewaterhouseCoopers (see Endres et al., 2007) See also Oestreicher and Spengel (2007).

41 For more details see Hommel and Wüstemann, 2006: 118-130, Oestreicher, 2003b: 171-173.

completed contract method is an issue of timing (see Oestreicher and Spengel, 2007: 8). In principle, revenues are recognised earlier under the percentage of completion method than under the completed contract method. Revenue recognition according to the percentage of completion method is consistent with the accrual principle. However, it requires reliable estmitates concerning the outcome of a transaction. If for reasons of legal certainty and with respect to liquidity issues revenue recognition should be aligned more closely to cash payments, the completed contract method seems more appropriate (see Kahle, 2001: 1205-1206).

IFRS grant companies an option to revalue non-financial assets that qualify for accounting under IAS 16/IAS 40 (if they are tangible) or under IAS 38 (if they are intangible) on a regular basis. In contrast to tangible assets, revaluation of intangible assets has to be made by reference to an active market (IAS 38.8). Since an active market does not exist for many intangible assets, revaluation of intangible assets is uncommon (see Hommel and Wüstemann, 2006: 50-51). If this approach is chosen, however, it has to be applied to an entire class of assets in order to avoid selective revaluation (IAS 16.29, 40.30). Revaluation cannot ensure an objective determination of income (see Baetge, Zülch and Matena, 2002: 367-372, 417-422; Hommel, 2005: 293). However, it is not arbitrary. Its application requires that all the assets of a given class can be valued reliably. The revalued carrying amount of an asset is the fair value at the date of the revaluation less any subsequent depreciation and impairment losses. If an asset's carrying amount increases as a result of a revaluation, the increase is credited directly to equity under the heading of revaluation surplus. However, the increase is taken to profit and loss to the extent that it reverses a devaluation of the same asset previously charged against revenue (IAS 16.39). A gain or loss arising from a change in the fair value of investment property is recognised in profit or loss for the period in which it arises (IAS 40.38). The member states' tax practice deviates from this accounting concept. Most member states' tax accounting practice follows the realisation principle and denies a revaluation of assets for tax purposes. With respect to plant and equipment, only France taxes unrealised revenues from revaluation. Belgium, Estonia, Hungary, Ireland and the United Kingdom permit revaluation; taxable income, however, is not affected. None of the member states imposes a tax on revenues resulting form revaluation beyond acquisition costs of intangibles. Revaluation of land and buildings is only taxable in France and Greece. In this respect, IFRS does not appear to be an appropriate starting point for a common tax base.

Both IFRS (Framework 95) and member states' tax practice follow the matching principle and require require the costs incurred to acquire or create an asset with an expected useful lifetime of more than one period to be capitalised. The differences are in the determination of the period in which the corresponding revenues are generated. In the framework of the IFRS an asset is defined as a source of probable future economic benefits obtained or controlled by the entity as a result of a past transaction or event (Framework 49). Decisive attributes are the probability of an inflow of future benefits and reliable assessment. A probable future economic benefit is also a key feature of the definition of an asset used in the member states (see section 4.1.1.2.3, table 5). Differences, however, can be identified concerning the criteria used to objectify the recognition of an asset. While IFRS require the source of probable future benefits to have a cost value that can be measured with reliability, some member states rely on civil law and other criteria indicating that there is a distinct value associated with and a potential to sell the asset. With respect to internally developed intangibles, IFRS draw a distinction between research and development costs (IAS 38.52). While research costs are treated as an immediate expense (IAS 38.54), development costs are capitalised if several conditions indicating the completion of the project and a future inflow of economic benefits are met (IAS 38.57). If the research and development phase cannot be distinguished, research and development costs are expensed when they are incurred (IAS 38.53). Member states' tax practice tends to follow IFRS (see section 4.1.1.2.3, table 6 and 7). While capitalisation of research expenses is only mandatory in two countries, development costs have to be capitlised in ten countries. However, the rules governing the capitalisation of research and development costs differ between member states to a great extent. Thus, a uniform concept is required. In order to provide legal certainty and objectivication, research and development costs shoul be expensed when they are incurred.

For the initial measurement of assets, both IFRS and taxation practice in the member states broadly follow the full cost approach. Thus, matching is recognised as a general principle in financial and tax accounting.

IFRS define a liability as a present obligation of the company arising from past events, the settlement of which is expected to result in an outflow from the enterprise of resources embodying economic benefits (Framework 49, IAS 37.10). An item that meets the definition of a liability should be recognized on the face of the balance sheet if it is probable that the obligation will be settled and if its amount can be reliably measured (Framework 91). A provision is defined as a liability of uncertain timing or amount (IAS 37.10). It has to be recognised on the balance sheet if it is more likely than not that an outflow of resources embodying economic benefits will be required to settle the obligation and a reliable estimate can be made of the amount of the obligation (IAS 37.23). IFRS basically refer to legal or constructive obligation. From the survey in section 4.1.1.2.6 it has become obvious that tax practices differ across the EU. In many countries, there is no legal definition of the term liability. However, the actual tax practice is very similar to IFRS. A main difference stems from the fact that IFRS require the probability of occurrence to exceed 50% for an uncertain liability to be recognized (IAS 37.23) (see Moxter, 1999: 520) while in many member states some serious evidence that a claim will be asserted is sufficient. Accounting for provisions is not widely accepted, particularly not in the eastern member states. Provisions for future operating losses, for contingent losses and for future expenses such as restructurings or deferred repair and maintenance are not accepted either in a number of member states, if these expenses do not reflect an obligation towards a third party. However, tax accounting rules in most member states allow for recognizing a provision even if there is no legal obligation, such as provisions for future expenses. The corresponding wording of the rules often refers to specified types of expenses, such as deferred repairs and maintenances or, as with IFRS (IAS 37.70), certain specified business-restructuring expenses. However, provisions relating to future expenses that are not based on a legal or constructive obligation such as provisions for maintenance and deferred repair seem to be not in line with the accrual principle.

With respect to the subsequent measurement of depreciable assets, both IFRS and taxation practice recognise the historical cost as a basis (starting point) for regular depreciation. With respect to the method and rate of depreciation, there is, however, also a considerable gap between IFRS and taxation practice in the member states. Whereas the general approach of IFRS is to allocate depreciation or capital allowances with respect to the economic profile of the asset, not considering any consequences for a neutral allocation, tax accounting in the member states aims instead to allocate these expenses on a fixed pro rata basis to subsequent periods. This deviation may be traced back to different reasons, such as public policy and simplification. Restrictive rules for regular depreciation may express a tax policy of tax-rate-cut-cum-base-broadening, which seeks to attract direct investment. Favourable depreciation rules may be indended to grant tax incentives for new investments. Depreciation rates fixed by national law promote simplicity and objectivity. Simplification may also be the reason for an application of a pool depreciation scheme, which is applied in Denmark,

Finland, Latvia and the United Kingdom. Under the pool depreciation scheme, the allocation of the amount to be amortised is basically not dependent upon the useful life of the depreciable assets. Therefore, it is easily manageable, straightforward to control, and has the advantage that neither taxpayer nor tax authority have to justify their assessment of the relevant period of the expected useful life. On this note, one has to bear in mind that according to IFRS, the straight-line method should at least be applied in the case that reliable estimates about the economic profile of the asset being depreciated do not exist. Therefore, IFRS also include elements of simplification in the area of regular depreciation and could be used here as a blueprint.

The accounting for potential losses is a common principle of IFRS and taxation practice. Impairment and lower of cost or market valuation is accepted by both certain IFRS and taxation practice in most member states. However, considerable variation exists in the fields of provisions and the recognition of bad debts. While these items are recognised under IFRS and affect income as expenses, they are limited and restricted for tax purposes in most member states. This is true in particular with respect to provisions.

All member states do not fully refund losses in the period they are incurred. Instead, losses can be carried back or carried forward to be offset against profits. These limitations can be traced back to the aims of accounting objectivity and the stabilisation of member states' tax revenues. The carrying back and carrying forward of losses is an important element of the tax base. They link the tax bases of different periods and compensate limitations and restrictions of the recognition of losses in tax accounting. The rules governing the inter-period loss relief differ across the EU. Many member states do not provide for a loss-carry back. If a common European tax base is introduced, common standards for loss offset will be necessary. As a general rule, the loss offset should be more liberal, the greater the limitations on the recognition of potential losses in tax accounting.

The comparison of IFRS and corresponding tax practice in the member states suggests that many IFRS accounting rules can provide guidance for the design of a Common Corporate Tax Base. Although the objectives of financial accounting and tax accounting differ to some extent, a broad basis of clearly defined accounting rules exists, which is in accordance with the current tax practice. However, in some areas, IFRS are not suitable for defining the tax base. The rules concerning the recognition of internally generated intangible assets and provisions as well as fair value accounting are of utmost importance. In these areas, the tax principles of legal certainty and simplicity call for different rules. Further differences arise with respect to amortisation. This area of accounting is influenced by fiscal policy. Accelerated depreciation may be seen as an incentive for new investment rather than a measure to ensure equity and neutrality.

6.3.1.4 Proposals of the Common Consolidated Corporate Tax Base Working Group (Common Consolidated Corporate Tax Base WG)

The design of a Common Corporate Tax Base has been at the centre of the work conducted by the working group concerned with the Common Consolidated Corporate Tax Base (Common Consolidated Corporate Tax Base WG) so far. Three main structural elements of the tax base have been addressed: the taxable income, fixed assets and depreciation (including capital gains) as well as reserves, provisions and liabilities.

A formal link between IFRS and a common tax base has constantly been rejected by the working group (see European Commission, 2007d: 5). However, the working group has considered IFRS as a usefull starting point for the design of a number of elements of the tax base, such as the definition of income, the recognition of revenues or the definition of liabilities. Only recently, possible elements of a technical outline of a common tax base have been published in a paper by the working group (see European Commission, 2007d).

As regards the determination of taxable income, the profit and loss method is preferred. Accordingly, taxable income would be calculated as the "difference between income subject to tax less exempt income; and deductible expenses and other deductible items" (European Commission, 2007d: 7). Thus, a separate tax balance sheet is not required. However, the choice between the balance sheet method and the profit and loss method is not decisive, since both methods – as a general rule – lead to the same taxable income.

There is an agreement that the definition of taxable income should be as wide as possible (see European Commission, 2006b: 3). In this respect, IAS 18 is considered as a useful starting point. Accordingly, the working group has defined income as the "gross inflow of economic benefits of an entity when those inflows result in the increase of equity, other than increases relating to contributions from equity participants" (European Commission, 2006g: 2). Income should include not only trading income but also proceeds from disposal of assets and rights, interest, dividends and other profit distributions, royalties, subsidies and grants, gifts, compensations and ex-gratia payments (see European Commission, 2007d: 8). A broad tax base as defined by the working group would promote simplicity and reduce tax avoidance and evasion. Furthermore, it would allow member states to obtain constant revenues with lower tax rates. Thereby, the attractiveness of the EU from a tax point of view could be improved.

IFRS are also the preferred reference point when determining the point of time at which revenues arising from the sale of goods and the rendering of services should be recognised for tax purposes (see European Commission, 2005d: 3-4; European Commission, 2006g: 3-4). Hence, the accrual principle is followed. However, with respect to revaluation, the Commission Services and the member states seem to reject IFRS rules. Most member states and the Commission Services emphasised the importance of the realisation principle in the design of the tax base. If the aim is to measure the tax capacity of a company, only realised revenues should be taxable. Thus, any revaluation of an asset due to the change of its fair value should not in principle influence the tax base or the tax residual value of an asset (see European Commission, 2005e: 6). Regarding long-term contracts IAS 11 is followed. Income and expenditure should be recognised with reference to the stage of completion, either on the basis of the ratio of costs of the year to the overall estimated costs or on the basis of an expert valuation of the stage of completion at the end of the tax year (see European Commission, 2007d: 11-12). A long-term contract is defined as "a contract for manufacturing, installation or construction, or the performance of related services, the terms of which exceeds or is likely to exceed 12 months" (European Commission, 2007d: 12).

The working group defined expenses as "decreases in economic benefits in the form of outflows or depletions of assets or incurrence of liabilities that result in decreases of equity, other than those relating to distributions to shareholders, which are made for business purposes and are incurred during the taxable period, constitute deductible expenses for their justified amount, to the exclusion of expenses shown in a special list" (see European Commission, 2006g: 5). In this context, the adoption of a business purposes test for the deductibility of expenses was deemed to be appropriate. Only "expenses incurred by the taxpayer for business purposes in the production, maintenance or securing of income including costs of research and development or in the raising of equity or debt for business purpose" are tax deductible (see European Commission, 2007d: 8). Furthermore, it seems to be generally accepted that expenses connected to exempt or non-taxable income and corporate income tax should not be deductible (European Commission, 2007d: 9).

In accordance with the matching principle, expenses associated with an asset are not tax deductible when incurred but instead have to be capitalised. The asset definition by the working group incorporates tangible assets, intangible assets, financial assets and proprietary benefits acquired by bearing expenditure (rights, monetary worth, actual conditions, specific possibilities) if under accepted standards they are capable of being valued independently and of generating a use for more than one taxable period (see European Commission, 2007d: 9). Although this definition should generally also apply to intangible assets, research and development costs should be expensed in the period in which they are incurred (see European Commission, 2007d: 9). Thus, a distinction is drawn between internally developed intangible assets and acquired assets. This distinction has the potential to violate the general principles of equality and neutrality. However, recognising research and development costs as an expense would promote simplicity and objectification of tax accounting, since it would be difficult to estimate future economic benefits and distinguish them from the overhead costs for the running of the business. Expensing research and development costs in the period in which they are incurred can be deemed as an incentive for taxpayers to engage in research and development. This corresponds to the objective of the European Commission to promote research and development activities throughout the EU.

As regards the amount of expenses included in the cost of an asset, IFRS are deemed to be a useful starting point. Thus, the full cost approach applies. However, some experts recommended that financial costs should never be included in the cost of an asset to be capitalised but instead be expensed when incurred. Concerning the valuation method for items taken out of the inventories, some delegates favour LIFO, FIFO or the average cost method, or even a combination of these methods. Indeed, the comparative analysis revealed that member states' tax practice in this area is far from being uniform (see section 4.1.1.2.4, table 9). In the Commission Services' view, the use of the FIFO or weighted average cost method is preferred (see European Commission, 2007d: 14). A single method within a consolidated group is of great importance as it ensures the consistency of the consolidated process (see European Commission, 2006h: 4). From a tax perspective, each option results in a potential conflict with the principle of equality. Whether valuation of inventory is neutral or not depends on the structure of the net payments. Therefore, there is no general solution determining which method should be used. Based on current member states' tax practice and IFRS, the FIFO method seems to be a reasonable approach.

Detailed depreciation rules have been issued by the Commission Services (see European Commission, 2007d: 14-19). Assets with a finite lifetime of more than one year are generally subject to depreciation. There is a consensus that the depreciable basis consists of historical acquisition or production costs. As regards the method of depreciation, the Commission Services suggest a system that distinguishes between long-term and short to medium term assets (see European Commission, 2007d: 14-19). Long-term assets are those with a useful lifetime of at least 25 years or with acquisition or production costs exceeding EUR 5,000,000. These assets should be depreciated individually on a straight line method. With respect to short to medium term assets, the Commission Services seem to favour to depreciate assets in pool. The pooling method is regarded to be simple and efficient since companies and tax authorities do not need to maintain and use detailed lists of individual assets and their estimated useful lifetimes. On the other hand, individual asset depreciation is deemed to be more accurate. The suggested approach is to use the reducing balance method at a rate of 20%. Disposal proceeds should be deducted from the available pool, thereby effectively deferring capital gains on assets. An exception applies to intangible assets, which should be depreciated individually on a straight line basis over the period for which the asset enjoys legal protection or for which the right is granted or, if that period cannot be determined, over 15 years.

The working group also considered special rules concerning assets with a minor value. If the value of an asset is less than EUR 1,000, the costs associated with these assets may be expensed when incurred instead of capitalising and depreciating them.

With respect to the accounting for provisions, the extant IAS 37 is regarded as a useful starting point. However, more detailed rules are required (see European Commission, 2005f: 5). Issues to be addressed in this context are whether the deduction of provisions arising from a constructive obligation should be admitted and whether third party criteria should be kept or taken out. A deduction should be allowed, if an amount arising from a legal obligation or a likely legal obligation relating to activities or transactions carried out in the current or previous tax years can be reliably estimated, the expense would be deductible in the current tax year. Consequently, obligations that have accrued in current or previous years in respect of future payments, such as pensions, would be deductible (see European Commission, 2007d: 10-11). This approach ensures a symmetric treatment of income and expenses. Recognition of both income and expenses would follow the accrual principle. Provisions should be calculated based on past experience and the amounts deducted should be reviewed and adjusted on an annual basis. Where an obligation would continue over future years, the deduction would be spread over the estimated duration of the activity. This is an issue of timing. Tax neutrality would be ensured, if the amount of an obligation is spread corresponding to the structure of the net payments. Thus, a general statement is not possible. If a full provision would be made in the period the obligation arises, the relevant accrual would exceed the amount that is necessary to fulfil the obligation at a later point of time, as the accrual will bear interest. Therefore, the deductible amount should be limited to the present value of the future obligation. As regards obligations that would continue over future years, a uniform allocation of the amount of the provision to the time span until payment is due seems reasonable, since reasons that may justify any specific allocation are lacking and evidence is difficult to attain. The Commission Services also propose to allow a deduction for bad debts if certain conditions are met (see European Commission, 2007d: 12). The deductibility of bad debts is based on the prudence principle. As pointed out above (see section 6.3.1.1), there should be a symmetric tax treatment of profits and losses. Since profits are only recognised upon realisation, losses should not be recognised unless they are realised. Thus, provisions for bad debts should not be essential for the determination of taxable income. Furthermore, as this approach would deviate from current member states' tax practice, it might not be accepted by the member states.

The exemption method seems to be the preferred method to relieve economic double taxation of dividends (see European Commission, 2007d: 30).[42] It applies, if the recipient taxpayer has an interest in the shareholding of at least 10% of either capital or voting rights and the participation has been held for an uninterrupted period of at least 12 months. These conditions correspond to those in the Parent Subsidiary Directive. If these requirements are not met, the credit method is applied. The credit method is also applied if the corporate tax rate in the source country is low. In general, both methods can avoid economic double taxation of dividends. An application of the exemption method would correspond to current member states' tax practice. The exemption method is currently applied by most member states (see section 4.1.1.2.7, table 14 and section 4.2.1, table 26). Furthermore, the exemption method has advantages from a pragmatic point of view. The credit method is complex to operate in practice especially in large business structures (see European Commission, 2007d: 31). Regarding

42 Dividends paid between companies, which meet the requirements for the application of the Common Consolidated Corporate Tax Base are dealt with in section 6.4.2.2.3. For a discussion of the tax treatment of dividends from third-countries see section 6.4.2.2.6.

individual equity and tax neutrality the credit method along with the residence principle is generally preferred to the exemption method along the source principle. However, even under the credit method, distortions to business decisions in an international context are going to remain (see section 3.3.2).

With respect to capital gains, the Commission Services propose to provide a tax relief for gains realised on the sale of shares and the disposal of pooled assets (see European Commission, 2007d: 8).[43] Capital gains on shares should be tax exempt. This relief is necessary in order to ensure tax neutrality regarding different modes of financing. If dividends and capital gains on shares are tax exempt, investment financing via new equity issues and retained earnings would be treated in the same way for tax purposes. Roll-over relief should be provided for the proceeds from the disposal of pooled assets. The capital gain is deducted from the balance of the pool to be depreciated in future years. In the year of the disposal the capital gain is tax exempt. However, since the capital gain reduces the balance of the pool, it is restored in the course of depreciation. Thus, the recognition of the gain is deferred until a later stage. The question on whether taxation of capital gains should be reliefed is a very controversial one. If comprehensive income should be taxed, capital gains should generally be included in the tax base. There should be no distinction between capital gains and other categories of income. This ensures that no individuals or groups receive preferential tax treatment relative to others who have the same ability to pay. However, there should be an allowance for inflation when computing capital gains. Otherwise, illusionary gains would be taxed. Regarding inter-temporal efficiency, i.e. two individuals should pay the same tax if their present discounted value of earnings is the same, capital gains taxation results in double taxation of investments. If capital gains are taxed, the deferral of consumption is subject to tax in a way that current consumption is not. As a result savings and investments may be discouraged. Most member states tax capital gains arising from the sale of assets other than shares with ordinary income but provide some form of relief (see section 4.1.1.2.8, table 15). Relief is provided in several ways. Some exempt capital gains, others provide an indexation for inflation or roll-over relief and some apply a special tax rate. If the Common Corporate Tax Base should include some form of relief for capital gains, it should be applied to all assets. Therefore, if only capital gains associated with pooled assets are subject to roll-over

---

43 For a discussion of the tax treatment of capital gains arising from intra-group transfers of assets in the context of the Common Consolidated Corporate Tax Base see section 6.4.2.2.2.

relief, this would place investments in assets which are depreciated individually at a disadvantage, thereby violating the principles of equity and neutrality.

With respect to inter-temporal loss relief, the preferable approach seemed to be the unrestricted loss-carry-forward, while the loss-carry-back was ruled out (see European Commission, 2006b: 4).[44] This corresponds to most member states' current tax practice (see section 4.1.1.2.9). The denial of a loss-carry-back would be compensated, if bad debts are deductible. Based on the principles of equity and neutrality, however, it would be preferable to restrict the accounting for potential losses and instead to provide for an unrestricted loss-carry-back and loss-carry-forward. Since a loss-carry-back would significantly affect tax revenues in some countries, an unrestricted loss-carry-forward without any loss-carry-back seems to be a reasonable compromise.

6.3.2 Effects of a Common Corporate Tax Base

In the previous chapter the design of a Common Corporate Tax Base was examined. The analysis revealed that IFRS provide a core set of accounting rules which are appropriate for tax purposes. Therefore, IFRS can be a starting point for common tax accounting rules, not in the sense of a formal linkage but as a basis providing a common language and common definitions. The working group concerned with the Common Consolidated Corporate Tax Base has introduced possible elements of a technical outline for a common tax base. Regarding a number of elements of the tax base, IFRS were considered as a useful starting point. The proposed tax treatment of development costs and depreciation rules, however, deviates from IFRS. Here, the rules rather correspond to member states' tax practice.

In the following, the consequences that the adoption of a common tax base would have on the size of the corporate tax bases of companies resident in one of the member states are analysed. The methodology used is the European Tax Analyzer. Prior research into this topic has already been conducted. It has been restricted, however, to only some member states (see Wissenschaftlicher Beirat beim Bundesministerium der Finanzen, 2007; Spengel, 2006b; Spengel, 2003b; Oestreicher and Spengel, 1999).

The analysis comprises two steps. First, the effective corporate tax base as defined by current national tax provisions in each country is measured. Second, these effective tax burdens are compared with the results for these companies if the rules of a Common Corporate Tax Base apply. In this context, the question to what extent an exclusive harmonisation of the tax base will effectively reduce the current EU-wide differences of effective company tax burdens is also examined. The results of this analysis are interesting for businesses, as they indicate how the competitiveness of companies resident in one of the member states may change from a tax point of view. Furthermore, governments may gain estimations on whether a common tax base would broaden or reduce the tax base. This information may also resolve reservations of member states against a Common Corporate Tax Base.

6.3.2.1 Methodology – European Tax Analyzer

The European Tax Analyzer[45] is a forward-looking approach that calculates the effective average tax burdens based on the model firm approach. The calculations are based on an industry-specific mix of assets and liabilities, taking as a base case a typical medium-sized company. Based on this (in general, existing) capital stock, the future pre-tax profits are derived on the bases of estimates for the future cash receipts and cash expenses associated with this initial capital stock. In order to determine the post-tax profits, the tax liabilities are derived by taking into account the tax bases according to the national rules and then applying the national tax rates. As the model firms can easily be run under alternative sets of assumptions for key variables, such as pre-tax receipts and expenses or types and age of assets and sources of finance, they can provide reliable results, i.e. the EATRs, under different circumstances and even for different industries.

The European Tax Analyser is the result of a joint research project from the Centre for European Economic Research (ZEW) and the University of Mannheim. It is a model firm approach for calculating and comparing EATRs in respect of companies located in different jurisdictions. The current version covers the tax systems of 25 member states (all actual member states except Bulgaria and Rumania). For the sake of comparability and in order to analyse differing tax burdens in isolation, it is assumed here that the companies in each country show identical business data before any taxation. Due to this assumption, any differences between pre-tax and post-tax data in the model can be solely attributed to differing tax rules in the jurisdictions considered. The EATR is derived from a simulation of the development of a corporation over a ten-

44 For a discussion of intra-group loss relief see section 6.4.2.2.1.

45 For detailed descriptions of the model see Spengel, 1995; Jacobs and Spengel, 1996; Meyer, 1996; Jacobs and Spengel, 2002; Stetter, 2005; Gutekunst, 2005, Hermann, 2006.

year period. It is expressed as the difference between the pre-tax and the post-tax value of the firm at the end of the simulation period, i.e. in period ten. The value of the firm represents the equity, which includes the capital stock and the cumulative net income of each of the ten periods. Consequently, the value of the firm is independent of the distribution of profits. At the end of period ten, the tax value of assets and liabilities may differ from their fair value, depending on the tax rules to be applied. These hidden reserves and liabilities are added to the taxable income in period ten. As a consequence, only the effects of different tax accounting rules on the liquidity are taken into account.

The tax liabilities in the jurisdictions are derived from an assessment over the ten-year period under the tax rules, i.e. the tax code, of each jurisdiction effective on 1 January 2006. The calculations take into account all relevant taxes that may be influenced by investment and financing.

Since the model firm in this study is designed as a corporation, the tax burden can be calculated for both the corporation as well as for the level of the shareholders. However, the following concentrates only on the taxation of company taxes, since only modifications of the tax base are at the centre of interest.

With regard to the tax bases, the most relevant items concerning assets and liabilities are considered. Furthermore, the model allows analyses between accounting options, enabling a company to influence its taxable profits. The rules for profit computation cover:

- Depreciation, i.e. the methods and tax periods for all relevant assets;
- Inventory valuation, i.e. production cost, LIFO, FIFO and weighted average;
- Research and development costs (immediate expensing or capitalisation);
- Accounting for pensions schemes;
- Elimination and mitigation of double taxation on foreign source income, i.e. exemption, foreign tax credits and the deduction of foreign taxes.

With regard to tax rates, the calculations consider statutory linear and progressive tax rate structures. In respect of progressive rates or income brackets, the tax rates are entered into the model as functions of the relevant income or net assets, i.e. non-profit taxes, as under the tax laws.

6.3.2.2 Economic Structures of the Model Firms

The calculations with the European Tax Analyser are based on an industry-specific mix of assets and liabilities. The computations and comparisons of effective tax burdens are made in two stages. The first stage is to determine and compare the tax burden, taking as a base case data typical for a manufacturing company of medium size. Pre-tax data was derived from the Federal Reserve Bank of Germany.

Table 31. Model Firm's Structure of the Balance Sheet (Period 6)

Assets	in €	Liabilities	in €
A. Fixed Assets		A. Shareholder's Equity	
I. Intangible Assets	16,972	I. Share Capital	350,000
II. Tangible Assets		II. Profits brought Forward	741,221
1. Real Estate	925,126	III. Net Income	134,392
2. Machinery	697,857		
3. Office Furniture and Fixtures	39,675		
III. Financial Assets		B. Provisions	
1. Investments	40,000	I. Provisions for Pensions	408,874
2. Long-term Loans	30,000		
B. Current Assets		C. Creditors	
I. Stocks	1,538,959	I. Loans from Third Parties	550,000
II. Trade Debtors	1,453,156	II. Loans from Shareholders	720,000
III. Fund's Assets	408,874	III. Trade Creditors	836,445
IV. Deposits	750,296	IV. Short-term Debt	2,160,000
Total	5,900,915	Total	5,900,915

The use of German pre-tax data is simply a matter of the availability of the data. The base case model firm's structure in respect of the balance sheet at the end of year six (the mid-point of the ten year comparison) is established on the assumption of German taxation shown in table 31.

The use of German data, however, does not limit the scope of the model, which in principle makes it possible to start with any country specific pre-tax data. To increase the relevance of the results, the second stage elaborates how the results will be affected by alternative assumptions as regards the pre-tax data of the company. Accordingly, in addition to the base case model firm, the effective tax burdens of nine other industries are calculated. Table 32 sets out the most important financial ratios of these industries. Again, the data is derived from the Federal Reserve Bank of Germany.

Table 32. Financial Ratios of Companies from Differen Industries

	Base Case	Chemicals	Construction	Electric	Food
Profits in €	209,392	280,127	100,705	238,696	158,718
Balance Sheet Total in €	5,975,915	6,795,485	5,781,122	6,342,660	5,482,631
Turnover in €	8,073,091	9,840,933	6,287,129	9,249,152	9,989,077
Capital Intensity in %	27.82	31.86	17.56	17.34	31,40
Capital Ratio in %	19.51	27.88	10.04	26.86	19.02
Return on Sales in %	2.59	2.85	1.60	2.58	1.77
Return on Equity in %	19.19	16.15	19.17	15.26	16.40
Stocks on Balance in %	25.75	21.53	41.33	29.25	19.07
Labour Intensity in %	29.71	22.97	29.69	27.65	15.99
	Engineering	Metal	Motor Vehicle	Services	Trade
Profits in €	214,147	260,058	193,542	550,277	76,079
Balance Sheet Total in €	6,227,443	6,087,280	5,588,189	22,326,018	2,966,924
Turnover in €	8,285,231	9,431,544	8,887,880	6,547,318	6,741,779
Capital Intensity in %	18.58	28.64	25.71	13.49	19.64
Capital Ratio in %	21.47	21.98	17.85	31.17	16.28
Return on Sales in %	2.58	2.76	2.18	8.40	1.13
Return on Equity in %	17.67	21.70	21.56	8.20	16.99
Stocks on Balance in %	31.72	24.44	23.71	6.5	35.40
Labour Intensity in %	32.91	25.65	27.23	36.19	11.73

6.3.2.3 Comparison of International Tax Burdens Based on Domestic Accounting

To estimate the impact of common tax accounting rules on the size of the corporate tax base and the effective tax burden of companies resident in the EU, the effective tax burdens resulting from current tax rules are examined first. The comparison takes into account the tax rules implemented as of the fiscal year 2006 of 24 member states (see chapter 4). Estonia is not considered, since its tax system differens from all other member states. The tax base is not linked to profits, and retained profits are tax-exempt. Instead, tax is only levied on profits that are distributed or deemed to be distributed. Distributable profits are assessed according to IFRS, but there are no specific tax accounting rules. Therefore, a Common Corporate Tax Base will not affect distributable profits and thus, the tax burden.

6.3.2.3.1 Base Case

Figure 2 and table 33 present the effective tax burdens at the corporate level of a model firm with typical characteristics of the manufacturing industry (Base Case). It is obvious that there is a remarkable dispersion of effective tax burdens across the 24 member states considered. The tax burdens range from 671 thousand € in Ireland to 2,536 thousand € in France with an

Table 33. Comparison of Effective Tax Burdens (Corporate Level, 10 Periods)

Rank	Country	Tax Burden in €	Deviation from Average in %
24	FR	2,536,118	185.37
23	DE	1,854,493	135.55
22	ES	1,792,126	130.99
21	IT	1,741,721	126.53
20	AT	1,730,083	126.45
19	BE	1,670,170	122.07
18	MT	1,621,308	118.50
17	GR	1,502,147	109.35
16	DK	1,438,532	105.14
15	LU	1,396,263	102.05
14	HU	1,390,108	101.60
13	SL	1,383,574	101.13
12	NL	1,382,640	101.06
11	SE	1,311,047	95.83
10	PT	1,271,440	92.93
9	FI	1,253,989	91.66
8	UK	1,167,591	85.34
7	CZ	1,096,656	80.16
6	CY	996,525	72.84
5	LT	980,953	71.70
4	PL	960,131	70.18
3	SK	912,379	66.69
2	LV	791,269	57.83
1	IE	671,098	49.05
	EU-Ø	1,311,047	100.00
	σ	409,209	29.87

average tax burden of 1,311 thousand €. The standard deviation from the average is 29.87%. These findings suggest that the attractiveness of particular countries differs significantly from a tax point of view.

The model firm bears a comparably low effective tax burden in those member states, which joined the EU in 2005. The tax burdens in Latvia, Slovakia, Poland, Lithuania, Cyprus and the Czech Republic are significantly lower than the EU average. Only Malta and Slovenia display an effective tax burden above the EU average.

The large[46] member states France, Germany, Spain and Italy can be classified as countries imposing a relatively high tax burden on corporations. These findings are in line with the theory on tax competition, which predicts that larger countries have higher tax levels than smaller countries (see Bucovetsky, 1991). The United Kingdom is the only large member state displaying an effective tax burden below the EU average. Since a medium sized model firm is considered here, the United Kingdom benefits from its progressive tax rates structure.

Fig. 2. Comparison of Effective Tax Burdens – Deviation from the EU Average in % (Corporate Level, 10 Periods)

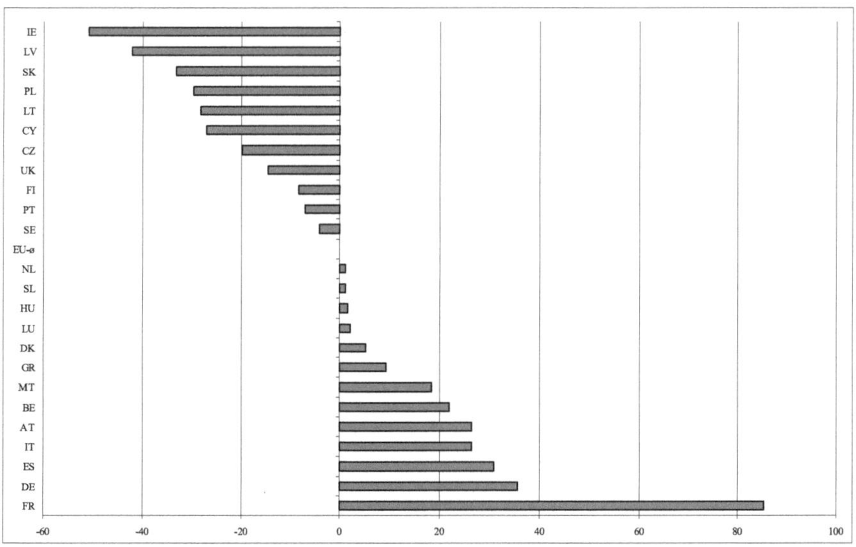

46 The size of a country is measured with respect to its population.

Effective tax burdens in the continental countries, such as Luxembourg, the Netherlands and Portugal, as well as in the Scandinavian countries Finland and Sweden can be deemed moderate.

The effective tax burden is influenced by the different kinds of taxes (see table 34). In general, the corporate income tax is the main determinant of the overall tax burden in all member states. Its share in the overall tax burden ranges between 47% in Cyprus and 100% in Malta. Besides corporate income tax, all member states except for Hungary, Malta and Slovenia levy real estate tax. The impact of real estate taxes on the overall tax burden however, is not significant. The impact of real estate taxes in Belgium, Ireland, Lithuania, Latvia, and especially in the United Kingdom is comparably high. In these countries, the share of the real estate tax on the overall tax burden amounts to more than 10%. In the United Kingdom, real estate tax makes up close to one-fifth of the overall tax burden.

Table 34. Impact of Particular Tax Categories on the Effective Tax Burden in %

Country	Real Estate Tax	Payroll Tax	Trade Tax on Income	Trade Tax on Capital	Net Wealth Tax	Corporate Tax (incl. Surcharges)
AT	5.31	28.21				66.48
BE	10.29					89.71
CY	3.80	43.80	5.23			47.17
CZ	1.34					98.66
DE	1.37		33.32			65.30
DK	7.07					92.93
ES	3.23			12.07		84.70
FI	5.20					94.80
FR	3.26	13.38		18.24		65.12
GR	1.45					98.55
HU	5.89		41.39			52.72
IE	11.34					88.66
IT	1.35		12.62			86.03
LT	12.29					87.71
LU	3.69		19.92		1.17	75.23
LV	14.01					85.99
MT						100.00
NL	1.83					98.17
PL	8.10					91.90
PT	3.13					96.87
SE	3.13					96.87
SK	4.64					95.36
SL		20.86				79.14
UK	18.18					81.82

Additional taxes are imposed in Austria, France, Germany, Hungary, Italy, Luxembourg and Slovenia. Germany, Luxembourg and Italy levy a trade tax on income. Since the real estate tax in Germany and Italy is negligible, the overall tax burden is almost only determined by profit taxes. The share of the real estate tax is below 2%. The same holds true in Luxembourg. Despite that Luxembourg has a net wealth tax besides a real estate tax, both non-profit taxes have only a minor impact on the tax burden of companies. Nearly 95% of the overall tax burden is determined by profit taxes.

A different picture is revealed for Austria, Cyprus, France and Slovenia. In these countries, the overall tax burden is substantially determined by non-profit taxes. All four countries impose a tax on payroll. Its share in the overall tax burden varies between 13.38% in France and 43.8% in Cyprus. France also levies a trade tax on capital, which amounts to 18.24% of the overall tax burden. Non-profit taxes play an important role in Austria, Cyprus and France. Thus, the tax system in Austria, Cyprus and France differs from the tax systems in the other member states.

6.3.2.3.2 Industry Specific Effective Tax Burdens

So far, the results shown have been based on a company with a structure typical for a medium-sized manufacturing business. To that extent, the differentials in tax burdens are the result of the specific underlying assumptions about the pre-tax data and should not be generalised. The conclusions heavily depend on the extent to which the factors are decisive for the application of the individual tax systems, the types of taxes, the tax accounting rules and the tax rates, which are relevant to the given business. Therefore, in the following, the effects on the effective tax burdens caused by altering the assumptions of the model company with respect to the industry to which it belongs are investigated. In addition to the manufacturing industry, the simulation includes chemical engineering, building and construction, electrical engineering, food and beverages, mechanical engineering, metal production, automotive vehicles engineering, and service and trade. The most important financial ratios for these industries are displayed in table 35.

The results in table 35 display the differences between the effective tax burdens with reference to the EU average, i.e. the EU average is the zero line. It becomes obvious that the differences between the countries' tax systems lead to different results depending on the relative weight placed on each factor relevant to taxation and therefore on the industry in which the business takes place. The simulation shows that the tax burden differentials of the EU average sometimes vary significantly. In Austria, Cyprus, France and Slovenia the overall tax burden is substantially determined by non-profit taxes. These countries impose payroll taxes, which have a significant impact on the overall tax burden. The impact of non-profit taxes is supposed to decrease in industries that are characterised by a high profitability. Furthermore, its impact should decrease due to low payroll expenses. The industry specific simulations provide evidence for these predictions. Compared to the base case, the chemical industry shows a lower labour intensity and higher profits. Consequently, Austria, Cyprus, France and Slovenia can improve their position in contrast to the base case. In Austria, Cyprus and Slovenia the relatively lower tax burden leads to an improved ranking position. France cannot improve its ranking position, because the difference compared to Germany is still too high. However, the difference between the effective tax burden of France and the EU average decreases. Austria, Cyprus, France and Slovenia can also improve the competitiveness from a tax point of view in the service industry. This industry is characterised by a very high profitability. Thus, the impact of non-profit taxes on the overall tax burden decreases significantly.

Profitability influences the relative competitiveness from a tax point of view of member states with a progressive tax rate structure. In this context, the United Kingdom, which applies a progressive tax rate structure, should improve their ranking position in industries with low profits. Accordingly, the simulations reveal that the United Kingdom shows a comparably lower effective tax burden in the building and construction industry, the automotive industry and the trade industry. All three industries are characterised by lower profits compared to the base case. The opposite result is obtained for the electrical engineering industry, and in particular the service industry, all of which show a comparably high profitability.

Table 35. Industry Specific Effective Tax Burdens – Deviation from the EU-Average

	Base Case			Chemicals			Construction			Electric			Food		
24	FR	2,536	185.4%	FR	3,367	172.3%	FR	1,447	184.8%	FR	3,130	164.8%	FR	2,223	187.3%
23	DE	1,854	135.5%	DE	2,655	135.9%	AT	1,081	138.1%	DE	2,664	140.3%	DE	1,604	135.2%
22	ES	1,792	131.0%	ES	2,651	135.7%	DE	1,039	132.7%	ES	2,633	138.6%	ES	1,585	133.6%
21	IT	1,731	126.5%	IT	2,530	129.5%	ES	963	123.0%	IT	2,462	129.6%	MT	1,497	126.1%
20	AT	1,730	126.5%	BE	2,452	125.5%	IT	952	121.6%	MT	2,358	124.2%	BE	1,456	122.8%
19	BE	1,670	122.1%	MT	2,344	120.0%	MT	935	119.3%	BE	2,338	123.1%	IT	1,449	122.1%
18	MT	1,621	118.5%	AT	2,269	116.2%	BE	912	116.5%	AT	2,267	119.4%	HU	1,397	117.7%
17	GR	1,496	109.4%	GR	2,158	110.5%	HU	911	116.3%	GR	2,157	113.6%	AT	1,380	116.3%
16	DK	1,439	105.1%	DK	2,058	105.4%	GR	884	112.8%	LU	1,993	105.0%	GR	1,287	108.5%
15	LU	1,396	102.1%	LU	2,026	103.7%	SL	859	109.7%	NL	1,985	104.5%	DK	1,237	104.3%
14	HU	1,390	101.6%	NL	2,000	102.4%	DK	811	103.5%	SL	1,962	103.3%	LU	1,202	101.3%
13	SL	1,384	101.1%	HU	1,942	99.4%	LU	769	98.1%	DK	1,958	103.1%	NL	1,181	99.5%
12	NL	1,383	101.1%	SL	1,931	98.8%	NL	761	97.1%	SE	1,883	99.2%	SE	1,129	95.2%
11	SE	1,311	95.8%	SE	1,904	97.5%	SE	740	94.5%	PT	1,843	97.1%	SL	1,124	94.7%
10	PT	1,271	92.9%	PT	1,864	95.4%	PT	707	90.2%	FI	1,781	93.8%	PT	1,098	92.6%
9	FI	1,254	91.7%	FI	1,821	93.2%	FI	702	89.6%	UK	1,692	89.1%	FI	1,089	91.8%
8	UK	1,168	85.3%	UK	1,773	90.8%	CY	675	86.2%	CZ	1,616	85.1%	UK	1,037	87.4%
7	CZ	1,097	80.2%	CZ	1,613	82.6%	UK	622	79.5%	HU	1,602	84.4%	CZ	950	80.1%
6	CY	997	72.8%	LT	1,420	72.7%	CZ	619	79.0%	PL	1,354	71.3%	PL	859	72.4%
5	LT	981	71.7%	PL	1,419	72.6%	LT	559	71.4%	LT	1,349	71.1%	LT	840	70.8%
4	PL	960	70.2%	SK	1,341	68.7%	PL	511	65.3%	SK	1,316	69.3%	SK	794	66.9%
3	SK	912	66.7%	CY	1,224	62.7%	SK	507	64.8%	CY	1,235	65.0%	CY	782	65.9%
2	LV	791	57.8%	LV	1,137	58.2%	LV	450	57.5%	LV	1,076	56.7%	LV	681	57.4%
1	IE	671	49.1%	IE	979	50.1%	IE	380	48.6%	IE	917	48.3%	IE	595	50.1%
	EU-Ø	1,368	100.0%	EU-Ø	1,953	100.0%	EU-Ø	783	100.0%	EU-Ø	1,899	100.0%	EU-Ø	1,187	100.0%
	σ	400	29.2%	σ	546	27.9%	σ	231	29.5%	σ	534	28.1%	σ	353	29.8%

Table 35. Industry Specific Effective Tax Burdens – Deviation from the EU-Average

	Mech. Engineering			Metal			Motor Vehicle			Services			Trade		
24	FR	2,756	168.6%	FR	3,110	174.8%	FR	2,449	195.3%	FR	4,431	147.2%	FR	991	161.4%
23	DE	2,239	136.9%	DE	2,447	137.5%	DE	1,689	134.7%	DE	4,221	140.2%	DE	853	138.9%
22	ES	2,189	133.9%	ES	2,421	136.0%	ES	1,674	133.5%	ES	4,133	137.3%	IT	794	129.3%
21	IT	2,132	130.4%	IT	2,293	128.9%	AT	1,614	128.7%	MT	4,117	136.8%	ES	786	128.0%
20	AT	2,031	124.3%	BE	2,206	123.9%	IT	1,601	127.6%	IT	4,008	133.2%	MT	778	126.6%
19	MT	1,980	121.1%	MT	2,159	121.3%	MT	1,571	125.3%	BE	3,961	131.6%	BE	756	123.1%
18	BE	1,978	121.0%	AT	2,134	119.9%	BE	1,494	119.1%	GR	3,454	114.8%	AT	746	121.4%
17	GR	1,790	109.5%	GR	1,986	111.6%	GR	1,373	109.5%	AT	3,306	109.8%	GR	692	112.7%
16	HU	1,753	107.2%	DK	1,877	105.5%	HU	1,320	105.3%	UK	3,257	108.2%	DK	647	105.4%
15	SL	1,698	103.8%	LU	1,842	103.5%	DK	1,269	101.2%	DK	3,251	108.0%	SL	634	103.2%
14	DK	1,675	102.5%	NL	1,831	102.9%	LU	1,267	101.0%	LU	3,141	104.3%	HU	633	103.1%
13	LU	1,675	102.4%	SL	1,796	100.9%	NL	1,263	100.7%	NL	3,086	102.5%	LU	633	103.0%
12	NL	1,663	101.7%	SE	1,733	97.4%	SL	1,251	99.7%	SE	3,010	100.0%	NL	618	100.6%
11	SE	1,585	97.0%	HU	1,705	95.8%	SE	1,179	94.0%	PT	2,914	96.8%	SE	608	99.1%
10	PT	1,542	94.3%	PT	1,690	95.0%	PT	1,160	92.5%	FI	2,839	94.3%	PT	588	95.8%
9	FI	1,498	91.6%	FI	1,653	92.9%	FI	1,143	91.2%	SL	2,836	94.2%	FI	574	93.5%
8	UK	1,445	88.4%	UK	1,531	86.0%	CZ	999	79.7%	HU	2,499	83.0%	CZ	510	83.1%
7	CZ	1,353	82.8%	CZ	1,473	82.8%	UK	988	78.8%	CZ	2,482	82.4%	UK	505	82.3%
6	LT	1,160	70.9%	LT	1,287	72.3%	CY	954	76.0%	LT	2,238	74.4%	PL	448	73.0%
5	CY	1,150	70.4%	PL	1,259	70.7%	PL	875	69.8%	PL	2,015	67.0%	LT	448	72.9%
4	PL	1,126	68.9%	SK	1,209	67.9%	LT	857	68.4%	SK	2,002	66.5%	SK	423	68.9%
3	SK	1,104	67.5%	CY	1,167	65.6%	SK	827	66.0%	LV	1,819	60.4%	CY	405	65.9%
2	LV	930	56.9%	LV	1,029	57.8%	LV	690	55.0%	CY	1,674	55.6%	LV	362	59.0%
1	IE	785	48.0%	IE	875	49.2%	IE	592	47.2%	IE	1,543	51.2%	IE	306	49.9%
	EU-Ø	1,635	100.0%	EU-Ø	1,780	100.0%	EU-Ø	1,254	100.0%	EU-Ø	3,010	100.0%	EU-Ø	614	100.0%
	σ	456	27.9%	σ	508	28.5%	σ	393	31.4%	σ	838	27.9%	σ	165	26.8%

Taxes on real estate and capital generally do not play a decisive role in the determination of effective tax burdens. For the base case, the highest impact of taxes on capital was found in France, where the share of real estate and trade tax on capital is 21.50%. In industries with comparably low capital intensity, France should improve its competitive ranking position. This prediction is affirmed for the service industry. Due to the low capital intensity and the high profits, the difference between the effective tax burden in France and the EU average decreases significantly compared to the base case. However, France still displays the highest effective tax burden among all member states considered.

To conclude, industry specific differentials can be traced back to four reasons:

- Profitability: When the profitability is low (high), the impact of non-profit taxes on the overall tax burden is high (low).
- Labour intensity: When the personnel intensity and thus personal expenses is high (low), the impact of payroll taxes is high (low).
- Capital intensity: When the capital intensity is low (high), the impact of taxes levied on capital is low (high).

In summary, the particular industry factor in which the business operates, has a decisive influence on the amount by which the overall tax burden differs between one country and another. However, the results for our base case manufacturing company are, on the whole, confirmed for the other industries. While France, Germany and Spain can be deemed high-tax countries in nearly all industries, Ireland and Latvia can be deemed low-tax countries in nearly all industries. Moreover, the results reveal a considerable dispersion of effective tax burdens across industries. The standard deviation remains nearly constant over all industries.

6.3.2.4 A Comparison of International Tax Burdens in Case IFRS Serves as a Starting Point for the Tax Bases

6.3.2.4.1 Scenario of a Common Corporate Tax Base

In the following the impact of common tax accounting rules on the size of the tax base is analysed. The harmonised tax accounting rules considered here are based on the proposals of the working group concerned with the Common Consolidated Corporate Tax Base working group (see section 6.3.1.4). For those elements of the tax base for which the working group does not provide information, IFRS are assumed to apply. However, IFRS are not followed in every respect. Fair value accounting is not taken into account, since this would violate the realisation principle. The following elements of a common tax base are considered:

- Production costs: in contrast to current country practice, which optionally allows accounting for partial costs, full costs are used in general.
- Valuation of inventories: IFRS rules are followed. Therefore, the FIFO method is prescribed as a benchmark.
- Provisions for pensions: national legal requirements prevail. With respect to the calculation of pension provisions, IFRS rules are followed. This implies a harmonisation of the discount rate and rules regarding the projection of future developments.
- Depreciation rules: The proposals of the working group are followed (see table 36). Accordingly, a distinction is made between long-term and short to medium term assets. Special rules apply to buildings and intangible assets.

Table 36. Assets of the Model firm and their tax depreciation

Type of Asset	Useful lifetime	Tax depreciation	
		Method	Rate
Intangibles	5 years	Straight-line	5 years
Machinery	5-10 years	Pool	20%
Buildings	50 years	Straight-line	2.5%
Factor and Office Equipment	4/9 years	Pool	20%

For the assessment of the impact of common tax accounting rules on the size of the tax base, it is assumed that all EU member states uniformly adopt the common rules. Since the current version of the European Tax Analyser covers – regarding the corporate tax base – only depreciation, computation of production costs, valuation of stocks and provisions for pensions, the outlined modifications of the tax bases result in an identical common tax base in all countries covered in this study. The remaining differences between the effective tax burdens are therefore the result of the different tax systems, kinds of taxes and their interactions, and the tax rates. Since in some countries certain taxes are deductible from the tax base as a business expense, (e.g. real estate tax and other local taxes) one has to bear in mind that the tax bases still differ to a certain extent even if the rules for tax accounting were harmonised.

6.3.2.4.2 Base Case

The changes in the effective tax burdens of the base case company of the manufacturing industry in case of a common tax base, as assumed here, are presented in table 37. In all member states except for Cyprus, IFRS based common tax accounting rules would result in a higher effective tax burden. This clearly indicates a broadening of the tax base. The increases of the effective tax burdens range from 0.01% in Greece to 8.1% in Latvia. On average, the effective tax burden increases by 3.4%. Belgium, the Czech Republic, France, Italy, Lithuania, Latvia, Portugal, Sweden, Slovakia, Slovenia and the United Kingdom worsen their position from a tax point of view, because the effective tax burden in these countries increases more than on average.

However, these changes rarely translate into a change of the ranking position. Austria, Cyprus, Denmark, Hungary, Luxembourg and Spain can improve their rank by one position. Belgium, Italy and Lithuania worsen their competitive position by one rank. Slovenia worsens its position even by three ranks. Overall, the impact of a common tax base on the ranking of the countries from the highest to the lowest effective tax burden seems rather limited. Although the tax base is almost identical in all member states considered here, there is a large dispersion of effective tax burdens. A common tax base therefore seems to have only a minor impact on the effective tax burden. By contrast, the nominal tax rates on corporate profits are in fact the most important factor in determining the effective tax burden. This result is also confirmed by other studies (see Spengel and Lammersen, 2001; Schreiber, Spengel and Lammersen, 2002; Devereux and Griffith, 2003).

Table 37. Changes in the Effective Tax Burden in Case of a Common Corporate Tax Base (Base Case)

Country	National Rules		Common Rules		Deviation	
	Tax burden in thousand €	Rank	Tax Burden in thousand €	Rank	in %	Rank
AT	1,730	20	1,757	19	1.6%	-1
BE	1,670	19	1,768	20	5.9%	+1
CY	997	6	987	5	-1.0%	-1
CZ	1,097	7	1,150	7	4.8%	-
DE	1,854	23	1,901	23	2.5%	-
DK	1,439	16	1,458	15	1.4%	-1
ES	1,792	22	1,830	21	2.1%	-1
FI	1,254	9	1,290	9	2.8%	-
FR	2,536	24	2,683	24	5.8%	-
GR	1,496	17	1,497	17	0.1%	-
HU	1,390	14	1,431	13	3.0%	-1
IE	671	1	678	1	1.0%	-
IT	1,731	21	1,834	22	6.0%	+1
LT	981	5	1,029	6	4.9%	+1
LU	1,396	15	1,435	14	2.8%	-1
LV	791	2	856	2	8.1%	-
MT	1,621	18	1,650	18	1.8%	-
NL	1,383	12	1,397	12	1.1%	-
PL	960	4	984	4	2.5%	-
PT	1,271	10	1,331	10	4.7%	-
SE	1,311	11	1,355	11	3.3%	-
SK	912	3	948	3	3.9%	-
SL	1,384	13	1,478	16	6.8%	+3
UK	1,168	8	1,211	8	3.7%	-
EU-Ø	1,341		1,414		3.4%	

So far, the cumulative effects of common tax accounting rules on the effective tax burden have been analysed. Rules regarding depreciation, inventory valuation, the determination of production costs and provisions for pensions are considered. In what follows, the isolated effects of the different elements of the Common Corporate Tax Base considered here are determined. Each of the simulations is based on a particular element of the tax base being harmonised across the EU. This analysis helps to identify the effect and importance of specific elements of a Common Corporate Tax Base.

– The first simulation consideres an isolated harmonisation of rules governing tax depreciation. Depreciation is an important element in determining the size of the tax base. Deviations between current depreciation rules and common depreciation rules are caused by different depreciation methods and rates. In figure 3, the changes of the effective tax burden due to common tax depreciation rules are displayed for the base case. It becomes evident that tax depreciation as proposed by the working group leads to a broadening of the tax base and thus, to a higher effective tax burden in all member states. Increases range from 0.45% in Greece to 8.58% in Slovenia. The highest increases of the effective tax burdens are reported for the Latvia and Slovenia. Thus, the current depreciation rules in these countries can be deemed comparably favourable. In contrast, the tax depreciation rules in Cyprus, Denmark, Greece and Malta are rather unfavourable. In these countries, the effective tax burden would only increase by about 1% if common tax depreciation rules are introduced. Overall, the impact of common depreciation rules on the effective tax burden is rather limited. On average, the effective tax burden increases only by 3.27%.

Fig. 3. Impact of Common Rules Regarding Depreciation on the Effective Tax Burden in %

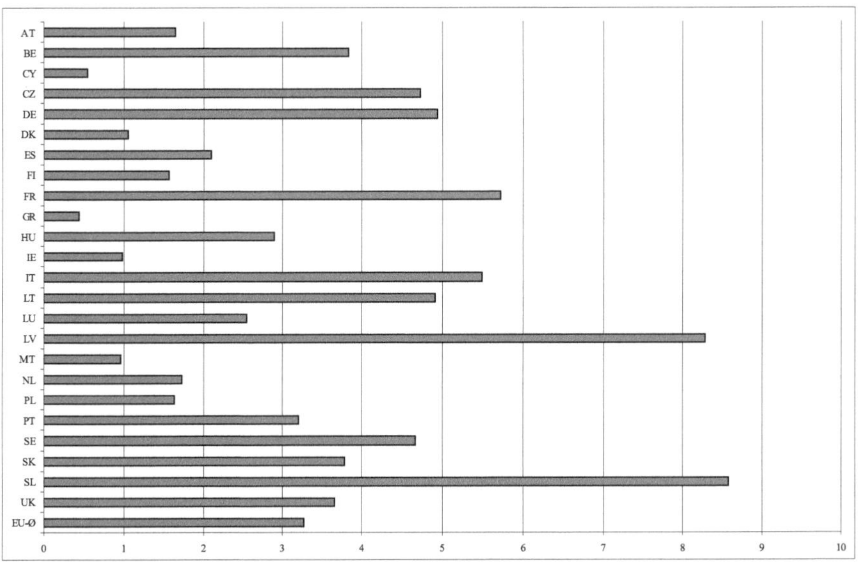

– The second simulation analyses the effect of an isolated harmonisation of methods for simplified valuation of inventories on the effective tax burden. In line with IFRS, the FIFO-method is used in the Common Corporate Tax Base. According to this method, the value of inventory is assessed based on those costs incurred for the inventory items, which were produced or acquired last. Given inflation and increasing costs over time, as assumed for the calculations here, inventory is valued comparably high. However, production costs do not necessarily increase over time. Instead, they may vary from period to period depending on the the amount of indirect costs, such as depreciation, and the number of units produced. Therefore, the effects of an introduction of the FIFO-method may vary. Changes of the effective tax burden

Fig. 4. Impact of Common Rules Regarding a Simplified Valuation of Inventory on the Effective Tax Burden in %

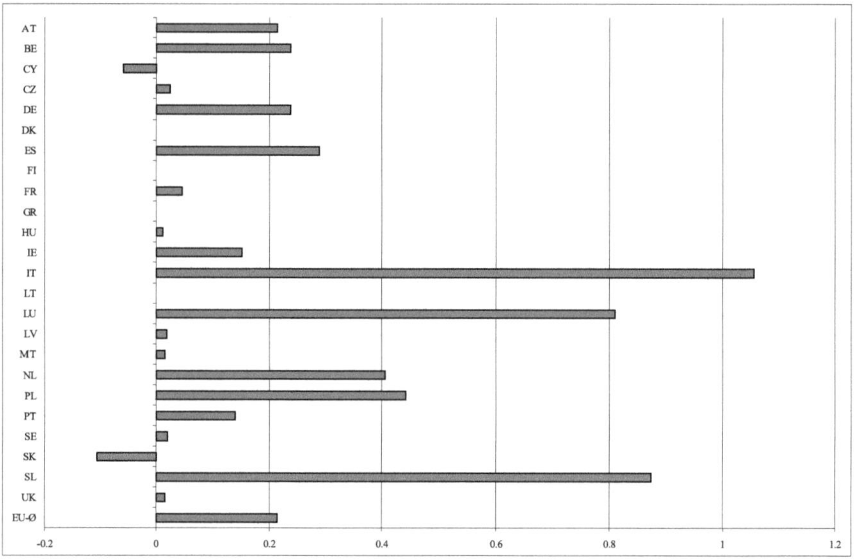

resulting from the introduction of the FIFO-method are displayed in figure 4. Compared to the LIFO-method and average-method, which prevail in most member states, the FIFO-method results in a comparably broad tax base in most countries. It is obvious that the method used for the assessment of inventory has a rather limited impact on the size of the tax base and the resulting effective tax burden. Changes range from -0.1% in Slovakia to 1.06% in Italy. The decrease of the effective tax burden in Cyprus and Slovakia can be explained as follows: According to current national tax law, both countries require inventory to be assessed according to the average-method. The application of the FIFO-method leads to comparably higher tax payments. Due to the higher tax payments, the liquidity of the model firm is not sufficient to pay a dividend, at least in some periods. Thus, the higher tax payment is compensated by a lower dividend payment. Furthermore, the hidden liabilities built up under the FIFO-method reduce the tax payment in period ten. Taken together, these effects lead to a lower effective tax burden in Cyprus and Slovakia.

- The third simulation investigates the effect of common rules for the determination of production costs. Depending on the rules for the determination of production costs, expenses are either tax deductible in the period in which they are incurred or capitalised and their deduction is deferred to the period in which the asset is sold. According to IFRS the full-cost approach is used to determine the production costs. Accordingly, not only direct costs but also indirect costs associated with the production

Fig. 5. Impact of Common Rules Regarding the Determination of Production Costs on the Effective Tax Burden in %

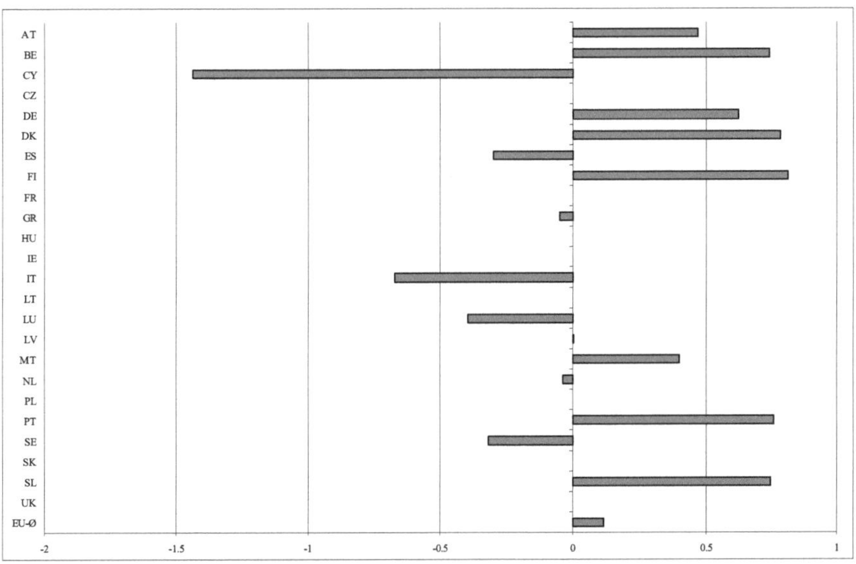

process have to be included in production cost. This approach is assumed to apply to the Common Corporate Tax Base. From the results presented in figure 5 it becomes evident that the effective tax burden would not change significantly. In the Czech Republic, France, Greece, Hungary, Ireland, Lithuania, Poland, Slovakia and the United Kingdom, the effective tax burden does not change at all. This indicates that the current tax practice in these countries is already in line with IFRS. Increases of the effective tax burden are presented for Austria, Belgium, Denmark, Finland, Germany, Latvia, Malta, Portugal and Slovenia. In these countries' current tax practice, not all indirect costs are currently included in the production costs. In contrast, the effective tax burden decreases in Cyprus, Italy, Luxembourg, the Netherlands, Spain and Sweden. These countries prescribe research and development costs to be capitalised. Thus, production costs according to the current tax law are higher compared to the production costs under the Common Corporate Tax Base.

- The last simulation deals with the effect of common rules regarding provisions for pensions. In this field, the member states' tax practices differ significantly. Funded retirement benefits are common in most member states. With respect to unfunded retirement benefits, only Austria, Germany, Luxembourg and the Netherlands allow for tax-effective pension provisions. The majority of member states require a funded retirement plan to be established. Only if this requirement is fulfilled, are the contributions tax-deductible. The amount of tax-deductible contributions to a pension fund or a pension provision depends on several factors. Most decisive are the pension scheme, the structure of personell, and consequences of the interest yield arising from the accumulated capital.[47] According to IAS 19, the obligation should be calculated based on actuarial assumptions, taking into account probabilities of entrance and future salary increases. The obligation should be allocated to the expected length of the service period (IAS 19). With respect to the discount rate there are no legal requirements. An important reference point should be the rate of high quality corporate bonds (IAS 19.78). Here, a discount rate of 3% is assumed. Most member states' tax practice is conform to IAS. The simulations indicate that common tax accounting rules concerning pensions based on IAS would result in a change of the effective tax burden only in Austria, Germany and the Netherlands (see figure 7). In these three countries, a common tax base would lead to a reduction of the effective tax burden. This result stems mainly from different discount rates. Austria and Germany require a discount rate of 6%. The discount rate in the Netherlands is fixed at 4%. Furthermore, in Austria and Germany, future salary increases are not taken into account. Thus, the obligation as determined under national law is lower than under the common tax accounting rules considered here.

---

47 For a detailed description of the assumptions made in the European Tax Analyser, see Spengel, 1995: 177-190.

Fig. 6. Impact of Common Rules Regarding Pension Provisions on the Effective Tax Burden in %

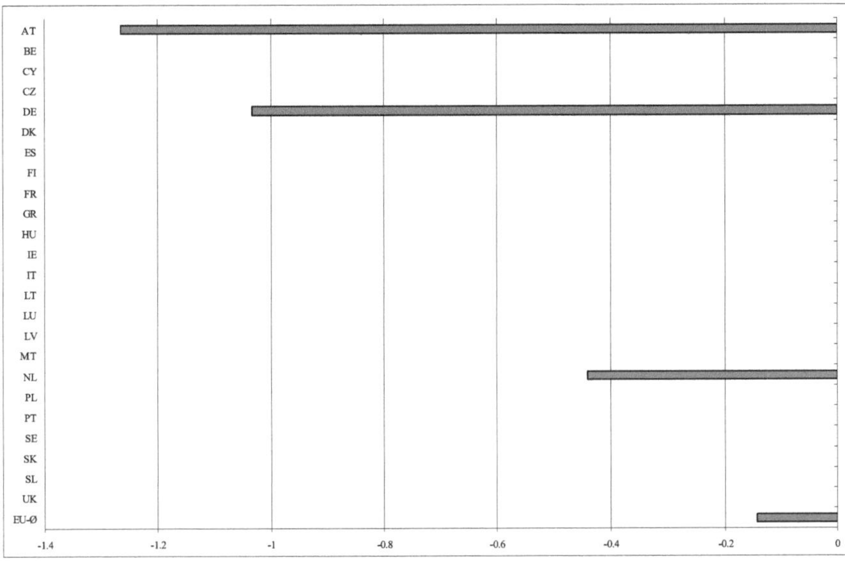

To conclude, the introduction of a Common Corporate Tax Base does not have a significant impact on the effective tax burden. Thus, tax accounting rules are less important. Instead, the main determinant of the effective tax burden is the nominal tax rate on profits. Other kinds of taxes have only a minor effect on the tax burden. The most significant changes of the tax burden are caused by the different tax depreciation methods and rates.

Although there are only slight changes in the tax burden for the base case, this result should not be generalised, since it is derived for a company with economic characteristics typical for the manufacturing industry. The changes concerning the different elements of the tax base will lead to different effects on the tax burden, depending on the characteristics of the model firm. As an example, a change of the depreciation rules will have a more significant effect on the tax burden for a model firm with a high capital intensity. Similarly, the rules governing a simplified valuation of inventory will become more important for a model firm with a high stock level on balance. To generalise the effects of a common tax base on the effective tax burden found for the model firm of the base case, different industries are taken into account in the following.

6.3.2.4.3 Sensitivity Analysis: Effects in Different Industries

The following shows the impact on the overall effective tax burden of a common tax base for the other industries (see table 38). The results of the simulations for the different industries correspond to those for our base case company. In nearly all considered member states, a common tax base results in higher effective tax burdens. The most significant increases in tax burdens can be observed in Latvia, Italy and Belgium with up to 15.4%, as opposed to Cyprus, Denmark and Greece, where increases are below 3%. On average the effective tax burden increases 8.8% in Latvia, 6.6% in Italy and 5.9% in Belgium, while it increases only 0.2% in Cyprus, 0.4% in Greece and 0.7% in Denmark. A reduction in tax burdens can be observed for the majority of industries in Cyprus ranging between -0.1% and -1%. Decreases can also be found in Denmark for companies of the food and automotive sector and in Ireland for companies of the services sector. On average, however, non of the considered member states displays a decrease.

If the focus shifts to the industries with their different characteristics, the highest overall increase is found in the automotive industry. This result stems mainly from comparably high intensities of inventory and capital in combination with a comparably low profitability. A high capital intensity increases the effect of common depreciation rules. Similarly, a high level of stock on balance leads to a stronger effect of common rules concerning the valuation of inventories. These effects are further increased in sectors with a low profitability, because the impact of the tax base on the effective tax base increases as well. The relationship between the capital intensity and tax depreciation becomes particularly obvious in Latvia. The increase of the tax burden caused by the common tax base is lower in industries with a comparably low capital intensity and a higher profitability, such as the electric industry and the service industry. As analysed in the previous chapter, Austria and Germany benefit from common tax accounting rules concerning pension provisions. These benefits increase with an increasing labour intensity. This reasoning becomes evident for companies in the service sector.

Table 38. Changes in the Tax Burden Resulting from a Common Corporate Tax Base for Different Industries in Each Country

	Base Case	Chemicals	Construction	Electric	Food	Mech. Eng.	Metal	Motor Vehicle	Services	Trade	Ø
AT	1.6%	1.6%	4.2%	0.8%	2.7%	1.2%	1.4%	2.6%	1.0%	1.6%	1.9%
BE	5.9%	5.3%	11.1%	2.1%	11.0%	4.5%	3.3%	11.6%	1.4%	2.9%	5.9%
CY	-1.0%	0.5%	-0.2%	-0.3%	0.3%	0.6%	-0.7%	3.0%	-0.6%	-0.1%	0.2%
CZ	4.8%	5.2%	6.2%	1.7%	11.1%	3.0%	2.7%	12.7%	1.4%	2.2%	5.1%
DE	2.5%	3.5%	7.2%	0.9%	7.5%	2.5%	1.5%	7.6%	1.0%	1.8%	3.6%
DK	1.4%	0.4%	1.1%	1.0%	-1.0%	0.8%	1.4%	-0.5%	0.6%	1.5%	0.7%
ES	2.1%	1.4%	4.5%	1.1%	2.1%	1.4%	1.7%	2.7%	0.8%	0.7%	1.9%
FI	2.8%	3.6%	4.9%	1.3%	7.3%	2.7%	1.9%	7.5%	1.2%	1.6%	3.5%
FR	5.8%	4.2%	7.6%	1.0%	8.1%	4.5%	2.3%	8.9%	0.7%	1.2%	4.4%
GR	0.1%	0.4%	2.2%	0.0%	0.6%	0.0%	0.2%	0.8%	0.0%	0.0%	0.4%
HU	3.0%	4.3%	5.7%	0.6%	6.0%	3.6%	0.6%	7.6%	0.8%	1.3%	3.4%
IE	1.0%	0.9%	1.4%	0.1%	3.1%	0.6%	0.0%	5.9%	-0.2%	0.8%	1.4%
IT	6.0%	6.1%	11.4%	3.2%	11.5%	4.5%	4.2%	11.6%	3.0%	4.2%	6.6%
LT	4.9%	5.3%	5.8%	2.2%	11.4%	3.3%	2.9%	11.7%	3.4%	3.6%	5.4%
LU	2.8%	3.0%	4.6%	1.5%	5.1%	2.2%	2.2%	5.7%	1.3%	1.1%	2.9%
LV	8.1%	9.6%	9.0%	4.6%	15.4%	5.5%	6.5%	14.2%	7.9%	7.5%	8.8%
MT	1.8%	2.7%	5.1%	0.9%	5.4%	2.3%	1.3%	6.3%	1.0%	0.4%	2.7%
NL	1.1%	2.2%	3.8%	0.7%	5.2%	1.5%	0.8%	4.8%	0.8%	1.7%	2.3%
PL	2.5%	3.7%	6.7%	1.2%	8.8%	2.8%	1.5%	9.4%	1.4%	1.8%	4.0%
PT	4.7%	4.5%	7.4%	2.2%	9.4%	3.8%	3.4%	9.9%	1.3%	2.4%	4.9%
SE	3.3%	3.7%	4.2%	1.8%	6.9%	2.5%	2.6%	8.6%	1.3%	0.8%	3.6%
SK	3.9%	4.4%	5.2%	1.8%	9.8%	2.7%	2.4%	10.3%	2.6%	2.9%	4.6%
SL	6.8%	3.4%	5.7%	3.1%	7.4%	4.2%	4.0%	11.9%	2.0%	1.7%	5.0%
UK	3.7%	6.5%	3.2%	1.4%	7.6%	3.1%	3.6%	8.7%	0.2%	1.0%	3.9%
EU-Ø	3.4%	3.5%	5.5%	1.4%	6.6%	2.7%	2.1%	7.4%	1.3%	1.8%	3.6%

6.3.2.4.4 Dispersions of Effective Tax Burdens across Industries

With respect to the future development of company taxation in Europe, it is interesting for policy makers to see the impact of a Common Corporate Tax Base on the dispersion of effective tax burdens across industries. Table 39 displays the differences of the effective tax burdens for the different industries from the EU average in case of a common tax base.

If one compares the industry-specific standard deviations across the EU for the two scenarios – i.e. current tax accounting (Table 35) and IFRS-based tax accounting (Table 39) – it becomes evident that a closer coordination of tax accounting rules is not likely to reduce cross-industry differences of effective tax burdens significantly. Under current member states' tax practice the standard deviations range between 26.8% and 31.4% and under a Common Corporate Tax Base the standard deviations range between 26.6% and 31.1%. Thus, a meaningful convergence of the tax competitive situation for different industries within the EU demands more than just the harmonisation of tax accounting rules. The remaining differences in tax burdens reflect the effects of the different tax systems, especially different kinds of taxes and tax rates. Thus, when harmonising the tax base, the characteristics of the tax schedule and the number and types of taxes determine a country's competitive international tax position.

It has already been pointed out above that the shift from domestic to common tax accounting would tend to increase effective company tax burdens in most member states. Thus, ideally, member states would have the opportunity to reduce their nominal tax rates at the same time without affecting the effective company tax burdens. A reduction of the tax rates therefore, would not only increase the attractiveness of member states as a place of location for companies. Assumingly it would reduce dispersions of effective tax burdens across industries at the same time, since the impact of accounting and of shifting profits to different periods respectively would decrease.

Table 39. Differences between the Effective Tax Burdens in Case of

	Base Case			Chemicals			Construction			Electric			Food		
24	FR	2,683	189.7%	FR	3,508	173.4%	FR	1,557	188.4%	FR	3,162	164.2%	FR	2,403	189.9%
23	DE	1,901	134.4%	DE	2,748	135.9%	AT	1,127	136.3%	DE	2,687	139.5%	DE	1,725	136.3%
22	IT	1,834	129.7%	ES	2,689	133.0%	DE	1,114	134.8%	ES	2,662	138.3%	ES	1,618	127.9%
21	ES	1,830	129.4%	IT	2,685	132.8%	IT	1,061	128.4%	IT	2,539	131.9%	BE	1,616	127.8%
20	BE	1,768	125.0%	BE	2,582	127.7%	BE	1,013	122.6%	BE	2,387	124.0%	IT	1,616	127.7%
19	AT	1,757	124.3%	MT	2,408	119.1%	ES	1,007	121.8%	MT	2,378	123.5%	MT	1,577	124.7%
18	MT	1,650	116.7%	AT	2,306	114.0%	MT	982	118.8%	AT	2,285	118.7%	HU	1,480	117.0%
17	GR	1,497	105.9%	GR	2,167	107.2%	HU	963	116.5%	GR	2,157	112.0%	AT	1,418	112.1%
16	SL	1,478	104.5%	LU	2,086	103.1%	SL	909	109.9%	LU	2,023	105.1%	GR	1,296	102.4%
15	DK	1,458	103.1%	DK	2,066	102.2%	GR	903	109.2%	SL	2,022	105.0%	LU	1,263	99.9%
14	LU	1,435	101.5%	NL	2,045	101.1%	DK	819	99.2%	NL	1,998	103.8%	NL	1,242	98.2%
13	HU	1,431	101.2%	HU	2,027	100.2%	LU	804	97.3%	DK	1,977	102.7%	DK	1,225	96.8%
12	NL	1,397	98.8%	SL	1,996	98.7%	NL	790	95.6%	SE	1,916	99.5%	SE	1,207	95.4%
11	SE	1,355	95.8%	SE	1,975	97.6%	SE	771	93.3%	PT	1,883	97.8%	SL	1,206	95.4%
10	PT	1,331	94.1%	PT	1,948	96.3%	PT	759	91.8%	FI	1,803	93.6%	PT	1,201	95.0%
9	FI	1,290	91.2%	UK	1,889	93.4%	FI	736	89.1%	UK	1,716	89.1%	FI	1,169	92.4%
8	UK	1,211	85.6%	FI	1,887	93.3%	CY	674	81.5%	CZ	1,644	85.4%	UK	1,116	88.2%
7	CZ	1,150	81.3%	CZ	1,697	83.9%	CZ	657	79.5%	HU	1,613	83.7%	CZ	1,056	83.5%
6	LT	1,029	72.8%	LT	1,495	73.9%	UK	642	77.7%	LT	1,379	71.6%	LT	936	74.0%
5	CY	987	69.8%	PL	1,471	72.7%	LT	592	71.6%	PL	1,371	71.2%	PL	935	73.9%
4	PL	984	69.6%	SK	1,401	69.3%	PL	545	66.0%	SK	1,339	69.5%	SK	872	68.9%
3	SK	948	67.0%	LV	1,246	61.6%	SK	534	64.6%	CY	1,231	63.9%	LV	786	62.1%
2	LV	856	60.5%	CY	1,230	60.8%	LV	491	59.4%	LV	1,125	58.4%	CY	784	62.0%
1	IE	678	47.9%	IE	988	48.8%	IE	386	46.7%	IE	918	47.7%	IE	613	48.5%
	EU-Ø	1,414	100.0%	EU-Ø	2,022	100.0%	EU-Ø	827	100.0%	EU-Ø	1,926	100.0%	EU-Ø	1,265	100.0%
	σ	420	29.7%	σ	563	27.8%	σ	251	30.4%	σ	539	28.0%	σ	376	29.7%

Table 39. Differences between the Effective Tax Burdens in Case of

	Mech. Engineering			Metal			Motor Vehicle			Services			Trade		
24	FR	2,880	171.5%	FR	3,182	175.0%	FR	2,666	198.0%	FR	4,462	146.3%	FR	1,003	160.5%
23	DE	2,294	136.7%	DE	2,484	136.6%	DE	1,817	134.9%	DE	4,265	139.8%	DE	868	138.9%
22	IT	2,228	132.7%	ES	2,463	135.5%	IT	1,787	132.7%	ES	4,165	136.6%	IT	828	132.5%
21	ES	2,220	132.2%	IT	2,390	131.5%	ES	1,720	127.7%	MT	4,158	136.3%	ES	791	126.6%
20	BE	2,066	123.0%	BE	2,278	125.3%	MT	1,670	124.0%	IT	4,128	135.3%	MT	781	124.9%
19	AT	2,055	122.4%	MT	2,186	120.3%	BE	1,667	123.8%	BE	4,017	131.7%	BE	778	124.5%
18	MT	2,025	120.6%	AT	2,162	119.0%	AT	1,655	122.9%	GR	3,454	113.2%	AT	758	121.2%
17	HU	1,816	108.2%	GR	1,990	109.5%	HU	1,420	105.5%	AT	3,340	109.5%	GR	692	110.7%
16	GR	1,790	106.6%	DK	1,902	104.7%	SL	1,400	103.9%	DK	3,270	107.2%	DK	657	105.1%
15	SL	1,768	105.3%	LU	1,882	103.5%	GR	1,384	102.8%	UK	3,265	107.0%	SL	644	103.1%
14	LU	1,712	101.9%	SL	1,868	102.8%	LU	1,339	99.4%	LU	3,181	104.3%	HU	642	102.7%
13	DK	1,689	100.6%	NL	1,846	101.6%	NL	1,324	98.3%	NL	3,110	102.0%	LU	640	102.4%
12	NL	1,688	100.6%	SE	1,778	97.8%	SE	1,280	95.1%	SE	3,049	100.0%	NL	628	100.5%
11	SE	1,625	96.8%	PT	1,747	96.1%	PT	1,275	94.7%	PT	2,952	96.8%	SE	613	98.2%
10	PT	1,600	95.3%	HU	1,716	94.4%	DK	1,263	93.8%	SL	2,894	94.9%	PT	602	96.4%
9	FI	1,539	91.6%	FI	1,685	92.7%	FI	1,229	91.3%	FI	2,873	94.2%	FI	584	93.4%
8	UK	1,490	88.8%	UK	1,587	87.3%	CZ	1,126	83.6%	HU	2,520	82.6%	CZ	521	83.4%
7	CZ	1,394	83.0%	CZ	1,512	83.2%	UK	1,074	79.7%	CZ	2,516	82.5%	UK	511	81.7%
6	LT	1,198	71.3%	LT	1,325	72.9%	CY	983	73.0%	LT	2,314	75.9%	LT	464	74.2%
5	CY	1,158	68.9%	PL	1,277	70.2%	LT	958	71.1%	SK	2,054	67.3%	PL	456	73.0%
4	PL	1,158	68.9%	SK	1,239	68.2%	PL	958	71.1%	PL	2,043	67.0%	SK	435	69.6%
3	SK	1,134	67.5%	CY	1,159	63.8%	SK	913	67.8%	LV	1,964	64.4%	CY	404	64.7%
2	LV	981	58.4%	LV	1,096	60.3%	LV	788	58.5%	CY	1,665	54.6%	LV	390	62.4%
1	IE	790	47.1%	IE	875	48.2%	IE	627	46.5%	IE	1,540	50.5%	IE	309	49.4%
	EU-Ø	1,679	100.0%	EU-Ø	1,818	100.0%	EU-Ø	1,347	100.0%	EU-Ø	3,050	100.0%	EU-Ø	625	100.0%
	σ	473	28.1%	σ	519	28.5%	σ	419	31.1%	σ	841	27.6%	σ	166	26.6%

6.3.3 Summary

IFRS can serve as a useful starting point for the design of a Common Corporate Tax Base. A formal link between IFRS and tax accounting is not appropriate. However, IFRS provide widely accepted accounting definitions and principles that can be used in designing an independent set of common tax accounting rules. The comparison of IFRS and member states' current tax accounting practice revealed that there is a broad basis of similar accounting rules. These areas cover the recognition of assets and liabilities, initial measurement (acquisition costs, production costs and simplified valuation of inventories) and subsequent measurement (regular depreciation).

The working group concerned with the design of a common tax base has also considered IFRS as the preferred reference point for several structural elements of the tax base, such as the definition of income, the recognition of revenues or the definition of liabilities.

Under the current tax law there is a wide range of effective corporate tax burdens within the EU member states. From the elements influencing the overall effective tax burden (i.e. different tax systems, types of taxes, tax bases and tax rates) the corporation tax and local profit taxes are of major importance. With respect to elements making up the effective corporate tax burden, the nominal tax rate is in fact the most important factor (in particular compared to the tax base).

A transition to tax accounting on the basis of IFRS within the EU, as examined here, only has minor effects on the effective corporate tax burdens. A major finding of the study reveals that the effective corporate tax burdens in all countries except Cyprus considered here tend to increase slightly (increases range from 0.1% in Greece to 8.1% in Latvia) since the tax bases tend to become broader. However, the considerable dispersions of effective tax burdens across industries would not change significantly (according to current tax law the hightest standard deviation amounts to 31.4% while under a Common Corporate Tax Base the highest standard deviation amounts 31.1%.

An exclusive harmonisation of the tax accounting rules cannot alleviate the current EU-wide differences of overall effective corporate tax burdens. For this purpose, additional measures are necessary, in particular the convergence of the nominal tax rates on profits. Ideally, a broader tax base offers the possibility to reduce the nominal tax rate, at the same time leaving the overall effective tax burden unchanged. A tax policy of tax cut cum base broadening would not only tend to increase the attractiveness of the member states as a location for companies. It would reduce dispersions of effective tax burdens across industries at the same time. Therefore, such a tax policy is in line with the long term Community goals to become more competitive in international terms.

6.4 Common Consolidated Corporate Tax Base

In the previous chapter options for a Common Corporate Tax Base have been elaborated and analysed. This section deals with the Common Consolidated Corporate Tax Base. In contrast to a Common Corporate Tax Base, a Common Consolidated Corporate Tax Base would also include a consolidation mechanism and formula apportionment. A Common Corporate Tax Base is a prerequisite for a consolidation mechanism. Therefore, this section focuses on issues related to consolidation and formula apportionment. Regarding tax accounting, reference can be made to the results of the previous section. Before the issues are addressed, general attributes of a Common Consolidated Corporate Tax Base are analysed.

6.4.1 General Attributes of a Common Consolidated Tax Base

The concept of a Common Consolidated Corporate Tax Base builds on the notion that multinational enterprises form an integrated economic unit. Although each group corporation is a legal distinct entity, a group of affiliated corporations is regarded as an economic entity for tax purposes. The consolidation mechanism as indented by the European Commission would provide multinational enterprises an intra-group loss relief, deferred taxation of intra-group transactions and avoidance of double taxation of intra-group dividend payments. Therefore, the Common Consolidated Corporate Tax Base is in general theoretically more consistent with the economic reality of a group of affiliated companies and has the potential to ensure tax neutrality with regard to the organisational structure of multinational enterprises. Both, permanent establishments and subsidiaries would be treated as an economic unit for tax purposes.

A consolidated tax base has also the potential to promote tax neutrality concerning different modes of investment financing. Via consolidation interest expenses and corresponding income would be netted out and intra-group dividend payments would be disregarded for tax purposes. Thus, the different modes of financing at the corporate level would be treated equally from a tax point of view and tax incentives to change the financial structure would be eliminated (see Schreiber, 2004: 219; Spengel, 2006a: G37).

Tax neutrality could also be promoted regarding cross-border business restructuring operations or the cross-border relocation of functions and risks. Under a consolidated tax base these activities would not trigger exit taxes, because the transferred assets and exchanged shares would be regarded as intra-group transactions and thus, be neutralised. Capital gains taxation would be deferred until the respective assets and shares are sold to an unrelated third party (see Spengel, 2006a: G38).

The Common Consolidated Corporate Tax Base has also the potential to overcome the deficits associated with the arm's length principle. It is incapable of determining the taxable income of a company separately from its affiliated companies in an objective and non-arbitrary way and entails the risk of double taxation if transfer prices are adjusted unilaterally. Under a consolidation mechanism as intended by the European Commission, there is no need to determine transfer prices at arm's length. Taxation of profits and losses arising from intra-group transfers of assets and provisions of services is deferred until these profits and losses have been affirmed in a market transaction with an unrelated third party. In addition, liabilities and provisions are only taken into account if they refer to an obligation with respect to a third party. Therefore, the consolidation approach avoids cases of double taxation and thus promots the principle of equity. A consolidation approach would also be consistent with the realisation principle, which is inherent to the principle of equity. The realisation principle aims to ensure the objective measurement of taxable income. According to the realisation principle profits and losses should only be recognized for tax purposes when they have been affirmed in a market transaction. With respect to an intra-group transaction, however, the realisation principle fails to achieve this objective. As pointed out before, the arm's length principle is difficult to apply in practice and entails scope for profit shifting. Considering an intra-group transfer as a realisation event would not promote an objective measurement of taxable income as intended by the realisation principle. If taxation of profits arising from intra-group transactions is deferred until they have been confirmed in a transaction with an unrelated party this would ensure an objectified determination of income in the sence of the realisation principle.

Although the Common Consolidated Corporate Tax Base focuses on the economic characteristics, a group of companies forming an economic entity is not treated as a single taxpayer. In contrast, the consolidated tax base is apportioned to each group member, which remains liable to tax with his share in the consolidated tax base (see

Kahle, 2006: 1405). The apportionment mechanism is a key element of a Common Consolidated Corporate Tax Base. It implies a significant change of the current international tax system, since it replaces the internationally accepted arm's length principle.

Formula apportionment does not seek to allocate income to its exact source. Instead, it is based on the notion that the source of an integrated multinational enterprise's overall profits cannot be determined reliable in economic terms. The rationale behind formula apportionment rather is to provide a pragmatic solution for profit allocation among jurisdictions in order to better cope with the issues of simplicity and enforceability (see Weiner, 2002: 523; McLure and Weiner, 2000: 258; Riecker, 1997:130). However, formula apportionment is not arbitrary. Depending on the choice of apportionment factors, this approach intends to ensure an allocation of the consolidated tax base to the profit generating activities. The elements of the formula should represent the factors that are deemed to generate the group's income. Thus, those countries in which there is a comparably larger share of the multinational enterprise's income generating production factors will be attributed a larger share of the consolidated tax base. Therefore, formula apportionment has the potential to satisfy the requirement of internation equity (for a detailed analysis see Paschke, 2007: 170-178; Argúndez-García, 2006: 32-85; Frebel, 2006: 122-179; Schäfer, 2006: 170-205).

In order to analyse the effects of formula apportionment suppose the following simplified example: Suppose a multinational enterprise, which operates production facilities in member state A and B. The consolidated tax base $P=P_A+P_B$ is apportioned using only a capital factor C with $C=C_A+C_B$. The tax liability in member state A would be

$$T_A = P\frac{C_A}{C}t_A,$$

and the tax liability in member state B would be

$$T_B = P\frac{C_B}{C}t_B,$$

where t_A is the tax rate in member state A and t_B is the tax rate in member state B. The overall tax liability T of the multinational enterprise in the EU would be

$$T = T_A + T_B = Pt_A\frac{C_A}{C} + Pt_B\frac{C_B}{C} = P\frac{t_AC_A + t_BC_B}{C}.$$

The example illustrates that the effective tax rate applied to the consolidated tax base is a weighted average of the tax rates in the different jurisdictions in which group entities operate, with the weights given by the presence of the apportionment factors of the firm in each jurisdiction relative to its total factors. Furthermore, under formula apportionment, the corporate income tax is transformed into a tax on the factors included in the formula (see McLure, 2004: 794-795; McLure, 1980: 327-346; Mintz, 1999: 406-407; Oestreicher, 2002: 354). In the example given above, the tax liability in country A can also be written as:

$$T_A = C_A \frac{P}{C} t_A .$$

Thus, the capital invested in country A is multiplied with the overall average profitability of capital of the multinational enterprises $\frac{P}{C}$ and taxed at the national tax rate t_A. Given a constant overall profitability of capital, an increase of capital in member state A would increase the tax liability in this country.

Formula apportionment has an impact on the role of the corporate income tax. Corporate income tax is generally thought to be a withholding tax, serving as a prepayment of the final taxes on the capital income originating in the corporate sector (see section 3.1.1). The final tax burden is determined by the personal taxes levied on dividends and capital gains, and these taxes will remain under the control of member state governments. Distributable profits at the corporate level are generally determined under separate accounting along with the arm's length principle. Formula apportionment replaces separate accounting and transforms the corporation tax into a tax on the factors entering the formula. The factors are multiplied with the multinational enterprise's average profitability of the respective factor. Thus, the tax base of a particular group entity is affected by attributes of the whole group. As a consequence, the corporate tax base calculated under formula apportionment may not correspond to the distributable profits calculated under separate accounting. This has an effect on the functioning of national corporate tax systems, which govern the integration of corporate and personal income tax. Under a full imputation system, the tax burden on dividends would be only determined by the personal income tax, since a tax credit is granted for corporate income tax. However, most member states do not apply a corporation tax system where the corporate income tax is fully integrated into the personal income tax. Instead, the vast majority provides a shareholder relief system, which ensures only partial relief from double taxation of distributed profits. Thus, member states do not seem to prefer a tight link between corporate and personal income tax. Under formula apportionment, this link will be further loosened.

Formula apportionment does not fit with the neutrality concepts that serve to assess fiscal policies in international taxation (see Argúndez-García, 2006: 66). Capital import neutrality requires an equal tax treatment of domestic and foreign investors. All investments in a location should be subject to the same taxes. In principle, this is achieved, if the source country levies the tax of local investments and the country where the investor is resident exempts the foreign income. Formula apportionment is conceptually aligned to the source principle. The consolidated tax base is apportioned to the involved member states and the share in the consolidated tax base attributed to a jurisdiction is ultimately taxed according to this country's rules (see Devereux, 2004: 83; Wissenschaftlicher Beirat beim Bundesministerium der Finanzen, 2007: 28). However, it is inconsistent with the concept of capital import neutrality. The tax burden on an investment not only depends on the tax rate in the source country, but also on the consolidated group income and the allocation of factors included in the apportionment formula.

$$T_A = (P_A + P_B) t_A \frac{C_A}{C_A + C_B}$$

Capital export neutrality is achieved if the investor is indifferent between an investment at home and abroad from a tax point of view. The residence country taxes foreign capital income and the state of source exempts local capital income of foreign investors. Under formula apportionment the tax burden of the investment does not only depend on the tax levied by the residence country. Instead, it depends on the effective tax rate of the corporate group which in turn depends on the allocation of factors and the tax rates applied by all member states the corporate group is engaged in business activities.

$$T = (P_A + P_B) \frac{t_A C_A + t_B C_B}{C}$$

Finally, formula apportionment is inconsistent with the concept of capital ownership neutrality, since the tax treatment of a foreign investment is not the same for all potential investors. Instead, it depends on the effective tax rate of the corporate group.

Consolidation and formula apportionment is not totally immune to strategic tax planning. If the apportionment factors are mobile across jurisdictions and the company controls them there is leeway for profit shifting. There might be an incentive for companies to relocate economic activities that comprise the factors to low tax jurisdictions in order to reduce the effective tax rate (see Agúndez-García, 2006: 59-69; Klassen and Shackelford, 1998: 385-406). Moreover, profitable investments in high tax member states might be avoided, since they would also result in a higher effective tax rate applied to the share in the consolidated tax base of other member states. In contrast, companies may invest in companies which are resident in low tax jurisdictions even if these companies are not profitable because due to the investment the effective tax rate applied to the consolidated tax base and thus the overall tax burden would decline (see Gérard and Weiner, 2003; Wellisch, 2004a: 274). However, an empirical study conducted by Mintz and Smart (2004) suggests that the elasticity of taxable income is greater under separate accounting than under formula apportionment.

The extent to which formula apportionment provides incentives for strategic tax planning depends on the apportionment factors. If apportionment factors are chosen that cannot be influenced by multinational enterprises, incentives for tax planning are eliminated. If firm-specific factors are used, the incentive for factor shifting depends on the degree of mobility of the factors and the possible incidence effects (see Wellisch, 2004a). Moreover, it depends on whether and to what extent the factors are aligned to location specific rents. If the taxes represent location specific rents, incentives for tax planning are reduced.

To summarise, the introduction of a Common Consolidated Corporate Tax Base has the potential to improve taxation of multinational groups of companies in the EU with respect to equity, neutrality as well as simplicity and enforceability. Whether and to what extent an improvement can be achieved depends on the design of the consolidated tax base. There are a number of issues related to consolidation and formula apportionment. First, a definition of what constitutes a group of companies for consolidation will be required. There are several different aspects to be considered in this context. In addition to defining criteria indicating whether a group of companies qualifies for consolidation, eligible entities and the spatial scope of the Common Consolidated Corporate Tax Base have to be specified. Second, a technique in computing the income of the group has to be found. Issues to be discussed in this context are the treatment of intra-group transactions, the mechanism of loss-relief, distinctions between different categories of income and the treatment of income arising on cross-border investments involving third countries. Furthermore, the formula used to apportion the consolidated tax base has to be determined.

6.4.2 Implementation Issues

6.4.2.1 Definition of the Taxable Unit

The definition of a consolidated group is a major issue in designing the Common Consolidated Corporate Tax Base. Criteria have to be determined according to which affiliated companies qualify for consolidation and formula apportionment. The fundamental question is whether to delineate the group in terms of legal criteria, economic criteria or a combination of both. In defining the group, the underlying rationale for the Common Consolidated Corporate Tax Base has to be kept in mind. Accordingly, economic interrelationships among affiliated companies that make it impossible to determine the source of profits on the basis of separate accounting using arm's length pricing should lay the foundation for the definition of the consolidated group (see Hellerstein and McLure, 2004: 204). The definition of the qualifying group of entities is a key element of the Common Consolidated Corporate Tax Base, since it implies the delineation of the income to be apportioned (see Agúndez-García, 2006: 10). In the following, alternative criteria for the definition of the consolidated group are considered.

6.4.2.1.1 Legal Ownership

Legal ownership is widely recognized as a key element in defining the taxable unit (see Agúndez-García, 2006: 11-15; European Commission, 2007b: 4). Currently, all member states providing a group taxation regime require qualifying group members to be aligned via ownership (see section 4.1.1.3, table 18). The underlying theoretic rationale is that legal ownership entails the ability to govern and control an affiliate's business activities in order to obtain economic benefits. For example, the controlling company may gain access to the subsidiary's patents or production techniques or realise economies of scale or scope. These economic benefits are difficult to allocate based on separate geographic accounting since these do not exist if transactions are coordinated via markets. Thus, legal ownership constitutes a necessary prerequisite for the existence of an economic entity that justifies replacing the arm's length principle with formula apportionment.

In general, legal ownership can be defined either with reference to voting stock or equity. As control requires voting power, ownership of voting rights seems more appropriate than ownership of equity (see European Commission, 2007b: 4). However, the distinction between the ownership of voting rights and ownership of equity is only relevant where they deviate from each other. This may be the case due to none-voting shares. To what extent these differences exist, depends on the company law of the respective member state.

Control is presumed to exist when the parent owns, directly or indirectly through subsidiaries, more than one half of the entity's voting power. Thus, a simple majority ownership of voting rights should be regarded as the minimum requirement. Alternatively, an ownership threshold of 75% or even 100% could be used to delineate the taxable unit. A high ownership percentage would correspond to member state's tax practice. In many member states the scope of group taxation currently includes only those entities where the parent entity owns 75% or even 95% or 100% (see section 4.1.1.3, table 18). Moreover, it is argued that entities connected to a high shareholding relationship might be more likely to be economically interdependent (see Agúndez-García, 2006: 12). Therefore, a high ownership percentage might better indicate whether a group of companies forms an economic entity the Common Consolidated Corporate Tax Base should be applied to. A high ownership threshold would also reduce the need for special provisions for minority shareholders (see Schön, 2007: 431). However, a threshold of 100% would be too restrictive, as the mere existence of a minority shareholder would cause an affiliate to fall out of the taxable unit (see Schreiber, 2004: 223).

A decisive disadvantage of a high-percentage ownership threshold delineating the taxable unit is its potential for tax planning strategies. Parent companies could adjust their ownership interest in other companies without losing control, depending on whether separate accounting using arm's length pricing or consolidation and formula apportionment is tax optimal. Furthermore, those subsidiaries that do not qualify for an application of the Common Consolidated Corporate Tax Base but are still controlled via a simple or qualified majority ownership may still be used for profit shifting (see Agúndez-García, 2006: 12; European Commission, 2004: 6; Oestreicher, 2005: 89). In order to reduce the scope for tax planning, the ownership threshold should be set sufficiently low as to ensure that a further reduction would be associated with a substantial loss of control (see Schön, 2007: 431). Accordingly, an ownership threshold of 50% or 75% seems appropriate for defining the taxable unit subject to taxation under the Common Consolidated Corporate Tax Base (see Schön, 2007: 431; Schreiber, 2004: 232).

6.4.2.1.2 Additional Criteria

A definition of the taxable unit based solely on legal ownership has the advantage of administrative simplicity, both for taxpayers and tax administrations. It provides a clear cut solution and certainty regarding the entities to be included (see European Commission, 2004: 5).

On the other hand, this definition does not necessarily represent the economic substance of the relationship among group entities (see Martens Weiner, 2001: 383; Schreiber, 2004: 223). A subsidiary might be under control but economically independent. If this is the case and the Common Consolidated Corporate Tax Base is applied, the consolidated tax base of these entities would be sourced using apportionment factors that would not have contributed to the production of the income in question (see Hellerstein and McLure, 2004: 205). Thus, although legal ownership is a prerequisite for economic integration, an extension of the definition of the taxable unit based on economic criteria seems conceptual more consistent with the concept of a Common Consolidated Corporate Tax Base (see Agúndez-García, 2006: 13; Jacobs, Spengel and Schäfer, 2005: 277-278; Martens Weiner, 2006: 71). For example, in economic terms, the delineation of the consolidated group could be based on entities of the company's organisational structure, such as organisational departments or value added processes (see Oestreicher, 2000: 208-217; 230). This approach may be appropriate where a group of companies is engaged in more than one activity.

Economic criteria may also by necessary to prevent tax planning strategies. These criteria could impede investments solely aimed to buy apportionment factors in a low tax jurisdiction in order to reduce the overall tax burden of the group.

However, economic criteria are less feasible, as they are rather subjective and do not provide legal certainty. Experience from the US state corporate income taxation has shown that problems exist in attempting to define what constitutes a unitary business (see Hellerstein and McLure, 2004: 203-206). There is no common definition of a unitary business, but tests are applied which are mainly based on economic criteria (see Oestreicher, 2000: 136-139). Against this background, reaching an agreement on economic criteria and applying them uniformly in the EU may become difficult and burdensome for taxpayers as well as for tax authorities (see Agúndez-García, 2006: 14). Therefore, the definition of the taxable unit should rely on legal criteria or bright-line tests indicating whether there are economic interdependencies between affiliated entities rather than on economic criteria. Reference can be made to those bright-line tests developed by McLure (see McLure, 1984) and Hellerstein (see Hellerstein, 1982: 48). Accordingly, the definition of a consolidated group could be based on a control test and tests determining whether there are economic interdependencies and a flow of value.

In addition to majority legal ownership, the test of control may be extended to cover arrangements that result in a different relationship of dependence as indicated by the ownership of voting rights. In this context, reference could be made to IFRS/IAS. The definition of control provided by IFRS does not refer to de facto control but only to legal arrangements indicating the power to control. According to IAS 27, control may arise through an agreement that gives the parent the right to control the votes of other shareholders, the power to govern the entity's financial or operating policies by agreement or statue, the right to appoint or remove the majority of the board of directors or other governing bodies or the power to direct their votes or a combination of factors such that control rests with the parent. However, consolidation of companies when the parent company owns only one half or less of a subsidiary's voting power seems not appropriate for tax purposes. This approach would be contrary to member states current tax practice and would intensify problems associated with minority shareholders. Therefore, a simple or qualified majority of ownership should be the minimum requirement. Additional legal criteria should only be used to prevent the application of the Common Consolidated Corporate Tax Base to companies where the majority ownership of an entity's voting rights does not constitute control of it.

Whether economic interdependencies or a flow of values between affiliated companies exist should be determined based on objective and easily administrable criteria. A key factor in explaining the presence of multinational enterprises is the intensity of headquarters services. Especially knowledge capital has turned out to be decisive. Accordingly, group entities engaged in research and development and those affiliated companies benefiting from these activities should form a group. Furthermore, the percentage of turnover realized on intra-group transfers of goods or provisions of services might serve as an indicator (see Hellerstein, 1993; Hellerstein and McLure, 2004: 205). A flow of goods, services, or intangibles could indicate whether commonly controlled entities constitute an economically integrated business and whether there is scope for profit shifting via transfer pricing. In determining the required turnover percentage attention has to be paid to the fact that the transaction volume may vary from

48 For a summary of test used to define a unitary business see Weiner, 1999: 29-34.

year to year. Therefore, the threshold may be defined as a weighted average for a certain period of time. Furthermore, the application of the Common Consolidated Corporate Tax Base could be restricted to group entities engaged in the same line of business. Thus, a test determining whether affiliated companies provide similar or a group of related products or services would have to be implemented.

6.4.2.1.3 Personal Scope of the Common Consolidated Corporate Tax Base

The personal scope of the Common Consolidated Corporate Tax Base should not be restricted to subsidiaries (i.e. corporations) as group members. Instead, it should also include permanent establishments (see Wissenschaftlicher Beirat beim Bundesministerium der Finanzen, 2007: 75-76). The difficulties caused by separate accounting if applied to an economically integrated group of companies are not only relevant for distinct legal entities but also for permanent establishments. In contrast, differentiating between subsidiaries and permanent establishments would entail scope for tax planning. Taxpayers could decide whether the Common Consolidated Corporate Tax Base or separate accounting applies simply by choosing the legal form of an investment. With respect to the principle of neutrality, this scope for strategic tax planning should be avoided. In contrast, under paragraph 2 of Article 7 of the OECD Model, the currently favoured method for allocating profits to a permanent establishment is the arm's length principle. As opposed to the proposals of the European Commission, the OECD strives harmonising the profit allocation for subsidiaries and permanent establishments using the arm's length principle. Moreover, an exclusion of permanent establishments could violate the freedom of establishment laid down in Article 42 of the EC Treaty. However, one has to bear in mind that the authorised OECD approach of profit attribution to permanent establishments is the separate entity approach based on the arm's length principle. As opposed to the concept of the Common Consolidated Corporate Tax Base, the OECD intends to harmonise the profit allocation of permanent establishments and subsidiaries using separate accounting under the arm's length principle (see section 4.2.2).

An important issue regarding the personal scope of the Common Consolidated Corporate Tax Base concerns the treatment of transparent entities. This issue was already addressed by the Working Group of the European Commission (see European Commission, 2007b: 5). The general view so far is that transparent entities should not qualify as parent companies of a consolidated group. Although the principle of neutrality would call for an equal tax treatment of transparent entities and corporations, there are good reasons to exclude transparent entities from the application of the Common Consolidated Corporate Tax Base. As outlined above, corporations are distinct legal entities which are taxed separately from their shareholders. In most countries the corporate income tax is not fully integrated into the personal income tax of the shareholders (see section 4.1.2). The vast majority of member states tax profits at the company level and the shareholder level. The shareholder is granted a partial relief in order to reduce double taxation on dividends. In contrast, partnerships are not regarded as distinct legal entities. Not the partnership itself but, according to the transparency principle, each partner is subject to tax with his share in the total profits. If transparent entities would qualify as a parent of a tax group for Common Consolidated Corporate Tax Base purposes, the share of the Common Consolidated Corporate Tax Base apportioned to the transparent entity would be allocated directly to the partners and would be subject to personal income tax. This would contravene the distinction between corporate income tax and personal income tax drawn by corporate tax systems. Therefore, transparent entities should be excluded from the personal scope of the Common Consolidated Corporate Tax Base in order to prevent national corporate tax systems from being evaded in the context of the Common Consolidated Corporate Tax Base. However, member states could be granted an option whether to extend the personal scope of the Common Consolidated Corporate Tax Base to transparent entities.

An inclusion of transparent entities would also affect revenues from personal income tax. The fiscal effects of consolidation and formula apportionment could not be limited to corporate income tax. These effects are not intended by the European Commission, as the proposals for a consolidated tax base focus on corporate income tax rather than on personal income tax. According to the Commission, the personal income tax should remain in the sole responsibility of the member states (see European Commission, 2001a: 17).

Although transparent entities should not qualify for the application of the Common Consolidated Corporate Tax Base, they are still relevant. If a corporation included in the personal scope of the Common Consolidated Corporate Tax Base is a partner of a transparent entity, its share of the income of the transparent entity should be included in the Common Consolidated Corporate Tax Base. Accordingly, the relevant percentage of the factors of such transparent entities should be considered with respect to formula apportionment (see European Commission, 2007b: 5).

When defining the personal scope of the Common Consolidated Corporate Tax Base the question arises whether the mere existence of apportionment factors or a corporation or permanent establishment is required to attribute a share of the Common Consolidated Corporate Tax Base to the respective country. From a theoretical point of view, it seems consistent with the method of formula apportionment to assign the taxing right to those jurisdictions in which at least one of the factors of the formula exists (see OECD, 2003: sec. 295). This approach would also prevent strategic tax planning such as splitting off activities in order to avoid a permanent establishment and thus, a taxing nexus in a certain country. Moreover, if the factor "sales by destination" is included in the apportionment formula, doing direct business would be taxed in the source country according to the supply-demand approach. This would promote tax neutrality because the intended allocation of the consolidated tax base to the profit generating activities would be applied irrespective of whether a company is doing direct business or doing business via a permanent establishment or a subsidiary.

However, assigning taxing rights to jurisdictions only due to the existence of an apportionment factor would be a very far reaching change, because according to current international tax practice a company becomes only liable to tax in the country in which it is resident or a permanent establishment exists. Furthermore, this approach is supposed to be difficult to administer (see OECD, 2003: sec. 295).

To conclude, the Common Consolidated Corporate Tax Base should be applicable to subsidiaries and permanent establishments as group members. The decision whether transparent entities can qualify as parent companies or not should be left to the member states. Assignment of taxing rights on corporate income should not be based on the mere existence of apportionment factors. Instead the minimum threshold should be the existence of a permanent establishment in one country. As a response, member states might broaden their definition of a permanent establishment in order to extent their taxing rights. Therefore, a common definition of permanent establishment and nexus is needed.

6.4.2.1.4 Territorial Scope

An important issue to be analysed is the territorial scope of the Common Consolidated Corporate Tax Base (see Agúndez-Garcia, 2006: 20-30). This issue arises because the application of the Common Consolidated Corporate Tax Base has to be limited to the territory of the internal market. With reference to the concept of unitary taxation in the United States this limitation of the territorial scope of the Common Consolidated Corporate Tax Base is also described as the "water's edge". The limitation of the territorial scope is necessary, because the OECD member states have chosen the arm's length principle as the predominant method for profit allocation at the international level.

Due to the water's edge approach, the traditional separate accounting under the arm's length principle continues to apply for business activities with respect to third countries. Thus, profit-shifting opportunities will exist via relationships with affiliates outside the EU.

The first issue to be addressed in designing the territorial scope is to determine a corporation's residence and the existence of a permanent establishment. A starting point could be current member state's tax practice. However, the definitions provided by national tax law and tax treaties differ between member states (see European Commission, 2005c). These differences may give scope for tax planning. Foreign companies resident in third countries could locate their subsidiaries in a member state with a restrictive definition of tax residency in order to avoid the application of the Common Consolidated Corporate Tax Base. In addition, different definitions of residency and permanent establishment may contradict the objective of the Common Consolidated Corporate Tax Base to introduce common tax rules in order to reduce compliance costs. Therefore, at least in the long run, common definitions of tax residency and permanent establishment should be introduced. This is also recommended by the European Commission (see European Commission, 2006b: 4-5). In this regard, the work carried out by the OECD is supposed to be a good starting point (see European Commission, 2006b: 5-6).

A second important issue is to determine which entities of a multinational group are eligible to apply the Common Consolidated Corporate Tax Base, either as an option or as an obligation. As a general rule, the Common Consolidated Corporate Tax Base should not encompass non-EU group entities. A parent company or subsidiary resident in a third country as well as a permanent establishment located outside the EU are not eligible. Although it is theoretically appealing to extend the scope of the Common Consolidated Corporate Tax Base to all group entities irrespective of whether they are located in the EU or outside, an inclusion of non-EU group entities seems not realistic, at least in the short run. As mentioned above, at the international level separate accounting under the arm's length principle is the agreed method for profit allocation regarding subsidiaries and permanent establishments. Therefore, the application of consolidation and formula apportionment has to be restricted to corporations and permanent establishments located in the EU.

Despite the general rule that EU group entities should be eligible to apply the Common Consolidated Corporate Tax Base, there are several issues that have to be addressed when designing the territorial scope of the Common Consolidated Corporate Tax Base. An important question to be addressed in this context is whether the Common Consolidated Corporate Tax Base should apply to EU group entities which are ultimately controlled by a corporation resident in a third country. Attention should be paid to several typical settings.

Fig. 7. Setting 1

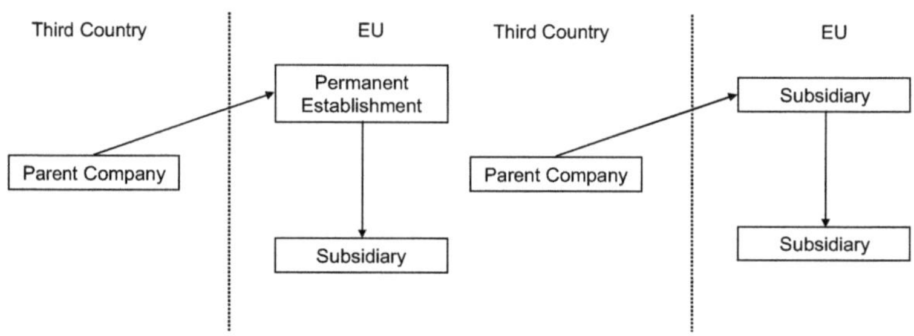

A typical setting is a non-EU corporation that controls an EU subsidiary which in turn is the controlling head of an EU tax group. Alternatively, the non-EU corporation could maintain a permanent establishment that controls EU subsidiaries (see Figure 11). The issue in these two settings is whether the EU subsidiary and the EU permanent establishment respectively are eligible for the application of the Common Consolidated Corporate Tax Base together with their EU subsidiaries. With respect to the criterion of neutrality, the application of the Common Consolidated Corporate Tax Base to economically integrated affiliates located in the EU should not depend on whether the ultimately controlling parent company is resident in the EU or in a third country. Accordingly, the Common Consolidated Corporate Tax Base should apply to an EU tax group with an EU entity at its head that is ultimately controlled by a non-EU corporation. Otherwise, there would be scope for tax planning. Companies could avoid the application of the Common Consolidated Corporate Tax Base to EU group entities simply by moving the controlling entity in a third country (see Agúndez-García, 2006: 30). Moreover, a different treatment of qualifying EU entities depending on whether the parent company is resident in the EU or a third country might violate article 24 of the OECD Model on non-discrimination. With respect to subsidiaries, article 24 Paragraph 5 of the OECD Model prohibits treating a subsidiary which is wholly or partly owned or controlled by a parent company of another country in a way which is other or more burdensome than the treatment of a similar subsidiary. An EU company controlled by a non-EU corporation and an EU company controlled by an EU corporation should be considered as similarly situated companies, if both have a relationship to another EU company that meets the requirements of the Common Consolidated Corporate Tax Base. Therefore, at least in settings to which a treaty with a non-discrimination article is applicable, EU group entities which are ultimately controlled by a non-EU company should be eligible for the application of the Common Consolidated Corporate Tax Base. Concerning permanent establishments, article 24 Paragraph 3 of the OECD Model could be relevant. According to this non-discrimination article, taxation of a permanent establishment of a foreign corporation shall not be less favourable than the taxation of an enterprise carrying on the same activities. Thus, a permanent establishment located in the EU should qualify as the head of an EU tax group subject to the Common Consolidated Corporate Tax Base.

Fig. 8. Setting 2

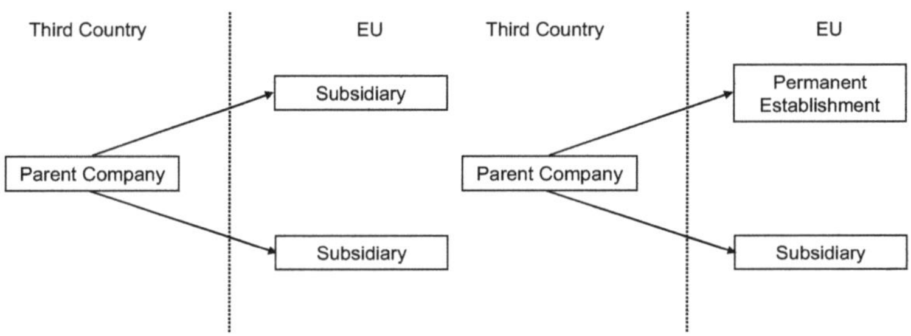

A different typical setting is a scenario involving a non-EU corporation controlling two subsidiaries resident in the EU or a non-EU corporation controlling an EU subsidiary and maintaining a permanent establishment located in the EU. These settings are illustrated in Figure 12. In both scenarios it has to be clarified whether those group entities located in the EU shall be able to apply for the Common Consolidated Corporate Tax Base. With respect to tax planning it seems advisable to allow those EU group entities to apply for the Common Consolidated Corporate Tax Base. Otherwise companies may decide to avoid the application of the Common Consolidated Corporate Tax Base simply by moving the controlling parent company outside the EU. Furthermore, as economies of integration may also occur between group entities on the same level in the ownership chain, they should be also consolidated from a conceptual point of view. Whether the non-discrimination article of the OECD Model is applicable to this setting, however, is questionable. Considering only those two entities located in the EU, there is no controlling relationship. In the absence of the controlling entity these two entities do not form an economic unit and thus, would not be eligible for the application of the Common Consolidated Corporate Tax Base. As a consequence, if two entities controlled by a non-EU corporation are not eligible for the application for the Common Consolidated Corporate Tax Base, this is not a case of discrimination because two sister companies controlled by an EU company would not be eligible either.

Fig. 9. Setting 3

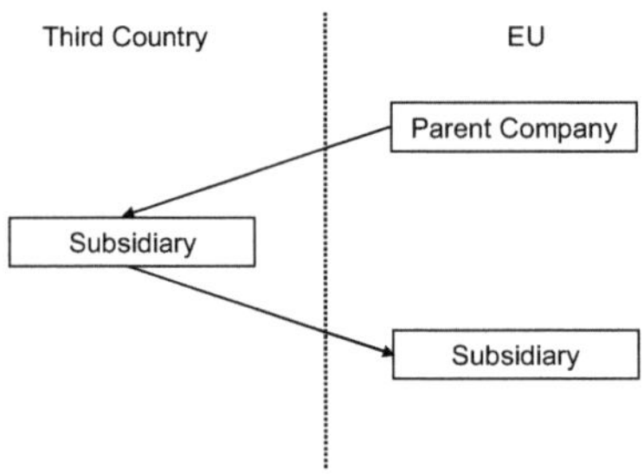

A final setting is an EU parent company controlling a non-EU subsidiary that in turn controls an EU subsidiary (see Figure 13). The question arising in this setting is whether the Common Consolidated Corporate Tax Base is applicable to the EU parent company and its EU subsidiary without taking into account the non-EU intermediary. In order to decide on this issue, reference has to be made to the general definition of the consolidated group. As considered above (see section 6.4.2.1.1), the definition of the consolidated group should mainly rely on legal ownership. The required ownership threshold can be reached either directly or indirectly through subsidiaries. The same rules should apply in this setting. With respect to the criterion of neutrality, two EU group companies aligned via indirect ownership should be eligible for the application of the Common Consolidated Corporate Tax Base irrespective of whether the intermediary is a tax resident in a member state or a third country. Otherwise, there would also be scope for tax planning, since companies could prevent the application of the Common Consolidated Corporate Tax Base by moving the intermediary outside the EU.

However, consolidation of group entities without taking into account the intermediary may get complex.

6.4.2.2 Consolidation

A key element essential to the concept of the Common Consolidated Corporate Tax Base is that of consolidation – i.e. cross border profit and loss offset and deferral treatment on gains (and/or losses) at the time of intra-group transfer. Since the EU-Regulation on consolidated accounts from 2002[49] obliges companies listed on an EU stock market to establish their consolidated accounts based on IFRS from 2005 onwards, for reasons of simplicity and practicability, consolidated IFRS-accounts could be used as a suitable starting point for the determination of the Common Consolidated Corporate Tax Base. This possibility was also considered by the European Commission (see European Commission, 2003c). There are, however, certain arguments against this strategy (see Spengel, 2004). Both, the definition as well as the territorial scope of the consolidated group are not satisfactory for tax purposes. Moreover, the method of consolidation is unlikely to be compatible with tax principles and current member states' tax practice. Adjusting IFRS-group statements would be complex and is unlikely to reduce compliance costs, as intended by this approach. Therefore, consolidated IFRS-accounts cannot serve as a starting point for the Common Consolidated Corporate Tax Base. By contrast, a tax-specific method of consolidation using the individual accounts as a starting point is preferable. This view follows member states' practice with regard to consolidated taxation of domestic groups and has now been shared by the European Commission (see European Commission, 2003c: 21).

All members of the taxable unit should calculate their own tax bases separately first. In this respect, common tax accounting rules as outlined in section 6.3.1 should apply. Entities that have a different currency from the group's currency have to translate their individual tax base into the group's currency. In this respect, the controlling parent's currency should be decisive. In general, the exchange rate of the respective tax accounting date should be used to translate the taxable income.

Taxable income of group members can only be consolidated with the taxable income of other group members of a corresponding accounting period. Otherwise, companies could defer taxation changing their reporting period. Therefore, where the accounting periods of entities differ, adjustments are necessary. Two approaches can be distinguished. One alternative would be to align the tax accounting period of each group member to the accounting period of the parent company. By contrast, if the accounting period remains unchanged, the taxable income of each company has to be time apportioned. Adjustments could be restricted to situations where the difference in the accounting dates does not exceed a certain period, e.g. three months.

6.4.2.2.1 Intra-group Loss Relief

In their study on company taxation, the European Commission pointed out, that the current limits to cross-border loss relief within the EU, in particular as regards subsidiaries, can lead to double taxation and constitute significant obstacles to economic activity in more than one member state (see European Commission, 2001b: 242-255). Therefore, the offset of losses and profits between members of the taxable unit is a key feature of the Common Consolidated Corporate Tax Base. Loss relief is achieved via consolidation. Adding together the individual tax bases of each group entity, losses incurred by one group entity are automatically offset against profits of other group entities.

If the consolidated tax base is negative, the loss should be carried back to be offset against profits of prior years or carried forward to be offset against future profits. This is necessary to ensure taxation of the net income, a requirement inherent to the principle of equity. Two possible mechanisms for a loss carry over were discussed by the working group (see European Commission, 2006b: 12). The first approach would be to allocate the loss to each group member according to the apportionment mechanism. The allocated share of the group's loss may then be carried back or forward at the level of each individual group member and offset against shares of a positive consolidated tax base in prior or future years. The second approach would be to carry back or forward such losses at the group level.

The first approach seems to be more consistent with the concept of consolidation and formula apportionment. Although the approach of consolidation is based on the notion that a group of companies forms an economic unit, under the concept of the Common Consolidated Corporate Tax Base each of the group members remains liable to tax for its apportioned share of the consolidated tax base on an individual basis. The first approach leads to a symmetric treatment of profits and losses. Not only a positive but also a negative consolidated tax base is apportioned to each group member. In con-

---

49 Regulation (EU) 1606/2002, OJ EU L 243/1 dated 11 September 2002.

trast, the second approach results in an asymmetric treatment of profits and losses. Whereas a positive group income is subject to formula apportionment in the period it is earned, a negative consolidated tax base is carried forward at the group level and reduces future profits. As a consequence, losses are apportioned according to the allocation of apportionment factors in the period in which they are offset at the group level. This allocation of apportionment factors, however, may not lead to an allocating of the consolidated tax base to the loss generating activities as intended by formula apportionment.

Moreover, with respect to international aspects, the second approach may cause problems. These may occur, if the credit method to foreign income earned by resident group members from sources outside the EU is applied. Without apportioning a negative consolidated tax base, the tax burden caused by the foreign income may be too high as the compensating effect of the losses is disregarded at the level of the receiving company. Loss relief is only achieved at the group level in subsequent years.

A drawback of the first approach, however, is its leeway for tax planning. Companies may re-locate apportioning factors in order to allocate group's losses to those member states with high tax rates. According to the second approach, the offset of a negative consolidated tax base does not depend on the apportionment mechanism. Therefore, possibilities for tax planning are reduced. However, the scope for tax planning occurs also in years with a positive consolidated tax base. Thus, these tax planning possibilities are inherent to the Common Consolidated Corporate Tax Base.

Taking all these arguments together, a negative Common Consolidated Corporate Tax Base should be apportioned to each group member, as this approach is in line with the concept of the Common Consolidated Corporate Tax Base and could prevent problems concerning international aspects.

If a negative consolidated tax base is to be apportioned to the involved group entities and offset against shares of a positive consolidated tax base in prior or future years, common rules for loss carry-back or loss carry forward in the EU are necessary in order to reduce incentives for tax planning. As outlined in section 6.3.1.4 the European Commission prefers to allow only for an unrestricted loss carry forward. A loss carry back should not be provided.

Special rules are required in order to prevent companies from utilizing losses more than once. Losses may not only be consolidated at the group level but also be carried over in previous or subsequent years to be offset against profits in the individual account of the respective group member. There are two alternative approaches to avoid this so called "double dip". Either, any carry-forward or carry-back of losses at the company level is added back to the consolidated tax base at the group level or the separate taxable income before compensation for loss carry forwards of each group member enters the consolidation. Both approaches would ensure that once losses are offset via consolidation, these losses cannot be used at the company level.

6.4.2.2.2 Adjustment of Intra-group Transfers

A systematic elimination of tax obstacles to cross-border EU-wide activities requires not only loss relief but also a deferred taxation of gains and losses realized on intra-group transactions. Transfer pricing issues arising from separate accounting could be eliminated or would practically disappear for transactions between companies participating in the Common Consolidated Corporate Tax Base. There would be considerably less scope for income shifting, if intra-group transactions are eliminated for tax purposes. Furthermore, the current complexity of Guidelines on Transfer Pricing would cease to exist for activities within the EU. This is considered one of the main potential advantages of the Common Consolidated Corporate Tax Base (see European Commission, 2001b: 420). Moreover, deferred taxation of intra-group transactions would be a potential solution to high tax costs and international double taxation when entering into cross-border business restructuring, for example in case of a merger, a division or a transfer of assets (see Spengel and Braunagel, 2006: 47-48).

Recapture of gains realized on intra-group transactions depends on the type of the respective asset. Gains and losses regarding intra-group transfers of non-depreciable assets should generally be deferred until the asset leaves the group, either by a sale or other disposition to a nonmember. Intra-group income regarding depreciable assets is either restored in the course of depreciation or if the asset leaves the group.

Special rules for recapture are required, if a group member moves its residence to another member state or assets and liabilities are transferred to an extent, that no permanent establishment remains in the transferring member state and thus, it looses its entitlement to tax a share of the consolidated tax base. In each case, taxing rights of member states are at risk.

According to the principle of inter-nation equity each member state should have the right to tax hidden capital gains built up in its territory. Therefore, recapture of deferred capital gains may be justified if taxing rights are at risk. However, a group member moving its residence or business restructuring do not represent realization events. Moreover, exit taxes may violate the fundamental freedoms of the EC Treaty. Therefore, an approach has to be found, which on the one hand ensures tax neutrality and individual equity and on the other hand ensures that the transferring member state remains its right to tax deferred gains realized on previous intra-group transfers.

First, this approach would require the recording of all gains and losses realized on an intra-group transfer in the individual accounts. Second, if taxing rights of a member state are at risk, the intra-group income attributable to this jurisdiction should be restored and apportioned to all involved member states. The share allocated to the receiving member states remains deferred. Similarly, the share of the transferring member state loosing its taxing nexus to the Common Consolidated Corporate Tax Base should not immediately tax the restored capital gains. Instead, the restored gain may be taxed pro rata over the useful lifetime of the respective asset or a certain period of time. It might be also reasonable to tax this income upon its actual disposal to a third party. However, one has to recognize that with this approach transfer pricing issues do not disappear. Companies may strategically determine transfer prices taking into account the allocation of apportionment factors in the year of recapture.

There are several different techniques with respect to the adjustments necessary to neutralize intra-group transactions:

A first approach would be to ignore intra-group transactions for tax purposes. According to this approach, the seller's basis in the asset would carry over to the buyer in the intra-group sale. The company receiving the assets is obliged to compute any new depreciation and any gain or loss in respect of the asset transferred according to the seller's basis in the asset ultimately before the transfer. As a result, gains or losses realized on an intra-group transaction are not documented for tax purposes.

A second approach is to record intra-group transfers at their internal transfer price, both in the seller's as well as the purchaser's account. Any gain or loss realized on the transaction is recorded as a balance sheet item and thus neutralized for tax purposes in the seller's account. The acquiring company computes new depreciation or a capital gain on a subsequent transfer on the basis of the transfer price. If the intra-group gain or loss has to be restored because of a subsequent transfer or in the course of depreciation, the balance sheet item is dissolved.

According to a third approach, each group member computes its individual taxable income taking into account all gains and losses realized on an intra-group transfer. Thus, group member's accounts correspond to those of unrelated companies. Instead of adjusting the individual accounts of the group members involved in intra-group transfers, gains and losses realized on an intra-group transfer may be neutralized in a separate combined report. Taxable income of each group member is calculated as between unrelated companies. These individual results are combined and adjusted, eliminating intra-group gains or losses and any excess depreciation. This approach prevails in France for domestic group taxation (see Jacobs and Spengel, 1994). The following example illustrates the effects of the three approaches.

Example: Company A and company B belong to the same tax group. Each company's annual profit amounts to 100,000 EURO. It is supposed now, that company A acquires a machine for 30.000 EURO. The machine has a useful lifetime of three years. The machine is depreciated according to the straight-line method over the course of the useful lifetime. At the end of period one, company A sells the machine to company B at a price of 30,000 EURO.

Table 40. Intra-group income is ignored

	Year 1	Year 2	Year 3
Company A			
Profits	100,000	100,000	100,000
Depreciation	-10,000	-	-
Capital Gains	-	-	-
Deferred Intra-group Gains	-	-	-
Restored Intra-group Gains	-	-	-
Adjusted Speparate Income	90,000	100,000	100,000
Company B			
Profits	100,000	100,000	100,000
Depreciation	-	-10,000	-10,000
Adjusted Separate Income	100,000	90,000	90,000
Consolidated Tax Base			
Combined Income	190,000	190,000	190,000
Adjustments	-	-	-
Consolidated Tax Base	190,000	190,000	190,000

It becomes evident from the example that all three approaches lead to the same consolidated tax base in each period (i.e. 190,000 EURO). Only the separate tax bases of each group member differ depending on the approach that is applied. According to the second and third approach, intra-group transfers are recorded at their transfer price in the individual accounts. This seems beneficial in cases where intra-group income has to be restored, for example if a company involved in an intra-group transfer ceases to be a group member or taxing rights of a member state are at risk due to business restructuring.

Table 41. Intra-group income is realized but adjusted in the seller's account

	Year 1	Year 2	Year 3
Company A			
Profits	100,000	100,000	100,000
Depreciation	-10,000	-	-
Capital Gains	10,000	-	-
Deferred Intra-group Gains	10,000	-	-
Restored Intra-group Gains	-	5,000	5,000
Adjusted Speparate Income	90,000	105,000	105,000
Company B			
Profits	100,000	100,000	100,000
Depreciation	-	-15,000	-15,000
Adjusted Separate Income	100,000	85,000	85,000
Consolidated Tax Base			
Combined Income	190,000	190,000	190,000
Adjustments	-	-	-
Consolidated Tax Base	190,000	190,000	190,000

The third approach has another advantage. As each group member's separate account is determined as though the company is independent, the separate accounts may remain the basis for the claim of minority shareholders. In contrast, the other two approaches require that adjustments take place in the separate accounts. On applying the second approach, all adjustments take place at the level of the transferring company. In contrast, the purchasing group member's account is determined as if it belonged to a nonmember. Both, the individual account of the seller and the purchaser have to be adjusted, if intra-group transactions are ignored for tax purposes. As a result, there are good reasons for adjusting intra-group transactions in a separate combined report and determining the individual accounts using the method of separate accounting (third approach).

Table 42. Intra-group income is realized but adjusted in a combined report

	Year 1	Year 2	Year 3
Company A			
Profits	100,000	100,000	100,000
Depreciation	-10,000	-	-
Capital Gains	10,000	-	-
Deferred Intra-group Gains	-	-	-
Restored Intra-group Gains	-	-	-
Adjusted Speparate Income	100,000	100,000	100,000
Company B			
Profits	100,000	100,000	100,000
Depreciation	-	-15,000	-15,000
Adjusted Separate Income	100,000	85,000	85,000
Consolidated Tax Base			
Combined Income	190,000	185,000	185,000
Adjustments	-10,000	5,000	5,000
Consolidated Tax Base	190,000	190,000	190,000

6.4.2.2.3 Other Adjustments

In addition to the intra-group loss-relief and deferred taxation of gains realized on intra-group transfers, further adjustments are necessary to prevent double or minor taxation. Intercompany dividends are paid out of taxable income. In order to avoid double taxation, they should be tax exempt. This follows from the idea of a Common Consolidated Corporate Tax Base with formula apportionment. Correspondingly, a write-down of an investment in a group member should not be tax deductible. Moreover, any withholding taxes on intercompany payments should be avoided. As a general rule, this is already achieved due to the Parent Subsidiary Directive as well as the Interest and Royalties Directive.

6.4.2.2.4 Distinction between Different Types of Income: Business and Non-business Income

A guiding principle for allocation of profits is to assign income to the source country. The source of profits is defined as the location where the profits are created (see Jacobs, Spengel and Schäfer, 2004: 270). If the source of certain categories of income can be precisely determined, there is a strong argument to exclude this income from consolidation and apportionment and instead to assign this income to the tax jurisdiction having its source within its borders. The application of formula apportionment should be restricted to income arising from transactions and activities in the course of the economically integrated business, as the arm's length principle fails to allocate the benefits from economic integration.

A distinction between different categories of income is also made in the United States and Canada. In these countries the application of formula apportionment is restricted to the so called business income (see Weiner, 2005: 66). Business income is generally referred to as any income arising from transactions and activities in the regular course of the business. Non-business income typically includes income such as royalties, dividends, interest receipts and rents. Whereas business income is consolidated and apportioned, non-business income is directly assigned to a tax jurisdiction.

Despite that a distinction between different types of income seems justified from a theoretical point of view, there are some disadvantages to this approach (see Argúndez-Garzía, 2006: 17-20). Separation between categories of income can get difficult and might be subject to manipulations, as deciding whether activities and resulting income belong to the economic unit is not an easy task. Moreover, a consequent application of this approach would require a separation of expenses aligned to the different categories of income as well. Taxing interest and licenses according to the current member states practice would enable companies to maintain their strategies of shifting income thus assigning expenses to high tax countries and corresponding income to low tax countries. A final problem linked to the distinction approach is that it removes one of the advantages of consolidation, namely the fact that loss offset disregarding the categories of income. Instead, losses incurred from the non-apportionable categories of income, excluded from the consolidated base, would not benefit from general intra-group cross-border loss compensation and therefore an additional system of loss transfers might be required.

Taking all these arguments into account, it might be more apt not to differentiate between different categories of income.

6.4.2.2.5 Consolidation in Case of Less than 100%-owned Affiliates

If the parent holds less the 100% of the shares in a subsidiary, the question arises if consolidation should be limited to part of the profits and losses in proportion to the share ownership. This issue was already addressed by the European Commission (see European Commission, 2006c: 7; Argúndez-Garzía, 2006: 14). From a theoretical point of view, full consolidation seems to be the superior approach. Economies of scale and scope and the excess profit associated with economic integration are not only realized in proportion to an ownership percentage. Instead, if control can be exercised and the affiliates are economically integrated all of the achieved excess profits should be allocated to the economic group (see Argúndez-Garzía, 2006, 15). Furthermore, if group member's income should be consolidated in proportion to their ownership, transfer pricing as an income shifting device and compliance costs associated with transfer pricing would prevail. Therefore, a potential advantage of the Common Consolidated Corporate Tax Base could not be achieved in case of proportional consolidation.

The idea of limiting loss-relief to the extent of the actual economic risk of bearing the loss does not justify proportional consolidation, because the economic risk of bearing a loss does not directly correspond to the ownership percentage but rather to the investment.

There is another issue related to the question whether to apply full or proportional consolidation. If the parent holds less than 100% of the shares in a subsidiary, consideration has to be given to the treatment of minorities (see European Commission, 2006c: 9). The question is how to ensure fair treatment of majority and minority shareholders if the tax paid by the companies they own is potentially determined by the companies' relationship with the group. As the consolidated tax base is apportioned, the tax liability of each group member may differ from the tax liability faced by the company if it were independent. If the tax liability according to formula apportionment is higher, minority shareholders might be entitled to compensation. However, this issue not only arises if all of the subsidiary's income is consolidated, but also if this applies only to those parts of the subsidiary's income that corresponds to the majority shareholders' profits. The following example illustrates this issue.

Example: Suppose a taxable group consists of a parent company that owns 60% of a subsidiary. Based on separate accounting, the parent is earning a profit of 1,000. In contrast, the subsidiary is incurring a loss that amounts to 500 under separate accounting. Under the assumption that there are no intra-group transactions, the consolidated tax base is 500. Assuming furthermore, that the tax base is apportioned equally, the share in the group's tax base for each company is 250. If the subsidiary's income is only consolidated in proportion to the ownership percentage the consolidated tax base amounts to 700 (1,000 + (-500 x 60%)). Combining the share in the consolidated tax base of 350 with the loss that corresponds to the minority shareholders' income results in a tax base of the subsidiary of 150 (350 + (-200)). As a result, independent of whether full or proportional consolidation is applied, the tax liability faced by minority shareholders can be higher applying the Common Consolidated Corporate Tax Base compared to separate accounting.

Therefore, the Common Consolidated Corporate Tax Base has to be based on full consolidation and should be accompanied with rules concerning compensation for minority shareholders. The treatment of minority shareholders should be ignored for tax purposes and left to company law of the member states. Therefore, tax law would only have to deal with compensation of minority shareholders for any negative consequences arising from consolidation and the apportionment mechanism (see European Commission, 2006b: 12-13).

6.4.2.2.6 Income arising on cross-border investments in third countries

6.4.2.2.6.1 Necessity of Common Rules

The application of the Common Consolidated Corporate Tax Base is limited to the boundaries of the EU (see European Commission, 2001b: 482-486, 498). For those cross-border business activities between member states and third countries, separate accounting using arm's length pricing remains.[50] With respect to third countries, outbound and inbound investments can be distinguished. Typical patterns for outbound investments are an EU parent company doing direct investment in a third country, i.e. an EU parent company maintaining a permanent establishment or having a subsidiary in a third country. Between parent and subsidiary different income flows may arise. The parent company may receive dividends, interest income, or royalties. Typical settings for inbound investments are a non-EU company doing either direct investment maintaining a permanent establishment or a subsidiary. Again, the non-EU parent company may receive dividend payments, interest income or royalties from its EU subsidiary.

A starting point for the tax treatment of inbound and outbound investment with respect to third countries is the current tax practice as codified in the national tax laws

[50] Separate accounting under the arm's length principle would also have to be applied to EU affiliates resident in member states that do not apply the Common Consolidated Corporate Tax Base and to EU affiliates excluded from the consolidated group.

and existing tax treaties. In contrast, any renegotiation or amendment to existing tax treaties is regarded as last resort solution (see European Commission, 2006i: 3).

At present, tax rules concerning inbound and outbound investments differ to a substantial degree (see section 4.2.1). Differences exist regarding various aspects. On the one hand, member states treat the same category of income differently. For instance, with respect to foreign permanent establishments some member states apply the exemption method either with or without loss relief while other member states apply the credit method to avoid double taxation (see section 4.2.1, table 25). Similarly, dividends on shares in a foreign subsidiary are either tax exempt or taxed and foreign tax credit is granted (see section 4.2.1, table 26). On the other hand, member states apply different approaches depending on the category of income. Interest on loans or royalties on intellectual property are subject to residence based taxation while source based taxation is rather applied to profits of a foreign permanent establishment or subsidiary. With respect to inbound investments, withholding taxes are levied at source with different rates. Furthermore, member states know different anti-avoidance rules in order to prevent the erosion of the tax base.

Due to these differences, it seems appropriate to exclude foreign income earned in third countries from the Common Consolidated Corporate Tax Base and instead, to assign the taxing right solely to the jurisdiction of residence of the group member receiving the income. Otherwise, member states would have to accept each other's tax rules regarding cross-border investment. For example, if one member state grants cross-border relief of losses incurred by a foreign permanent establishment, foreign losses would be consolidated thereby reducing the apportionable consolidated tax base and thus, the share in the consolidated tax attributable to other involved countries. Similar conflicts may arise, if the exemption method is meant to relief double taxation in one member state while the credit method is applied in another member state.

Although, maintaining current tax practice seems attractive from a pragmatic point of view, there are good reasons to strive for common rules with respect to third country issues, at least in the long run. If different national rules are to be followed with respect to cross-border investments between EU group entities and non-EU group entities, this may facilitate strategic tax planning. EU companies might reorganize their business organization within the EU in such a way that cross-border investments in third countries are subject to the most beneficial rules provided by a member state. For instance, direct investment in a low-tax country via a permanent establishment or a subsidiary would be undertaken from a company resident in a member state providing the exemption method as a means to avoid double taxation. Similar tax planning strategies might occur with respect to non-EU companies investing in the EU. Therefore, a Common Consolidated Corporate Tax Base maintaining differing current tax practice with respect to third country issues is not neutral.

As companies can reorganize their business in order to realize tax advantages, anti-avoidance rules applied by some member states are likely to be evaded. Thin-capitalization rules, for instance, could by evaded, if a non-EU company first grants a loan to a subsidiary resident in a country without thin-capitalization rules, and afterwards this loan is directed to the relevant company via intra-group transactions. This is facilitated by consolidation, as intra-group transactions are netted out and thus, are not subject to tax. As a consequence, it becomes difficult for member states to enforce their tax rules, especially if they are less favorable than comparable rules of other member states applying the Common Consolidated Corporate Tax Base. Moreover, with different national tax rules regarding third country issues, multinational companies doing business not only within the internal market but also in third countries would still have to cope with 27 different tax systems.

To conclude, at least in the long run common rules for taxing inbound and outbound investments with respect to third countries are recommended (see also Hellerstein and McLure, 2004: 207; Mintz, 2004: 228).

6.4.2.2.6.2 Outbound Investments

Basically, there are two alternative approaches for the taxation of income which results from cross-border business activities: source-based taxation and residence based taxation.

According to the source principle, foreign profits generated in the source country would have to be finally taxed according to the rules of the source country, since the income is exempted from taxation in the residence country. Thus, business profits attributable to a permanent establishment or a subsidiary located in a third country are not included in the Common Consolidated Corporate Tax Base but exempt from taxation in the EU. The same should apply to other categories of income, such as interest on loans, dividends on shares, or royalties on intellectual property. These categories of income should be exempt from taxation in those member states where the receiving company is resident. However, pure source-based taxation seems to be unrealistic, as it would contradict current tax conventions. According to the OECD Model, the right of the source country to tax interest income and royalties is only limited. Therefore, in order to prevent double non-taxation of these kinds of passive investment income the residence jurisdiction should maintain its right to tax these kinds of income received by a resident company and provide a credit for the underlying foreign taxes.

The residence principle calls for taxation of an investor's worldwide income according to the rules of the residence country, regardless of the geographical source of the income. This approach would imply that income earned through a permanent establishment or a subsidiary outside the EU, dividends on shares, interest income on loans, or royalties on intellectual property should be taxed by the residence member state. To avoid international double taxation, the residence jurisdiction grants a credit for taxes paid abroad. Similar to the source principle, pure residence based taxation seems not feasible as it would not be in line with current international tax practice. Two restrictions to a pure residence approach are necessary. First, taxation of profits attributed to a foreign subsidiary has to be deferred until the time of repatriation. Second, the foreign tax credit has to be limited to the amount of domestic tax payable on the foreign income.

There are two possibilities how to introduce the residence principle in conjunction with the Common Consolidated Corporate Tax Base (see Argúndez-García, 2006: 23-26).

The first possibility is to include foreign income from sources outside the EU earned by EU-resident group entities in the consolidated tax base for later apportionment across the corresponding member states. A credit for taxes paid abroad is granted by those member states receiving a share of the foreign income. The foreign tax credit is limited to the amount of domestic tax payable on the share of the foreign income.

The second possibility is to exclude income earned outside the EU from consolidation and instead to attribute it to the EU group entity earning that foreign income. Thus, income earned outside the EU would follow the same attribution rules as at present and would be taxed in the particular residence jurisdiction. The foreign income is added to the share in the consolidated tax base apportioned to the respective company. A foreign tax credit is granted by the member state where the group entity earning that foreign income is a tax resident.

The source principle is conceptually consistent with the concept of the Common Consolidated Corporate Tax Base (see Hellerstein and McLure, 2004: 207). Under the Common Consolidated Corporate Tax Base concept, the consolidated income is apportioned according to the distribution of the group's income generating activities and finally taxed according to the rules of the respective jurisdiction. A major difference, however, remains. While EU group entities are subject to consolidation and formula apportionment, non-EU group entities have to apply separate accounting using arm's length pricing. In contrast, application of the residence principle to cross-border investments involving third countries would imply not only a different method of allocating profits but also a different assignment of taxing rights compared to the concept of the Common Consolidated Corporate Tax Base. If the taxing right of income earned in a third country is assigned to the particular jurisdiction in which the company earning the foreign income is resident, this would be conform to the traditional interpretation of residence taxation. In contrast, by including foreign income from non-EU sources in the consolidated tax base subject to formula apportionment, each member state having a nexus to the consolidated tax base would be deemed to be a resident jurisdiction (see Argúndez-García, 2006: 23). On the one hand, this seems theoretically questionable, as those apportionment factors located within the EU do not reflect the activities generating the income outside the EU. On the other hand, this approach would promote the intention behind the Common Consolidated Corporate Tax Base to treat the EU as one internal market and to take into account that a group of affiliates forms an economic unit.

Although conceptually appealing, there are some shortcomings associated with the source principle in light of the principle of neutrality. As outlined in section 5.2, the combination of the source principle and the separate accounting approach facilitates profit shifting either by abusive transfer pricing or relocation of functions and risks. Moreover, as source principle is probably not going to be applied to debt financing, incentives to modify the financing structure in order to gain a tax advantage remain.

To prevent an erosion of the tax base due to strategic tax planning, the EU could introduce common anti-avoidance rules in international situations in conjunction with third countries (see European Commission, 2005c: 13-15). Rules regarding controlled foreign companies (CFC) located in tax havens, and rules to cope with abusive transfer pricing could be taken into consideration. However, these rules would lead to distortions of business decisions which are not conform to the principle of tax neutrality.

Compared to the source principle, residence based taxation is rather supposed to promote neutrality, since the decisions where to invest as well as the decisions on the finance structure and the legal structure are unaffected by taxation (see section 3.3.2). However, due to the possibility to move the residence of the parent company to a low-tax country and due to the deferral principle and the limitations of the foreign tax credit tax induced distortions of business decisions remain even under the residence principle.

When evaluating the effects of the residence principle in light of the principle of neutrality, a distinction has to be made between attributing income earned outside the EU to the whole group or only to the group member doing business outside the EU. If foreign income is attributed to a particular group entity, the individual tax rate of the residence jurisdiction is applied. This approach will give a tax incentive for multinationals to change the residence of group entities doing business in a third country. Direct investments outside the EU would be relocated to affiliated companies in a low-tax member state or group companies investing in a third country may move their residence to a low-tax country. Additionally, if the tax rate in the residence jurisdiction is lower than the effective tax rate applied to the consolidated tax base, there is an incentive to shift profits to a third country, as these profits are subject to the lower tax rate in the jurisdiction of residence. Instead, if foreign income is consolidated and apportioned, it is subject to the effective tax rate determined by the allocation of apportionment factors and the tax rates of the corresponding member states. Thus, the effective tax rate applied to the group's EU income determines the tax burden of foreign income, irrespective of where the company doing business outside the EU is a tax resident. This would eliminate incentives to move the residence of EU group entities investing in a third country. However, incentives to change the inter-jurisdictional allocation of apportionment factors will increase, as the effective tax rate applied to the consolidated tax base will also determine the tax burden of the world wide income of EU multinationals.

To ensure a symmetric treatment of profits and expenses, source based taxation would require a distinction to be drawn between expenses associated with tax exempt non-EU income and expenses associated with EU apportionable income. Those expenses related to exempt income should not be tax deductible. A similar distinction is required, if the residence principle is followed and foreign income is attributed to the residence jurisdiction. Corresponding to the tax treatment of income, expenses associated with this income should be separated from the consolidated tax base and directly ascribed to the residence country. These presumably complex distinctions are not necessary, if income earned outside the EU is included in the consolidated tax base. The residence principle is generally supposed to require a higher administrative effort than the source principle. Therefore, with respect to the criterion of simplicity, the source principle should be favored.

To summaries, in order to reduce scope for tax planning and compliance costs, the EU should strive for common rules with respect to outbound investments of EU group companies in third countries. The application of the source principle would be consistent to the concept of the Common Consolidated Corporate Tax Base and has administrative advantages. Regarding tax neutrality, however, income earned outside the EU should be included in the Common Consolidated Corporate Tax Base and shared by the involved member states (see Gérard, 2006).

6.4.2.2.6.3 Inbound Investments

Taxable income of EU group affiliates which are ultimately controlled by a non-EU company should be consolidated and apportioned. This should apply to both subsidiaries and permanent establishments located in the EU. Between the non-EU company and the EU group entities, separate accounting under the arm's length principle should prevail to determine the individual tax base to be included in the Common Consolidated Corporate Tax Base.

Regarding payments of dividends, interest, and royalties by EU group companies to a company resident in a third country most of the existing tax treaties allow the imposition of a withholding tax. According to the OECD Model, the withholding tax rate is limited. Although, a consequent application of the source principle guiding the Common Consolidated Corporate Tax Base would allow for an unlimited taxation of these kinds of passive income, withholding taxes should fall in to the range agreed by the individual tax treaties of the countries involved. Pure source based taxation seems unrealistic.

When imposing a withholding tax, the question arises, whether the taxing right is assigned only to the jurisdiction in which the paying company is resident or to the whole EU group. This question is closely linked to the issue whether non business income should be excluded from consolidation. If a distinction between different types of income is refused, as favored here, the amount paid is deducted from the consolidated tax base and therefore reduces the income to be apportioned to member states. Accordingly, the withholding tax levied by the member state where the payer is a tax resident should be also subject to formula apportionment (see European Commission, 2006e: 3). Instead, if dividends, interest or royalties are excluded from consolidation, these payments are tax deductible only in the jurisdiction where the paying company is a resident. In this case, the withholding tax received by the member state should not be shared by other member states.

6.4.2.2.6.4 Treatment of Companies Entering the Group

Another issue that has to be discussed with respect to losses refers to pre-consolidation losses (see European Commission, 2007b: 6). In general, there are three approaches for the treatment of pre-consolidation losses. These losses can be treated as part of the group losses and offset against profits of other group members. Another approach is to exclude these losses from consolidation and to prohibit their compensation during the time group taxation applies. This is, for example, the current German approach for domestic group taxation. Thus, losses may only be used against profits when the company that has incurred these losses leaves the taxable group. An intermediate approach would provide that pre-consolidation losses do not enter consolidation but can be offset against the positive share of the consolidated tax base of the respective company.

As pre-consolidation losses of a company are not incurred by the taxable group, it seems reasonable to exclude such losses from consolidation. Since under the concept of the Common Consolidated Corporate Tax Base each group entity remains liable to tax with its share in the consolidated tax base on an individual basis, such losses should remain with the company that has incurred them and offset on a stand-alone-basis (see European Commission, 2007b: 6). This approach is consistent with the source principle inherent to the Common Consolidated Corporate Tax Base and corresponds to current member states' tax practice (see section 4.1.1.3). However, to deny the offset of these losses during the consolidation phase would be too restrictive. This might prevent companies with loss carry forwards from opting for the Common Consolidated Corporate Tax Base. In order to separate these losses from consolidation, pre-consolidation losses should be carried forward and subtracted from the consolidated tax base after formula apportionment.

Another issue refers to the tax treatment of hidden capital gains build before a company joins the group. These gains do not belong to the group, but to the company and the country of residence. Taxing rights of the source country may be at risk since if these hidden gains are realized in a subsequent year they are apportioned to all group members. According to IFRS, all identifiable assets acquired, and liabilities and contingent liabilities assumed in a business combination are initially recorded in the consolidated financial statements at fair value (IFRS 3.36). For tax purposes, however, it should be avoided, that member states tax companies applying the Common Consolidated Corporate Tax Base the first time on the difference between the fair value of their assets and liabilities and their value for tax purposes. Should a company opt for the application of the Common Consolidated Corporate Tax Base, this does not lead to a realization of hidden capital gains. Taxation of these gains would probable keep companies from applying the Common Consolidated Corporate Tax Base. The difference between the fair value of assets and liabilities and their value for tax purposes could rather be treated like an intra-group transaction. Group members are not to be taxed at the time of the transaction. If the intra-group income is restored in subsequent years, an amount equal to the hidden capital gains assessed in the year the Common Consolidated Corporate Tax Base is applied the first time should be directly allocated to the respective tax jurisdiction. As a consequence, there is a need for separate accounting to allow for a systematic tax treatment of hidden capital gains build before a company joins the group.

6.4.2.2.7 Treatment of Companies Leaving the Group

If a company leaves the group or the group terminates, losses apportioned to each group member during the group phase should remain with each company.

Moreover, if one of the group companies engaged in an intra-group transfer afterwards leaves the group, this should be deemed as a restoration event. If the internal purchaser of the asset afterwards leaves the group, not only the purchaser but also the asset leaves the group. Therefore, this event should be treated in the same way as a sale of the asset to an unrelated party. Furthermore, this approach would prevent tax planning strategies aimed to avoid taxation of capital gains by transferring assets into a subsidiary and selling the shares of the subsidiary with full participation exemption (see European Commission, 2007c: 9). If the seller leaves the group, this should generally not deamed to be a realization event regarding previously deferred intra-group gains and losses. Only gains and losses associated with the assets of the leaving group entity are realized. However, a previously deferred intra-group gain or loss should still become subject to tax. As the seller and the buyer do not belong to the same group, the requirement for deferred taxation is not met anymore. Another reason for this provision again refers to tax planning. Companies might avoid taxation of capital gains in a certain country by joining the group, transferring assets into other group members and afterwards leaving the group. In order to ensure that taxing rights of the country of residence are not at risk, the leaving company has to be subject to tax on the gain which is assessed as the difference between the seller's basis in the asset and the arm's length price at the time of the original transfer. Here, a distinction has to be made between those hidden capital gains assessed in the year the Common Consolidated Corporate Tax Base is applied the first time and those capital gains assessed in a subsequent year, when the intra-group transfer occurred. The latter capital gains should be subject to formual apportionment, since they belong to the group. The hidden capital gains built before the entity joined the group should be directly attributed to this entity. Subject to tax should be the leaving group entity with the capital gains attributed to this company, not those companies remaining in the group. To conclude, arm's length prices are still relevant under a Common Consolidated Corporate Tax Base.

6.4.2.3 Formula Apportionment

The apportionment mechanism can be based on different factors (see European Commission, 2001b). A general distinction can be drawn between macro-based factors and mirco-based factors.

A macro-based apportionment scheme would decouple an individual company's tax liability in a member state and its business activities in that country. Instead of company-specific attributes, the consolidated tax base would be allocated in proportion to aggregated economic data at the level of the member state. For instance, the gross domestic product (GDP) could be used as a macro-based factor (see Sørensen, 2004: 96). Since the allocation of profits does not depend on company specific attributes, a macro-based apportionment scheme is prone to tax planning (see Argúndez-García, 2006: 42; Wellisch, 2004b: 271). However, such a scheme could lead to a mismatch between the income generating activities of a company and its tax liability in a particular member state (see Hellerstein and McLure, 2004: 211; Sørensen, 2004: 96; Wellisch, 2004b: 271). Only a small fraction of the consolidated tax base may be allocated to a group member in a member state, even if the group has most of its income generating production facilities in that country. It is obvious, that especially large member states might benefit from a marco-based apportionment scheme. Such an allocation of international income would be inconsistent with the principle of inter-nation equity, because it neither based on the supply approach nor on the supply-demand approach (see Argúndez-García, 2006: 41; Frebel, 2006: 126). It is therefore questionable whether the member states will accept distribution rules that are divorced from the activities of a resident enterprise and thus also completely detached from existing conventions of source taxation (see Sørensen, 2004: 96; Wellisch, 2004a: 37).

In contrast to macro-based apportionment schemes, a micro-based allocation maintains a link between firm specific attributes and the tax liability. The best known apportionment mechanism using micro-data is formula apportionment, which has a long tradition in Canada and the United States at the state level (see Wellisch, 2004b: 269-270; Weiner and Mintz, 2002: 349; Riecker, 1997: 130-133). Formula apportionment is generally based on three factors: labour factor, capital/property factor and sales factor. The labour factor and the capital factor are meant to reflect the contribution of labour and capital as production factors in the generation of income.

The labour factor can be measured by employee compensation, including for example salaries and commissions. Alternatively, the labour factor may be determined using the number of employees (see Wellisch, 2004b: 273). When choosing between the two alternatives one has to take into account that labour costs differ significantly across member states. On the one hand, these differences may be the result of differences in labour productivity. On the other hand, they may be the result of the different general levels across member states (see Wellisch, 2004b: 273; Bökelmann, 1997: 262). Companies make use of these factor price differences across countries. They set up production plants in low factor-price countries, thereby reducing their productivity cost and increasing their profits. As mentioned in chapter 2, differences in factor price endowments across countries can explain the presence of foreign direct investment. If the number of employees is chosen to reflect the labour factor, an equal productivity of labour is implicitly assumed. This assumption seems unrealistic, since employees might indeed have different levels of productivity (see Wellisch, 2004b: 273). If group units with an identical number of employees have different levels of productivity, potential distortions of the division of taxable income may occur. Therefore, the labour factor should not be measured by the number of employees. In order to take account of the wage level differentials across countries, payroll could be adjusted using a cross-country labour cost index provided by an official international organisation. It seems however questionable whether the member states would be able to reach an agreement on such an index. One has to bear in mind that issues associated with different wage levels across member states do already arise in determining the consolidated tax base. Since labour costs are deductible against the consolidated tax base, the share of all participating member states will decrease. Therefore, mutual recognition of different national wage levels seems to be a prerequisite not only with respect to the income allocation but also with respect to the determination of the consolidated tax base.

The capital factor could include tangible and intangible assets. Moreover, it could be measured as a stock or as a flow (see Oestreicher, 2000: 190-192; Musgrave, 1984: 241). From a theoretical point of view, it seems essential to take into account intangible assets, since they are an important factor for the generation of profits especially for multinational enterprises. In practice, however, it may be difficult to value and locate intangible assets (see Frebel, 2006: 149-153). Valuation problems are especially relevant with regard to internally generated intangibles. Since their assessment entails scope for discretion, expenses associated with intangible assets are tax deductible in the period in which they occur in many member states (see section 4.1.1.2.3). In this context, it also has to be kept in mind that the working group concerned with the design of a common tax base recommends to expense research and development costs in the period in which they occur (see section 6.3.1.4). The 'stock' approach to the measurement of capital would be based on the current market value or original cost of assets less accumulated depreciation, whilst the 'flow' approach would be based on economic depreciation and interest, which is the user cost of capital (see Oestreicher, 2000: 190-192; Musgrave, 1984: 241). An asset may be defined as the source of future economic benefits. Accordingly, its fair value is generally determined by the discounted value of the anticipated income inflow associated with the asset. Thus, the property factor measured as a ‘stock’ would rather reflect estimated future income than the generation of income within one period. The mismatch between the recognition of the property factor and the annual income associated with the property may result in a misallocation of the consolidated tax base. For instance, since new machines have a higher fair value than old machines, a larger share of the consolidated tax base is attributed to group members using comparably new machines. With respect to the generation of income within one year, however, both new and old machines may be used with the same productivity. If the property factor is measured as a ‘flow’, the annual costs of capital would be matched with the income generated within the same period. This approach would better reflect the contribution of assets as an income producing factor for a given year (see Musgrave, 1984). It also seems logical since all other variables of the tax system are measured on an annual basis as flow variables (i.e., income, payroll, sales, are 'flow' and not 'stock' variables). On the other hand, to a certain extent, if there was some correlation between 'flow' and 'stock' of capital (i.e., if the first was a constant percentage of the second), the two measures could be equivalent in estimating the annual contribution of capital to the generation of profits.

The idea behind the reference to sales is that profits are only generated by the interaction between supply and demand (supply-demand approach), so that in the case of cross-border transactions both the production location and the state where there is demand for the product have a claim on the company's profits (see Oestreicher, 2000: 183-184; Salzberger, 1999: 101; McLure, 1997: 863). The sales factor has to be located at the place of demand, since only a destination-based sales factor would be a counterpart of the payroll and the property factor both representing origin-based factors (see Oestreicher, 2000: 182). However, the place of use might in various cases not be easy to determine (see McLure and Weiner, 2000: 270). Particularly with the ongoing decentralisation and internationalisation and the increase in digital transactions, the localisation of the destination of sales and services provided becomes more complex (see Schäfer, 2006: 194). It is thus more and more difficult to identify the place of demand in an exact and, at the same time, cost-effective way. Also in the United States, the sales factor has generated the most practical controversy of all three factors (see Hellerstein and McLure, 2004: 213; Weiner, 2001: 385; Coffill and Willson, 1993: 1109-1110).

Value-added has been proposed as an alternative micro-factor (see Lodin and Gammie, 2001). Compared to company-specific production factors, value-added has the advantage that companies activities are recorded more broadly. Moreover, value-added can be derived comparatively simply from the value-added-tax base, which is harmonized throughout the EU (see Hellerstein and McLure, 2004: 215). However, the distribution of group profits according to the value-added of the group members causes problems if goods and services are delivered within the taxable unit. This is because, in this case, the determination of value-added presupposes that the services exchanged by the group companies are valued. This in turn requires transfer prices, which is precisely what the Common Consolidated Corporate Tax Base is supposed to avoid (see Hellerstein and McLure, 2004: 215; Sørensen, 2004: 97; Wellisch, 2004b: 273; Oestreicher, 2002: 350).

To conclude, for the apportionment of group income the allocation formula should be based on a broad set of company-specific production factors such as proportional property, payroll, and sales which must be defined uniformly across member states. A uniform definition of these factors is necessary to exclude situations of both double taxation and lower taxation. Theory provides no clear answer for the weight of the company-specific production factors. A political agreement is therefore required on the weighting of these factors. Macro-factors and micro-factors, if derived from value-added, do not seem to be appropriate. Factors which are deemed to represent profit generating activities are typically property, payroll and sales. In this context it has to be kept in mind that in an economically integrated entity consisting out of separate legal entities it is not possible to determine the source of profits on an economic rationale.

6.4.2.4 Related Issues

6.4.2.4.1 Optional or Mandatory?

As a general rule, the Common Consolidated Corporate Tax Base should be mandatory for those companies belonging to the taxable unit. With respect to the principle of neutrality companies should not have an option whether to be taxed according to the method of separate accounting or formula apportionment. Otherwise, there would be scope for tax planning which might also increase complexity (see Herzig, 2006: 162; Mintz, 2004: 226; Sørensen, 2004: 102; Weiner, 2003: 695). However, the European Commission intends to implement the Common Consolidated Corporate Tax Base as an optional system (see European Commission, 2007b: 2). Their decision is based on the notion that the Common Consolidated Corporate Tax Base provides companies with rules allowing them to benefit from the single market (see European Commission, 2007b: 2). Furthermore, the Common Consolidated Corporate Tax Base is a very far reaching reform. Currently, consolidation including a deferred taxation of gains arising on intra-group transfers is only available in seven member states (see section 4.1.1.3). Consolidation and formula apportionment could be very complex and associated with high administrative costs. Therefore, companies should have the option of remaining with the current tax system in order to avoid compliance costs associated with the Common Consolidated Corporate Tax Base. If the Common Consolidated Corporate Tax Base is applied as an optional scheme, the option should be obligatory for a certain period of time in order to prevent taxpayers from having the choice between the two systems each year (see European Commission, 2007b: 3).

Two contrasting approaches exist regarding the choice of members in the election. One requires an "all-in or all-out" treatment. If the group decides to apply for the regime, all members that meet the shareholding and other requirements must join. Another treatment allows "cherry-picking" of some members among the potential members that meet the shareholding requirements. If the application of the Common Consolidated Corporate Tax Base is optional, all eligible entities should be consolidated. Cherry-picking as a means of tax planning should not be allowed.

The question of whether the application of the Common Consolidated Corporate Tax Base should be optional or mandatory is closely related to the definition of the consolidated group (see Schön, 2007: 431). If the criteria used to define the consolidated group can be adjusted without costs, companies would have a factual option regarding the group entities to be included in the Common Consolidated Corporate Tax Base. In this case, a compulsory scheme may not be effective. Similarly, if the application of the Common Consolidated Corporate Tax Base is optional, the importance of a definition of the consolidated group resistant to tax planning would decrease.

6.4.2.4.2 Local Profit Taxes, Non-profit Taxes and Social Security Contributions

In most countries, companies are subject to taxes other than the corporate income tax (see section 4.1.3). These taxes are either imposed on income (profit taxes) or business factors (non-profit taxes), such as payroll or property. A Common Consolidated Corporate Tax Base as proposed by the European Commission raises several issues regarding additional local profit and non-profit taxes. First, the consolidation and apportionment approach may affect the determination of the tax base of local taxes.

Local profit taxes would have to be levied on the share in the common tax base ascribed to the respective member state. This, however, will probably not cause conceptual problems, since both, the concept of the Common Consolidated Corporate Tax Base and the determination of the tax base of national local profit taxes follow the source principle.

In some member states, certain items of income have to be deducted or added back in order to calculate the tax base of local taxes. For instance, in Hungary the taxable base is the net sales income decreased by the acquisition costs of goods sold, costs of mediated services and material costs. To provide information on these items of income, intra-group income may have to be taken into account. Similar issues may arise concerning non-profit taxes. The tax base may comprise business assets valued at their standard tax value. In this context, deferred taxation of gains realized on intra-group transfers would lead to a lower tax base. Therefore, it seems necessary to maintain separate accounting for determining the group member's individual accounts and to adjust them in a separate combined report.

Another issue to be considered refers to the deductibility of additional local taxes (see European Commission, 2006f: 4-7). At present, most member states allow companies to deduct additional taxes from the corporate income tax base (see European Commission, 2006f: 4).

Subgroup 3 on taxable income of the Common Consolidated Corporate Tax Base Working Group has elaborated a definition of deductible expenses in general. Deductible expenses are defined as decreases in economic benefits in the form of outflows which are made for business purposes and are incurred during the taxable period (see European Commission, 2006g: 5). Exceptions to this definition are to be shown in a special list. Regarding taxes, there seems to be a consensus to exclude the corporate income tax and VAT (see European Commission, 2006g: 6).

Local taxes represent a mandatory cost incurred in the course of business. Thus, with reference to the definition of deductible expenses, these taxes should be deductible. There are two alternative approaches to deducting local taxes. They can either be deductible against the Common Consolidated Corporate Tax Base before apportionment or they can be deductible against the share of the Common Consolidated Corporate Tax Base after apportionment (see European Commission, 2006f: 6).

If local taxes are deducted from the Common Consolidated Corporate Tax Base before apportionment, the share of all participating member states will decrease. Therefore, mutual recognition of the different national practices as regards the division of competences and the methods of raising revenues seems to be a prerequisite. However, member states may not accept to provide relief for taxes levied by another member state. Moreover, there is also an incentive inherent to this approach for funding public needs by imposing local taxes, because these taxes are effectively paid not only by the company resident in the respective jurisdiction but also by other participating countries.

In order to avoid mutual agreement of different national tax systems, local taxes should be deductible against the share of the Common Consolidated Corporate Tax Base after apportionment. This approach would be also consistent with the source principle and the principle of inter-nation equity. Local taxes are generally used for funding of public goods, such as infrastructure. Therefore, these taxes can be characterised as costs for infrastructure that facilitates income generating activities conducted in a certain jurisdiction. As these taxes are closely linked to income generating activities in a certain jurisdiction, they can be directly attributed to the jurisdiction in which the group entity is resident. Accordingly, local taxes should be deducted from the share of the Common Consolidated Corporate Tax Base after apportionment. This is especially relevant regarding local taxes levied on property and payroll, as these taxes are closely related to apportionment factors.

Similar issues regarding the deducibility of expenses arise in the context of social security contributions (see European Commission, 2006f: 4). Generally, these social security contributions should be tax deductible. However, it seems questionable whether member states would accept each other's practice and level of social security system. Member states may not accept to provide relief for higher social standards provided in other countries. Therefore, similar to local taxes, social security contributions should be deductible from the consolidated tax base after apportionment.

However, one has to bear in mind, that mutual recognition is already implied regarding different national levels of expenses such as wages or rental fees, since these expenses may be influenced by national regulations. Thus, it would make conceptual sense not to distinguish between different kinds of expenses and instead to deduct social security contributions as well as local taxes from the consolidated tax base before apportionment.

To conclude, local profit and non-profit taxes as well as social security contributions should be tax deductible against the consolidated tax base. Whether these expenses reduce the Common Consolidated Corporate Tax Base before or after apportionment mainly depends on the willingness of member states to accept each others national practices concerning the level and methods of raising revenues. As regards the determination of the base of local taxes, the introduction of a Common Consolidated Corporate Tax Base would not lead to serious problems. However, there might be a need to maintain separate accounting in order to provide information on certain income items needed for the determination of the tax base.

6.4.3 Summary

The scenario of a Common Consolidated Corporate Tax Base is related to the scenario of a Common Corporate Tax Base. Both scenarios require common tax accounting rules. In addition to common tax accounting, the Common Consolidated Corporate Tax Base also includes a consolidation and formual apportionment approach. Consolidation raises several issues to be addressed. The consolidated group of corporations has to be defined and an approach for computing the income of the group has to be found. Several issues are also related to formula apportionment. The key question in this context is how to design the formula used to apportion the consolidated tax base to the involved member states.

As regards the definition of the consolidated group, a simple or qualified majority of ownership should be a key element. Ownership should be defined with reference to voting power and can be reached both, directly or indirectly through subsidiaries. Additional legal criteria indicating whether there are economic interdependencies are preferable, although they may be difficult to enforce. The Common Consolidated Corporate Tax Base should be applicable to corporations and permanent establishments as group members. The decision whether transparent entities can apply for the Common Consolidated Corporate Tax Base as parent company or not should be left to the member states. Assignment of taxing rights on corporate income should not be based on the mere existence of apportionment factors. Instead, the minimum threshold should be the existence of a permanent establishment. The territorial scope of the Common Consolidated Corporate Tax Base should be restricted to group entities located within the EU. Common definitions of tax residency and permanent establishment are required in order to avoid scope for tax planning and to reduce compliance costs. A group of EU entities ultimately controlled by a non-EU parent should be eligible for application of the Common Consolidated Corporate Tax Base. The same should apply to situations where a non-EU intermediary exists in the ownership chain connecting EU group entities.

Individual tax accounts should serve as a starting point for consolidation. These individual accounts should be consolidated, thus forming the consolidated tax base. Intra-group loss relief is a key feature of consolidation. A negative Common Consolidated Corporate Tax Base should be apportioned and offset against a future positive share of the Common Consolidated Corporate Tax Base. Deferred taxation of gains and losses realized on intra-group transactions is another essential element of consolidation. Instead of adjusting the individual accounts of group entities involved in the intra-group transfer, gains and losses realized on an intra-group transfer should be neutralized in a separate combined report. Individual accounts based on separate accounting are necessary with respect to claims of minority shareholders and recapture of gains in cases where group entities enter or leave the Common Consolidated Corporate Tax Base group or group entities move their residence.

With respect to group companies, which are resident outside the EU, common rules are necessary. Neither the source principle, nor the residence principle can be applied in a way as to avoid distortions of business decisions. An application of the source principle would be consistent to the concept of the Common Consolidated Corporate Tax Base and has administrative advantages. Regarding tax neutrality, however, the residence principle is more favourable.

Pre-consolidation losses and hidden capital gains do not belong to the group. Therefore, these losses and gains should be directly attributed to the jurisdiction where they have been built up. Losses may only be offset against the share of the Common Consolidated Corporate Tax Base after apportionment. Hidden capital gains are taken into account and taxation is deferred until the asset leaves the group or in the course of depreciation. If a company leaves the group, apportioned losses should remain with each company. Moreover, if a company involved in an intra-group transaction leaves the group, this should be deemed as a restoration event. If the internal purchaser afterwards leaves the group, the group is liable to tax with the deferred intra-group income. Instead, if the selling company leaves the group, this company is taxes on the deferred intra-group income. There should be no distinction between apportionable income and income excluded from formula apportionment, neither concerning different categories of income nor with respect to the ownership percentage.

The apportionment of group income should be based on a broad set of company-specific production factors such as property, payroll and sales, which must be defined uniformaly across member states. As regards the weight of the company-specific production factors, theory does not provide a clear solution.

If the requirements for the Common Consolidated Corporate Tax Base are met, its application should be mandatory to avoid tax planning. However, under this approach, a definition of the consolidated group resistant to tax planning becomes more important. If the application of the Common Consolidated Corporate Tax Base is optional, the importance of the definition of the group decreases.

Local profit and non-profit taxes as well as social security contributions should be tax deductible, either against the consolidated tax base or against the share of the consolidated tax base after formula apportionment.

As a conclusion, the Common Consolidated Corporate Tax Base has the potential to reduce tax obstacles induced by separate accounting under the arm's length principle. It is based on the notion, that a group of companies forms an economic unit. Consequently, it does not seek to allocate income to its economic source. The rationale behind is rather to provide a pragmatic solution for profit allocation among jurisdictions. Thereby transfer pricing issues can be solved to a great extent. However, multinational enterprises will still have to determine arm's length prices. The necessity arises due to minority shareholders, companies entering and leaving the consolidated group, local taxes and transactions to group corporations, which are resident outside the EU. Thus, transfer pricing issues will remain, at least to some extent. The Common Consolidated Corporate Tax Base can promote neutrality regarding cross-border restructuring, the financial structure and legal form of investments. Decisions regarding the allocation of the factors entering the apportionment formula, however, are distorted. Thus, incentives and scope for profit shifting are probably going to persist. In order to avoid these incentives, a harmonisation of the tax rate would be required.

7 Conclusions

Multinational enterprises have become increasingly important, especially between developed countries like the EU member states. Their presence is explained by the intensity of headquarter services, such as research and development, incomplete contracts and hold-up problems associated with market transactions, intra-industry heterogeneity and cross-country differences in factor endowments.

Taxation of multinational enterprises according to the current member states' tax practice is inappropriate with respect to the principles of equity and neutrality as well as administrative aspects. At present, EU-based multinational enterprises are confronted with 27 national tax systems, which are far from being uniform. Compliance with these different tax systems entails considerable compliance costs, which represents an obstacle to cross-border business activities. The allocation of profits between countries is based on separate accounting under the arm's length principle. This approach is theoretical questionable, since it ignores specific characteristics of multinational enterprises. Its application results in double taxation, leaves scope for profit shifting and turns out to be burdensome. Foreign income is either taxed according to the source principle or the residence principle, depending on the category of income. The separate entity approach and the coexistence of source-based and residence-based taxation facilitate tax planning aimed to make use of the existing international differences of tax burdens. Thereby, taxation distorts business decisions. Governments react and introduce provisions such as the denial of cross-border loss relief, thin-capitalisation rules and exit taxes in order to protect their tax bases. These measures are not only inconsistent with the principles of neutrality and equity but may also violate the fundamental freedoms of the EC Treaty.

A Common Consolidated Corporate Tax Base as intended by the European Commission would address these tax obstacles in a systematic way. The Commission distinguishes two reform scenarios.

The first scenario would consist of providing companies with the possibility to opt for a Common Corporate Tax Base for the determination of the taxable income resulting from their EU-wide activities. This scenario would not include a consolidation mechanism. A Common Corporate Tax Base would reduce compliance costs associated with having to deal with different tax codes in each country. Moreover, common tax accounting rules facilitate cross-border loss relief and have the potential to reduce tax charges arising in the context of cross-border business restructuring. However, transfer pricing issues and double taxation would remain.

The design of a common tax base can be based on IFRS. Although a formal link between IFRS and tax accounting does not appear to be appropriate, IFRS provide a broad basis of rules, which can be adopted for tax accounting. A comparison between IFRS and corresponding tax practice in the member states revealed that IFRS could provide a useful starting point concerning the recognition of revenues, the definition of assets and liabilities, the initial measurement of assets and regular depreciation. However, with respect to fair-value accounting, the recognition of internally generated intangible assets and provisions IFRS seem to be not suitable for defining the tax base. The working group concerned with the design of a Common Consolidated Corporate Tax Base has also considered IFRS as a useful starting point for the design of a number of elements of the tax base. Areas in which reference is made to IFRS include the definition of income and the recognition of revenues, the definition of liabilities and the initial measurement. The proposals concerning tax depreciation and the definition of assets, however, deviate from IFRS. These deviations result from tax accounting principles, such as simplification, objectification and legal certainty.

Calculations using the European Tax Analyzer revealed that a transition to a common tax base, as examined here, has only minor effects on the effective corporate tax burdens. At present there is a wide range of effective corporate tax burdens within the EU member states. Differences are mainly determined by the differences in nominal tax rates. Under a Common Corporate Tax Base the effective corporate tax burdens in all countries considered here except Cyprus tend to increase slightly since the tax bases tend to become broader. However, the considerable dispersions of effective tax burdens across countries would not change significantly. These results hold true for all industries considered in this study. As a conclusion, an exclusive harmonisation of the tax accounting rules cannot alleviate the current EU-wide differences of overall effective corporate tax burdens. In order to significantly reduce the dispersion of effective tax burdens within the EU, additional measures are necessary. Since the nominal tax rates are an important determinant of the effective tax burden, a convergence of the nominal tax rates on profits might be an efficient measure to reduce the differences in effective tax burdens across the EU.

The second scenario would be the Common Consolidated Corporate Tax Base as originally intended by the Commission. It is based on a Common Corporate Tax Base, but also includes some form of consolidation and formula apportionment. A Common Consolidated Corporate Tax Base would address most identified obstacles to cross-border business activities. It builds on the notion that a group of companies forms an economic unit. Thereby neutrality regarding the financial structure, the legal form and cross-border restructuring can be promoted. Since the consolidation and formula apportionment approach recognises that a multinational enterprise forms an economic unit, it does not seek to allocate income to its exact economic source. The rationale behind formula apportionment is rather to provide a pragmatic solution for profit allocation among jurisdictions and to reduce transfer pricing issues. Under formula apportionment, the role of the corporate income tax changes. Since the corporate income tax is transformed into a tax on the factors included in the allocation formula, the role as a benefit tax may be strengthened. At the same time, the role of the corporate income tax as a backstop for personal income tax loosens. The Common Consolidated Corporate Tax Base is conceptually aligned to the source principle. However, it does not fit with the neutrality concepts applied in an international context. Therefore, it is not totally immune against strategic tax planning. If companies can influence the cross-country allocation of apportionment factors, there is leeway for profit shifting. Given the dispersion of nominal tax rates across the EU, decisions on the location of investments and their expansion as well as the acquisition of companies might be distorted under formula apportionment.

The design of a Common Consolidated Corporate Tax Base raises several implementation issues. These issues refer to the definition of the consolidated group, the technique and scope of consolidation and the formula used to allocate the consolidated tax base among the involved member states. The definition of the consolidated group should be mainly based on legal criteria. A direct or indirect majority ownership should be a key element in this respect. Additional legal criteria circumscribing the economically integrated unit are preferable. The definition of the consolidated group is interrelated with the question, whether the application of the Common Consolidated Corporate Tax Base should be mandatory or optionally. If the application is mandatory, a definition resistant to tax planning becomes more important. In contrast, if the application is optional, the importance of the group definition decreases. The personal scope of the consolidated group should not only be restricted to corporations. Permanent establishments should also be included. Tax neutrality with respect to the legal form would also require it to include transparent entities. However, since an inclusion of transparent entities would also affect the personal income tax, this choice should be left to the individual member states.

Individual tax accounts should be the starting point for consolidation. An important feature of the consolidation mechanism is an intra-group loss relief. In order to ensure a symmetric treatment of profits and losses, a negative consolidated tax base should be apportioned to the group members and carried forward to be offset with future positive shares of the consolidated tax base. Pre-consolidation losses may only be offset against the share of the consolidated tax base after apportionment, since these losses are not economically aligned to the group. If a company leaves the group, the apportioned losses should remain with the leaving company. Another essential feature of the consolidation approach is deferred taxation of gains arising from intra-group transactions. These gains are restored, if the asset leaves the group, in the course of depreciation, if a company involved in an intra-group transaction afterwards leaves the group or group entities move their residence. Pre-consolidation capital gains have to be taken into account and taxation should be deferred until it is restored. All these measures of consolidation should not affect the individual accounts, since separate accounting is necessary with respect to claims of minority shareholders and recapture of gains in cases where group entities enter or leave the Common Consolidated Corporate Tax Base group or group entities move their residence. Instead, measures of consolidation should become effective in a separate combined report. As a consequence, consolidation and formula apportionment cannot fully avoid transfer pricing issues.

The territorial scope of the Common Consolidated Corporate Tax Base has to be restricted to group entities located within the EU. Thus, separate accounting using arm's length pricing will also prevail with respect to third countries. With respect to group companies, which are resident outside the EU, common rules are necessary. In this context a decision has to be made, whether the member states should uniformly apply the source or the residence principle. However, the analysis revealed that neither the source principle, nor the residence principle can fully avoid distortions of business decisions.

Consolidation and formula apportionment should encompass all categories of income. The apportionment should be based on a broad set of company-specific production factors, which should be defined uniformly across the EU. Local profit and non-profit taxes as well as social security contributions should be tax deductible, either against the consolidated tax base or against the share of the consolidated tax base after formula apportionment.

As long as there are differences in the nominal tax rates on corporate income across the EU, incentives to allocate capital or shift profits will remain under a Common Consolidated Corporate Tax Base. This raises the question, whether harmonisation efforts should concentrate on nominal tax rates. A harmonisation of tax rates, however, seems not feasible, since member states are reluctant to give up their sovereignty to set their tax rates independently. Moreover, an isolated harmonisation of nominal tax rates, would not address all existing obstacles to cross-border investments. Similarly, an isolated harmonisation of the tax base as implied by the introduction of a Common Consolidated Corporate Tax Base cannot resolve all distortions to business decisions in an international context, if nominal tax rates differ across the EU. Against this background, a solution might be to combine the Common Consolidated Corporate Tax Base with some form of harmonisation of nominal tax rates, such as a minimum tax rate or a tax-rate corridor (see Spengel, 2006a: G40; Wissenschaftlicher Beirat beim Bundesministerium der Finanzen, 2007: 72).

List of References

Altshuler, R. an T.S. Newlon (2003), The Effects of U.S. Tax Policy on the Income Repatriation Patterns of U.S. Multinational Corporations, in: Alberto, G., R.G. Hubbard and J. Slemrod (Eds.), Studies in International Taxation, Chicago, 77-115.

Anderson, E. and D. Schmittlein (1984), Integration of the Sales Force: An Empirical Investigation, in: Rand Journal of Economics, 385-395.

Antràs, P. (2003), Firms, Contracts, and Trade Structure, in: Quarterly Journal of Economics, 1375-1418.

Antràs, P. and E. Helpman (2004), Global Sourcing, in: Journal of Political Economy, 552-580.

Argúndez-Garzía, A. (2006), The Delination and Apportionment of an EU Consolidated Tax Base for Multi-Jurisdictional Corporate Income Taxation: A Review of Issues and Options, Taxation Papers, Brussels.

Ault, H.J. and D. Bradford (1990), Taxing International Income: An Analysis of the U.S. System and Its Economic Premises, in: Razin, A. and J. Slemrod (Eds.), Taxation in a Global Economy, Chicago/London.

Baetge, J., H. Zülch and S. Matena (2002), Fair Value-Accounting, in: Steuern und Bilanzen, 365-372, 417-422.

Bailey, E.E. and F. Friedlander (1982), Market Structure and Multiproduct Industries, in: Journal of Economic Literature, 1024-1048.

Baker & McKenzie (1999), Survey of the Effective Tax Burden in the European Union, Amsterdam.

Barba-Navaretti, G. and A.J. Venables (2004), Multinational Firms in the World Economy, Princeton.

Bauer, K., (1987), Die Besteuerung deutscher Konzerne: wirtschaftliche Einheit und Konzernsteuerrecht, Regensburg.

Becker, K., (2005), Rechnungslegung nach IAS/IFRS: IAS 39 – Europäischer Alleingang oder weltweite Konvergenz?, in: Der Konzern, 286-298.

Berry, C.H., D.F. Bradford and J.R. Hines (1992), Arm's-Length Pricing: Some Economic Perspectives, in: Tax Notes, 731-740.

Besley, T. and A. Case (1995), Incumbent Behaviour: Vote Seeking, Tax Setting and Yardstick Competition, in: American Economic Review, 25-45.

Besley, T., R. Griffith and A. Klemm (2001), Empirical Evidence on Fiscal Interdependence in OECD Countries, Mimeo.

Bird, R.M. (1996), Why Tax Corporations?, Working Paper Prepared for the Technical Committee on Business Taxation, Ottawa.

Boadway, R.W. and N. Bruce (1984), A General Proposition on the Design of a Neutral Business Tax, in: Journal of Public Economics, 231-239.

Bökelmann, J. (1997), Gewinnzurechnung im Körperschaftsteuerrecht – Die Worldwide Unitary Taxation U.S.-amerikanischer Einzelstaaten und ihre Anwendbarkeit durch die Europäische Union, Konstanz.

Bond, E.W. and L. Samuelson (1989), Strategic Behaviour and the Rules for International Taxation of Capital, in: The Economic Journal, 1099-1111.

Bordhag, K. (1997), Vergleich der Besteuerung deutscher und französischer Kapitalgesellschaften unter besonderer Berücksichtigung der ertragsunabhängigen Besteuerung, Frankfurt on the Main et al.

Bradford, D.F. (1986), Untangling the Income Tax, Cambridge.

Brainard, S.L. (1997), An Empricial Assessment of the Proximity-Concentration Trade-off between Multinational Sales and Trade, in: American Economic Review, 520-544.

Brown, E.C. (1948), Business-Income Taxation and Investment Incentives, in: Lloyd A. (Ed.), Income, Employment and Public Policy. Essays in Honor of Alvin H. Hansen, New York, 251-283.

Buckley, P.J. (1985), A Critical View of Theories of the Multinational Enterprise, in: Buckley, P.J. and M. Casson (Eds.), The Economic Theory of the Multinational Enterprise, London, 1-19.

Bucovetsky, S. (1991), Assymetric Tax Competition, in: Journal of Urban Ecnomics, 167-181.

Bucovetsky, S. and J. Wilson (1991), Tax Competition with Two Tax Instruments, in: Regional Science and Urban Economics, 333-350.

Busse von Colbe, W. (2001), Anpassung der EG-Bilanzrichtlinien an IAS, in: Zeitschrift für kapitalmarktorientierte Rechnungslegung, 199-205.

Busse von Colbe, W. (2002), Vorschlag der EG-Kommission zur Anpassung der Bilanzrichtlinien an die IAS – Abschied von de Harmonisierung?, in: Betriebs-Berater, 1530-1536.

Büttner, T. and M. Ruf (2006), Tax Incentives and the Location of FDI: Evidence from a Panel of German Multinationals, in: International Tax and Public Finance, 151-164.

Büttner, T., M. Overesch, U. Schreiber and G. Wamser (2006), Taxation and Capital Structure Choice – Evidence from a Panel of German Multinationals, ZEW Discussion Paper No. 06-067, Mannheim.

Caves, R.E. (1982), Multinational Enterprise and Economic Analysis, Cambridge.

Caves, R.E. (1996), Multinational Enterprise and Econometric Analysis, Cambridge.

Caves, R.E. and W.F. Murphy (1976), Franchising: Firms, Markets, and Intangible Assets, in: Southern Economic Journal, 572-586.

Coase, R.H. (1937), The Nature of the Firm, in: Economica, 386-405.

Coffill, E.J. and P. Jr. Willson (1993), Federal Formulary Apportionment as an Alternative to Arm's Length Pricing: From the Frying Pan to the Fire?, in: Tax Notes, 1103-1117.

Desai, M. and J. Hines (2003), Economic Foundations of International Tax Rules, A Paper Prepared for the American Tax Policy Institute, Washington D.C.

Desai, M., C. Foley and J. Hines (2004), A Multinational Perspective on Capital Structure Choice and Internal Capital Markets, in: Journal of Finance, 2451-2488.

Devereux, M. (2003), Measuring Taxes on Income from Capital, CESifo Working Paper No. 962, Munich.

Devereux, M. (2006), The Impact of Taxation on the Location of Capital, Firms and Profit: A Survey of Empirical Evidence, University of Warwick, unpublished manuscript, Warwick.

Devereux, M. and H. Freeman (1995), The Impact of Tax on Foreign Direct Investment: Empirical Evidence and the Implications for Tax Integration Schemes, in: International Tax and Public Finance, 85-106.

Devereux, M. and M. Pearson (1995), European Tax Harmonisation and Production Efficiency, in: European Economic Review, 1657-1681.

Devereux, M. and P. Sørensen (2006), The Corporate Income Tax: International Trends and Options for Fundamental Reforms, European Economy, European Commission, Directorate-General for Economic and Financial Affairs, Economic Papers No. 264, Brussels.

Devereux, M. and R. Griffith (1998), Taxes and the Location of Production: Evidence from a Panel of US Multinationals, in: Journal of Public Economics, 335-367.

Devereux, M. and R. Griffith (2003), Evaluating Tax Policy for Location Decisions, in: International Tax and Public Finance, 107-126.

Devereux, M. P. (2004), Debating Proposed Reforms of the Taxation of Corporate Income in the European Union, in: International Tax and Public Finance, 71-89.

Devereux, M., B. Lockwood and M. Redoano (2003), Do Countries Compete over Corporate Tax Rates?, in: CEPR Discussion Papers No. 3400, London.

Devereux, M., R. Griffith and A. Klemm (2002), Corporate Income Tax Reforms and International Tax Competition, in: Economic Policy, 451-488.

Diamond, P.A. and J.A. Mirrlees (1971), Optimal Taxation and Public Production I: Production Efficiency, in: The American Economic Review, 8-27.

Diamond, P.A. and J.A. Mirrlees (1971), Optimal Taxation and Public Production II: Tax Rules, in: The American Economic Review, 261-278.

Doernberg, R.L., L. Hinnekens, W. Hellerstein, J. Li (2001), Electronic Commerce and Multijurisdictional Taxation, The Hague.

Dunning, J.H. (1977), Trade, Location of Economic Activity and the MNE: A Search for an Eclectic Approach, in: Ohlin, B. (Ed.), The International Allocation of Economic Activity, Bath, 395-418.

Elschen, R. (1989), Institutionale oder personale Besteuerung von Unternehmensgewinnen?, Hamburg.

Elschner, C. and M. Overesch (2007), Trends of Corporate Tax Levels in Europe, in: Intereconomics, 127-132.

Endres, D., A. Oestreicher, W. Scheffler and C. Spengel (2007) The Determination of Corporate Taxable Income in the EU Member States, Frankfurt on the Main.

Ernst, C. (2001), EU-Verordnungsentwurf zur Anwendung von IAS: Europäisches Bilanzrecht vor weitreichenden Änderungen, in: Betriebs-Berater, 823-825.

Ethier, W. (1986), The Multinational Firm, in: Quarterly Journal of Economics, 805-833.

Ethier, W. and H. Markusen (1996), Multinational Firms, Technology Diffusion and Trade, in: Journal of International Economics, 1-28.

Europäische Wirtschaftsgemeinschaft (1962), Bericht des Steuer und Finanzausschusses, Brussels.

European Commission (1982), Proposal for a Directive of the Council on the Harmonization of the Corporation Tax Systems and the Regulations of the Withholding Tax on Dividends, in: Drucksache(n) des Deutschen Bundestages 7/3981, Berlin.

European Commission (1984), Vorschlag für eine Richtlinie zur Harmonisierung der steuerlichen Rechtsvorschriften der Mitgliedstaaten zur Übertragung von Unternehmensverlusten vom 20.9.1984, in: Amtsblatt der Europäischen Gemeinschaft, Nr. C 253/5 and Amtsblatt der EG, Nr. C 170/3, Brussels.

European Commission (1988), Proposal for a Directive on the Harmoization of the Regulations on the Determination of Taxable Profits, Brussels.

European Commission (1990a), Guidelines on Company Taxation, Communication from the Commission to the Council, the European Parliament and the Economic and Social Committee, SEC(90) 601 final, Brussels.

European Commission (1990b), Communication from the Commission to the Council, the European Parliament and the Economic and Social Committee, COM(1990) 595 final, Brussels.

European Commission (1992a), Report of the Committee of Independent Experts on Company Taxation, Brussels.

European Commission (1992b), Mitteilung an den Rat und das Europäische Parlament im Anschluss and die Schlussfolgerungen des unabhängigen Sachverständigenausschusses über die Leitlinien für die Unternehmensbesteuerung im Rahmen der Vertiefung des Binnenmarkts, in: Drucksache(n) des Deutschen Bundesrates 540/1992, Berlin.

European Commission (1996), Taxation in the European Union, COM(96) 546 final, Brussels.

European Commission (1997a), Towards Tax Co-ordination in the European Union, Communication from the Commission to the Council, the European Parliament and the Economic and Social Committee, COM(1997) 485 final, Brussels.

European Commission (1997b), A Package to Tackle Harmful Tax Competition in the European Union, Communication from the Commission to the Council, the European Parliament and the Economic and Social Committee, COM(1997) 564 final, Brussels.

European Commission (2001a), Tax policy in the European Union – Priorities for the Years Ahead, Communication from the Commission to the Council, the European Parliament and the European Economic and Social Committee, COM(2001), 260 final, Brussels.

European Commission (2001b), Company Taxation in the Internal Market, Communication from the Commission to the Council, the European Parliament and the European Economic and Social Committee, COM(2001), 582 final, Brussels.

European Commission (2001c), Towards an Internal Market without Tax Obstacles – A Strategy for Providing Companies with a Consolidated Corporate Tax Base for their EU-wide Activities, SEC(2001) 1681, Brussels.

European Commission (2003a), Taxation: Commission Welcomes Adoption of Package to Curb Harmful Tax Competition, Press Release IP/03/787, Brussels.

European Commission (2003b), Die Anwendung der International Accounting Standards (IAS) ab 2005 und ihre Implikationen für die Schaffung einer konsolidierten Steuerbemessungsgrundlage für die grenzüberschreigende Unternehmenstätigkeit in der EU – Workshop, 18.3.2003, Brussels.

European Commission (2003c), The Application of International Accounting Standards (IAS) in 2005 and the Implications for the Introduction of a Consolidated Tax Base for Companies' EU-wide activities, Consultation Document, Brussels.

European Commission (2003d), An Internal Market Without Company Tax Obstacles – Achievements, Ongoing Initiatives and Remaining Challenges, Communication from the Commission to the Council, the European Parliament and the European Economic and Social Committee, Brussels.

European Commission (2004a), European Tax Survey, Commission Staff Working Paper, SEC(2004) 1128/2, Brussels.

European Commission (2004b), Summary Report of the Workshop on the Allocation Mechanism, Brussels.

European Commission (2005a), Tackling the Corporation Tax Obstacles of Small and Medium-sized Enterprises in the Internal Market – Outline of a Possible Home State Taxation Pilot Scheme, Communication from the Commission to the Council, the European Parliament and the Economic and Social Committee COM(2005) 702 final, Brussels.

European Commission (2005b), Implementation of the Community Lisbon Programme, The Contribution of the Taxation and Customs Policies to the Lisbon Strategy, Communication from the Commission to the Council, the European Parliament and the Economic and Social Committee, COM(2005) 532 final, Brussels.

European Commission (2005c), Common Consolidated Corporate Tax Base Working Group – International Aspects in the CCCTB, Working Document, Brussels.

European Commission (2005d), Common Consolidated Corporate Tax Base Working Group (CCCTB WG) – An Overview of the Main Issues that Emerged at the First Meeting of the Subgroup on Taxable Income, Working Document, Brussels.

European Commission (2005e), Common Consolidated Corporate Tax Base Working Group (CCCTB WG) – Capital Gains and Losses, Working Document, Brussels.

European Commission (2005f), Common Consolidated Corporate Tax Base Working Group (CCCTB WG) – Intangible Assets and Tax Depreciation, Working Document, Brussels.

European Commission (2006a), Implementing the Community Lisbon Programme: Progress to Date and Next Steps towards a Common Consolidated Corporate Tax Base (CCCTB), Communication from the Commission to the Council. The European Parliament and the Economic and Social Committee, COM(2006) 157 final, Brussels.

European Commission (2006b), Common Consolidated Corporate Tax Base Working Group (CCCTB WG) – Progress to Date and Future Plans for the CCCTB, Working Document, Brussels.

European Commission (2006c), Common Consolidated Corporate Tax Base Working Group (CCCTB WG) – Issues Related to Group Taxation, Working document, Brussels.

European Commission (2006d), Tax Treatment of Losses in Cross-Border Situations, Communication from the Commission to the Council. The European Parliament and the Economic and Social Committee, COM(2006) 824 final, Brussels.

European Commission (2006e), Common Consolidated Corporate Tax Base Working Group (CCCTB WG) – An Overview of the Main Issues that Emerged at the Third Meeting of the Subgroup on International Aspects (SG4), Working Document, Brussels.

European Commission (2006f), Common Consolidated Corporate Tax Base Working Group (CCCTB WG) – An Overview of the Main Issues that Emerged at the Fourth Meeting of the Subgroup on Taxable Income (SG3), Working Document, Brussels.

European Commission (2006g), Common Consolidated Corporate Tax Base Working Group (CCCTB WG) – An Overview of the Main Issues that Emerged at the Third Meeting of the Subgroup on Taxable Income (SG3), Working Document, Brussels.

European Commission (2006h), Common Consolidated Corporate Tax Base Working Group (CCCTB WG) – An Overview of the Main Issues that Emerged at the Second Meeting of the Subgroup on Group Taxation (SG5 – 02&03 October 2006), Working Document, Brussels.

European Commission (2006i), Common Consolidated Corporate Tax Base Working Group (CCCTB WG) – An Overview of the Main Issues that Emerged at the First Meeting of the Subgroup on International Aspects, Working Document, Brussels.

European Commission (2007a), Summary Record by the Chair of the Meeting of the Common Consolidated Corporate Tax Base Working Group, held in Brussels on 12 December 2006, Brussels.

European Commission (2007b), Common Consolidated Corporate Tax Base Working Group (CCCTB WG) – An Overview of the Main Issues that Emerged at the Third Meeting of the Subgroup on Group Taxation (SG – 05&06 February 2007), Working Document, Brussels.

European Commission (2007c), Implementing the Community Programme for Improved Growth and Employment and the Enhanced Competitiveness of EU Business: Further Progress during 2006 and Next Steps Towards a Proposal on the Common Consolidated Corporate Tax Base (CCCTB), Communication from the Commission to the European Parliament, the Council and the European Economic and Social Committee, COM(2007) 223 final, Brussels.

European Commission (2007d), Common Consolidated Corporate Tax Base Working Group (CCCTB WG) – Possible Elements of a Technical Outline, Working Document, Brussels.

Flick, H. (1961), Recht und Gerechtigkeit im internationalen Steuerrecht, in: Finanz-Rundschau, 171-174.

Fohr, I. (2001), Besteuerungskonzept für Holdinggesellschaften: Eine systematische Analyse der Anforderungen an die Ertragsbesteuerung internationaler Holdingsgesellschaften unter besonderer Berücksichtigung des deutschen Steuerrechts, Frankfurt on the Main et al.

Frank, R.H. (2003), Microeconomics and Behaviour, 5th Edtition, New York.

Frebel, M. (2006), Erfolgsaufteilung und –besteuerung im internationalen Konzern, Lohmar.

Füllbier, R.U. and J. Gassen (1999), Wider die Maßgeblichkeit der International Accounting Standards für die steuerliche Gewinnermittlung – Erwiderung zu Oestreicher/Spengel (Der Betrieb, Seite 593-600), in: Der Betrieb, 1511-1513.

Gammie, M., S. Giannini, A. Klemm, A. Oestreicher, P. Parascandolo and C. Spengel (2005), Achieving a Common Consolidated Corpoarte Tax Base in the EU, Report of a CEPS Task Force, Brussels.

Gérard, M. (2006), Reforming the Taxation of Multijurisdictional Enterprises in Europe: A Tentative Appraisal, paper presented at the Workshop of the General Directorate Economic and Financial Affairs on Corporate Tax Competition and Coordination in Europe, 25th September, Brussels.

Gérard, M. and J. Martens Weiner (2003), Cross-border Loss Offset and Formulary Apportionment: How Do They Affect Multijurisdictional Firm Investment Spending and Interjurisdictional Tax Competition?, CESifo Working Paper No. 1004, Munich.

Girma, S., H. Görg and E. Strobl (2004), Exports, International Investment, and Plant Performance: Evidence from a Non-Parametric Test, in: Economics Letters, 317-324.

Girma, S., R. Kneller and M. Pisu (2005), Exports versus FDI: An Empirical Test, in: Review of World Economics, 193-218.

Griemla, S. (2003), Grenzüberschreitende Verschmelzung von doppelt ansässigen Kapitalgesellschaften im Ertragssteuerrecht, Lohmar/Cologne.

Grossmann, S. and O. Hart (1986), The Costs and Benefits of Ownership: A Theory of Lateral and Vertical Integration, in: Journal of Political Economy, 691-719.

Grubert, H. and J. Mutti (1991), Taxes, Tariffs and Transfer Pricing in Multinational Corporate Decision Making, in: Review of Economics and Statistics, 285-293.

Grünärml, F. (1975), Kritische Anmerkungen zu einer merkmalspezifischen Typologie multinationaler Unternehmen, in: Jahrbuch der Sozialwissenschaft, 228-243.

Gutekunst, G. (2005), Steuerbelastungen und Steuerwirkungen bei nationaler und grenzüberschreitender Geschäftstätigkeit, Lohmar.

Gutekunst, G., R.A. Hermann and L. Lammersen (2003), Deutschland ist kein Niedrigsteuerland – eine Replik auf den Beitrag von Hettich und Schmidt: Beitrag zur (Er)Klärung der Methoden zur Messung der Unternehmenssteuerbelastung, in: Perspektiven der Wirtschaftspolitik, 125-129.

Hahn, K. (2001): Deutsche Rechnungslegung im Umbruch – Stand und Entwicklungstendenzen der deutschen Rechnungslegung vor dem Hintergrund neuer EU-Vorgaben, in: Deutsches Steuerrecht, 1267-1272.

Haig, R.M. (1959), The Concept of Income – Economic and Legal Aspects, in: Americal Economic Association, Readings in the Economics of Taxation, London.

Haller, H. (1981), Die Steuern – Grundlinien eines rationalen Systems öffentlicher Ausgaben, Tübingen.

Hanson, G., R. Mataloni and M. Slaughter (2003), Vertical Production Networks in Multinational Firms, National Bureau of Economic Research Working Paper, Cambridge.

Harberger, A. (1962), The Incidence of the Corporation Income Tax, in: Journal of Political Economy, 215-240.

Hart, O. (1995), Firms, Contracts, and Financial Structure, Oxford.

Hart, O. and J. Moore (1985), Incomplete Contracts and Renegotiation, London.

Hay, D., F. Horner and J. Owens (1994), Past and Present Work in the OECD on Transfer Pricing and Selected Issues, in: Intertax, 423-439.

Hellerstein, J.R. (1982), Allocation and Apportionment of Dividends and the Delineation of the Unitary Business, in: Tax Notes, Special Report, 155-168.

Hellerstein, J.R. (1993), Federal Income Taxation of Multinationals: Replacement of Separate Accounting with Formulary Apportionment, in: Tax Notes, 1131-1145.

Hellerstein, J.R. and McLure (2004), The European Commission's Report on Company Income Taxation: What the EU Can Learn from the Experience of the US States, in: International Tax and Public Finance, 199-220.

Helpman, E. (1984), A Simple Theory of International Trade with Multinational Corporations, in: Journal of Political Economy, 451-471.

Helpman, E., J. Melitz and S.R. Yeaple (2004), Exports versus FDI with Heterogeneous Firms, in: American Economic Review, 300-316.

Hermann, R.A. (2006), Die Besteuerung von Personengesellschaften in den EU-Mitgliedstaaten und den USA, Lohmar.

Herzig, N. (1998), Globalisierung und Besteuerung, in: Die Wirtschaftsprüfung, 280-296.

Herzig, N. (2005), IAS und steuerliche Gewinnermittlung, in: Die Wirtschaftsprüfung, 211-235.

Herzig, N. (2006), Harmonisierung der steuerlichen Gewinnermittlung in der Europäischen Union, in: Steuer und Wirtschaft, 156-164.

Hey, B. (1996), Harmonisierung der Unternehmensbesteuerung in Europa, Cologne.

Higinbotham, H.N. and M.M. Levey (1998), When Arm's Length Isn't Really Arm's Length: Issues in the Application of the Arm's-Length Standard, in: International Tax Review, 235-244.

Hines, J.R. and E.M. Rice (1994), Fiscal Paradise: Foreign Tax Havens and American Business, in: Quarterly Journal of Economics, 149-182.

Homburg S. (2005), Wohnsitzprinzip, in: Endres, D., A. Oestreicher, W. Scheffler, U. Schreiber and C. Spengel (Eds.), Die internationale Unternehmensbesteuerung im Wandel, Munich, 14-27.

Homburg, S. (2007), Allgemeine Steuerlehre, 5th Edition, Munich.

Homburg, S. and A. Bolik (2005), BB-Forum: Auswirkungen des Kirchhofschen EStGB insbesondere auf die Unternehmensbesteuerung, in: Betriebs-Berater, 2330-2335.

Hommel, M. (2005), Die Neubewertungsmethode als Allowed Alternative Treatment für Sachanlagen und immaterielle Anlagewerte, in: Bieg, H. and R. Heyd (Eds.), Fair Value, Munich, 288-308.

Hommel, M. and J. Wüstemann (2006), Synopse der Rechnungslegung nach HGB und IFRS. Eine qualitative Gegenüberstellung, Munich.

Horstmann, I.J. and J.R. Markusen (1987), Strategic Investments and the Development of Multinationals, in: International Economic Review, 225-247.

Horstmann, I.J. and J.R. Markusen (1992), Endogenous Market Structures in International Trade, in: Journal of International Economics, 109-129.

Huizinga, H. and G. Nicodéme (2006), Capital Structure and International Debt Shifting in Europe, Mimeo, University of Tilburg, paper presented at the European Tax Policy Forum Conference "The Impact of Corporation Taxes Across Borders", London.

Huizinga, H. and L. Laeven (2007), International Profit Shifting within European Multinationals, in: CEPR Discussion Paper 6048, London.

Huizinga, H. and Laeven, L. (2005), International Profit Shifting within European Multinationals, Mimeo, University of Tilburg.

Huizinga, H., L. Laeven and G. Nicodème (2007), Capital Structure and International Debt Shifting, in: CEPR Discussion Paper 5882, London.

Hymer, S.H. (1976), The International Operations of National Firms: A Study of Direct Foreign Investment, Cambridge.

International Bureau of Fiscal Documentation (2006), European Tax Handbook, Amsterdam.

Jachmann, M. (2000), Steuergesetzgebung zwischen Gleichheit und wirtschaftlicher Freiheit – Verfassungsrechtliche Grundlagen und Perspektiven der Unternehmensbesteuerung, Stuttgart.

Jacobs, O.H. (1971), Das Bilanzierungsproblem in der Ertragssteuerbilanz, Stuttgart.

Jacobs, O.H. (1980), Empfiehlt sich eine rechtsformunabhängige Unternehmensbesteuerung? Betriebswirtschaftliche Überlegungen zum diesbzüglichen Thema des 53. Deutschen Juristentages, in: Zeitschrift für Unternehmens- und Gesellschaftsrecht, 289-319.

Jacobs, O.H. (2007), Internationale Unternehmensbesteuerung – Deutsche Investitionen im Ausland, Ausländische Investitionen im Inland, 6th Edition, Munich.

Jacobs, O.H. and C. Spengel (1996), European Tax Analyzer. EDV-gestützter Vergleich der Steuerbelastung von Kapitalgesellschaften in Deutschland, Frankreich und Großbritannien, Schriftenreihe des ZEW, Baden-Baden.

Jacobs, O.H. and C. Spengel (2000), Measurement and Development of the Effective Tax Burden of Companies – An Overview and International Comparison, in: Intertax, 334-352.

Jacobs, O.H. and C. Spengel (2002) Effective Tax Burden of Companies in Europe – Current Situation, Past Developments and Simulation of Reforms, ZEW Economic Studies 15, Heidelberg.

Jacobs, O.H., C. Spengel and A. Schäfer (2004), ICT and Profit Allocation within Multinational Groups, in: Intertax, 268-283.

Jäger, C. (2001), Die Körperschaftsteuersysteme in Europa: Eine europarechtliche und betriebswirtschaftliche Analyse, Lohmar.

Jakob, W. (1996), Einkommensteuer, 2nd Edition, Munich.

Johansson, S.-E. (1969), Income Taxes and Investment Decisions, in: Swedish Journal of Economics, 104-110.

Kahle, H. (2001), Bilanzierung der langfristigen Auftragsfertigung nach HGB und US-GAAP, in: Steuern und Bilanzen, 1201-1210.

Kahle, H. (2002), Maßgeblichkeit auf Basis der IAS?, in: Die Wirtschaftsprüfung, 178-188.

Kahle, H. (2006), Harmonisierung der Konzernbesteuerung in der EU, in: Die Wirtschaftsprüfung, 1401-1409.

Keen, M. and D. Wildasin (2004), Pareto-Efficient International Taxation, in: The American Economic Review, 259-275.

Keen, M. and H. Piekkola (1997), Simple Rules for the Optimal Taxation of International Capital Income, in: Scandinavian Journal of Economics, 447-461.

Keen, M. and J. King (2002), The Croatian Profit Tax: An ACE in Practice, in: Fiscal Studies, 401-418.

Keen, M. and M. Marchand (1997), Fiscal Competition and the Pattern of Public Spending, in: Journal of Public Economics, 33-53.

Kessel von, J. (1974), Die konsolidierte Konzernbesteuerung im Körperschaftsteuerrecht der USA, Munich.

Kiesewetter, D. (1997), Theoretische Leitbilder einer Reform der Unternehmensbesteuerung. Eine vergleichende Analyse der Reformmodelle Kroatiens, Österreichs und Skandinaviens, in: Steuer und Wirtschaft, 25-34.

Kiesewetter, D. (1999), Zinsbereinigte Einkommen- und Körperschaftsteuer. Die Implementierung im deutschen Steuersystem, Bielefeld.

Klassen, K.J. and D.A. Shakelford (1998), State and Provincial Corporate Tax Planning: Income Shifting and Sales Apportionment Factor Management, in: Journal of Accounting and Economics, 385-406.

Klein, B., R. Crawford and A. Alchian (1978), Vertical Integration Appropriable Rents and the Competitive Contracting Process, in: Journal of Law and Economics, 297-326.

König, R. (1997), Ungelöste Probleme einer investitionsneutralen Besteuerung, in: Schmalenbachs Zeitschrift für betriebswirtschaftliche Forschung, 42-63.

König, R. and M. Wosnitza (2004), Betriebswirtschaftliche Steuerplanungs- und Steuerwirkungslehre, Heidelberg.

Koop, M.J. (1993), Zur Gewinnbesteuerung von Körperschaften in der Europäischen Gemeinschaft, Tübingen.

Kraft, C. (1991), Steuergerechtigkeit und Gewinnermittlung, Eine vergleichende Analyse des deutschen und US-amerikanischen Steuerrechts, Wiesbaden.

Krebühl, H.-H. (2003), Konzernbesteuerung de lege ferenda, in: Herzig (Ed.), Organschaft, laufende und aperiodische Besteuerung, nationale und internationale Aspekte, Hinweise zum EU-Recht, Stuttgart, 595-612.

Kryzaniuk, M. and R. Musgrave (1963), The Shifting of the Corporation Income Tax, Baltimore.

Kutschker, M. and S. Schmid (2006), International Management, 5th Edition, Munich/Vienna.

Lammersen, L. (2005), Steuerbelastungsvergleiche, Anwendungsfelder und Grenzen in der Steuerplanung und der Steuerwirkungslehre, Frankfurt on the Main.

Li, J. (2002), Global Profit Split: An Evolutionary Approach to International Income Allocation, in: Canadian Tax Journal, 823-883.

Lodin S.O. and M. Gammie (2001), Home State Taxation, IBFD Publications, Amsterdam.

Markham, M.A. (2005), The Resolution of Transfer Pricing Disputes through Arbitration, in: Intertax, 68-74.

Markusen, J.R. (1984), Multinationals, Multi-Plant Economies, and the Gains from Trade, in: Journal of International Economics, 205-226.

Markusen, J.R. (1995), The Boundaries of Multinational Enterprises and the Theory of International Trade, in: The Journal of Economic Perspectives, 169-189.

Markusen, J.R. (1997), Trade versus Investment Liberalization, National Bureau of Economic Research Working Paper, Cambridge.

Markusen, J.R. (2001), Multinational Firms and the Theory of International Trade, Cambridge.

Markusen, J.R. and A. Venables (1998), Multinational Firms and the New Trade Theory, in: Journal of International Economics, 183-203.

Markusen, J.R. and A. Venables (2000), The Theory of Endowment, Intra-industry and Multinational Trade, in: Journal of International Economics, 209-234.

Martens Weiner, J. (1999), Using the Experience in the U.S. States to Evaluate Issues in Implementing Formula Apportionment at the International Level, Office of Tax Analysis Paper 83, Washington D.C.

Martens Weiner, J. (2001), The European Union and Formula Apportionment: Caveat Emptor, in: European Taxation, 380-388.

Martens Weiner, J. (2002), Would Introducing Formula Apportionment in the European Union Be a Dream Come True or the EU's Worst Nightmare?, in: ifo Studien, 519-532.

Martens Weiner, J. (2005), Company Tax Reform in the European Union. Guidance from the United States and Canada on Implementing Formulary Apportionment in the EU, New York.

Martens Weiner, J. and J.M. Mintz (2002), An Exploration of Formula Apportionment in the European Union, in: European Taxation, 346-351.

Masten, S. (1984), The Organization of Production: Evidence From the Aerospace Industry, in: Journal of Law and Economics, 403-418.

McLure Jr., C. E. (1984), Defining a Unitary Business: An Economist's View, National Bureau of Economic Research Working Paper Series W1125, Stanford.

McLure Jr., C. E. (Ed.), The State Corporation Income Tax: Issues in Worldwide Unitary Combination, Stanford, 89-124.

McLure Jr., C.E. (1980), The State Corporate Income Tax: Lambs in Wolves' Clothing, in: Aaron, H.J. and M.J. Boskin (Eds.), The Economics of Taxation, Washington D.C., 327-346.

McLure Jr., C.E. (1997), U.S. Federal Use of Formula Apportionment to Tax Income from Intangibles, in: Tax Notes International, 859-871.

McLure Jr., C.E. (2001), Globalization, Tax Rules and National Sovereignty, in: Bulletin for International Fiscal Documentation, 328-341.

McLure Jr., C.E. and J. Martens Weiner (2000), Deciding whether the European Union should adopt Formula Apportionment of Company Income, in: Cnossen, S. (Ed.), Taing Capital Income in the European Union – Issues and Options for Reform, Oxford, 243-292.

Meade Committee (1978), The Structure and Reform of Direct Taxation, London.

Meilicke, W. (2003), Die Niederlassungsfreiheit nach "Überseering", Rückblick und Ausblick nach Handelsrecht und Steuerrecht, in: GmbH-Rundschau, 793-809.

Meyer, R. (1996), Computergestützte Simulation von Steuerbelastungen, ZEW Schriftenreihe, Baden-Baden.

Mills, L. and K. Newberry (2004), Do Foreign Multinationals' Tax Incentives Influence Their U.S. Income Reporting and Debt Policy?, in: National Tax Journal, 89-107.

Mintz, J. (1996), Corporation Tax: A Survey, in: Fiscal Studies, 23-68.

Mintz, J. (1999), Globalization of the Corporate Income Tax: The Role of Allocation, in: Finanzarchiv, 389-424.

Mintz, J. and A. Weichenrieder (2005), Taxation and the Financial Structure of German Outbound FDI, in: CESifo Working Paper 1612, Munich.

Mintz, J. and J. Seade (1991), Cash Flow or Income? The Choice of the Base for Company Taxation, in: World Bank Research Observer, 177-190.

Mintz, J. and M. Smart (2004), Income Shifting, Investment, and Tax Competition: Theory and Evidence from Provincial Taxation in Canada, in: Journal of Public Economics, 1149-1168.

Mintz, J. M. (2004), Corporate Tax Harmonization in Europe: It's All About Compliance, in: International Tax and Public Finance, 221-234.

Monteverde, K. and D. Teece (1982), Supplier Switching Costs and Vertical Integration in the Automotive Industry, in: Bell Journal of Economics, 206-213.

Mooij de, R.A. and S. Everdeen (2006), What a Difference does it make? Understanding the Empirical Literature on Taxation and International Capital Flows, paper presented at the Workshop of the General Directorate Economic and Financial Affairs on Corporate Tax Competition and Coordination in Europe held on the 25th September 2006, Brussels.

Moxter, A. (1999), Rückstellungen nach IAS: Abweichungen vom geltenden deutschen Bilanzrecht, in: Betriebs-Berater, 519-525.

Mühlschlegel, G. (1971), Die steuerliche Gewinnermittlung für Konzerne, die Organschaftsbesteuerung in Deutschland, die konsolidierten Steuererklärungen in den USA. Gewinnermittlung mit Konzernsteuerbilanzen, Mannheim.

Müller, K. (2001), Verwirklichung von Gerechtigkeit und Entscheidungsneutralität in den Einkommen- und Körperschaftsteuersystemen der EU-Mitgliedstaaten, Lohmar.

Musgrave, P.B. (1972), International Tax Base Division and the Multinational Corporation, in: Public Finance, 394-413.

Musgrave, P.B. (1984), Principles for Dividing the State Corporate Tax Base, in: McLure Jr., C.E. (Ed.), The State Corporation Income Tax: Issues in Worldwide Unitary Combination, Stanford, 228-252.

Musgrave, P.B. (1987), Interjurisdictional Coordination of Taxes on Capital Income, in: Cnossen, S. (Ed.), Tax Coordination in the European Community, Amsterdam.

Musgrave, P.B. (2000), Interjurisdictional Equity in Company Taxation: Principles and Applications to the European Union, in: Cnossen, S. (Ed.), Taxing Capital Income in the European Union: Issues and Options for Reform, Oxford, 46-77.

Musgrave, P.B. and R.A. Musgrave (1989), Public Finance in Theory and Practice, 5th edition, New York/St. Louis et al.

Musgrave, R.A. and P.B. Musgrave (1989), Public Finance in Theory and Practice, 5th Edition, New York et al.

Neumark, F. (1970), Grundsätze gerechter und ökonomisch rationaler Steuerpolitik, Tübingen.

Newlon, T.S. (2000), Transfer Pricing and Income Shifting in Integrating Economies, in: Cnossen, S. (Ed.), Taxing Capital Income in the European Union: Issues and Options for Reform, Oxford, 214-242.

Nobes C. (2004), A Conceptual Framework for the Taxable Income of Business, and How to Apply it under IFRS, Association of Chartered Certified Accountants, London.

Oates, W.E. (1972), Fiscal Federalism, New York.

OECD (1995), Transfer Pricing Guidelines for Multinational Enterprises and Tax Administrations, Paris.

OECD (1996), Benchmark Definition of Foreign Direct Investment, 3rd Edition, Paris.

OECD (2003), Are the Current Treaty Rules for Taxing Business Profits Appropriate for E-Commerce?, Paris.

Oestreicher, A. (2000), Konzern-Gewinnabgrenzung: Gewinnabgrenzung – Gewinnermittlung – Gewinnaufteilung, Munich.

Oestreicher, A. (2002), Konzernbesteuerung in Europa. Zum Vorschlag einer konsolidierten körperschaftsteuerlichen Bemessungsgrundlage für die grenzüberschreitende Unternehmenstätigkeit in der EU, in: Steuer und Wirtschaft, 342-356.

Oestreicher, A. (2003a), Entwicklung und Rechtfertigung des Arm's length principle im Rahmen der Gewinnabgrenzung internationaler Konzerne, in: Oestreicher, A. (Ed.), Internationale Verrechnungspreise, Herne/Berlin, 1-51.

Oestreicher, A. (2003b), Handels- und Steuerbilanzen. HGB, IAS/IFRS, US-GAAP, EStG und BewG, Heidelberg.

Oestreicher, A. (2005a), Gewinnaufteilung, in: Endres, D., A. Oestreicher, W. Scheffler, U. Schreiber and C. Spengel (Eds.), Die internationale Unternehmensbesteuerung im Wandel, Munich, 73-91.

Oestreicher, A. (2005b), Konzernbesteuerung im Spannungsfeld zwischen wirtschaftlicher Einheit und rechtlicher Vielheit, in: Oestreicher, A. (Ed.), Konzernbesteuerung, Beiträge zu einer Ringveranstaltung an der Universität Göttingen im Sommersemester 2004, Herne/Berlin, 1-33.

Oestreicher, A. and C. Spengel (1999), Maßgeblichkeit der International Accounting Standards für die steuerliche Gewinnermittlung?, Baden-Baden.

Oestreicher, A. and C. Spengel (2001), Anwendung der IAS in der EU – Zukunft des Maßgeblichkeitsprinzips und Steuerbelastung, in: Recht der Internationalen Wirtschaft, 889-902.

Oestreicher, A. and C. Spengel (2007), The Determination of Corporate Taxable Income in the EU Member States, ZEW-Discussion Paper No. 07-35, Mannheim.

Owens, J. (1997), The Tax Man Comenth to Cyberspace, in: Tax Notes International, 1833-1852.

Paschke, D. (2007), Die „Unitary Taxation“ der US-Bundesstaaten, Leitbild für die Konzernbesteuerung in der Europäischen Union, Lohmar.

Portner, R. (2000), Steuerliche Probleme der internationalen Gewinnabgrenzung durch neue Formen der Medien (insbesondere Internet), in: Grotherr, S. (Ed.), Handbuch der internationalen Steuerplanung, Herne/Berlin, 889-906.

Razin, A. and E. Sadka (1991), International Tax Competition and Gains from Tax Harmonization, in: Economic Letters 37(1).

Redoano, M. (2004), Fiscal Interactions among EU Countries, in: University of Warwick Discussion Papers 680.

Riecker, A. (1997), Körperschaftsbesteuerung in der Europäischen Union und das US-amerikanische Modell der Unitary Taxation, Baden-Baden.

Rouselle, O. (2005), The EC Arbitratiuon Convention – an Overview of the Current Position, in: European Taxation, 14-18.

Rousslang, D.J. (1997), International Income Shifting by US Multinational Corporations, in: Applied Economics, 925-934.

Rupp, R. (1983), Die Ertragsbesteuerung nationaler Konzerne: Konzernsteuerbilanz oder Weiterentwicklung der körperschaftsteuerlichen Organschaft?, Frankfurt on the Main.

Sachverständigenrat zur Begutachtung der gesamtwirtschaftlichen Entwicklung (Council of Economic Experts in Germany) (2001), Für Stetigkeit – gegen Aktionismus, Jahresgutachten 2001/02, Stuttgart.

Sachverständigenrat zur Begutachtung der gesamtwirtschaftlichen Entwicklung (Council of Economic Experts in Germany) (2003), Staatsfinanzen konsolidieren – Steuersystem reformieren, Jahresgutachten 2003/04, Wiesbaden.

Sachverständigenrat zur Begutachtung der gesamtwirtschaftlichen Entwicklung (Council of Economic Experts in Germany) (2006), Die Chancen nutzen, Reformen mutig voranbringen, Jahresgutachten 2005/06, Wiesbaden.

Salanié, B. (1997), The Economics of Contracts: A Primer, Cambridge.

Salzberger, W. (1994), Die steuerliche Gewinnermittlung einer Konzernunternehmung in der Europäischen Union, Cologne.

Salzberger, W. (1999), Unitary Taxation – Vorbild für eine Konzernbesteuerung in der Europäischen Union?, in: Internationales Steuerrecht, 97-103.

Samuelson, P.A. (1964), Tax Deductibility of Economic Depreciation to Insure Invariant Valuations, in: Journal of Political Economy, 604-606.

Schäfer, A. (2006), International Company Taxation in the Era of Information and Communication Technologies. Issues and Options for Reform, Wiesbaden.

Schäfer, A. and C. Spengel (2003), The Impact of ICT on Profit Allocation within Multinational Groups, Arm's Length Pricing or Formula Apportionment?, ZEW Discussion Paper No. 03-53, Mannheim.

Schanz von, G. (1896), Der Einkommensbegriff und die Einkommensteuergesetze, in: Finanzarchiv, 1-87.

Schaumburg, H. (1998), Internationales Steuerrecht: Außensteuerrecht, Doppelbesteuerungsrecht, 2nd Edition, Cologne.

Scheffler, W. (2002), Besteuerung der grenzüberschreitenden Unternehmenstätigkeit, Munich.

Scherer, F. (1980), Industrial Market Structure and Economic Performance, Second Edition, Chicago.

Scheuchzer, M. (1994), Konzernbesteuerung in der Europäischen Union, Bielefeld.

Schneider, D. (1997), Betriebswirtschaftslehre, Volume 2, Rechnungswesen, 2nd Edition, Munich/Vienna.

Schneider, D. (1999), Ist die Einkommensteuer überholt? Kritik und Reformvorschläge, in: Smekal, C., R Sendlhofer and H. Winner (Ed.), Einkommen versus Konsum, Heidelberg, 1-14.

Schneider, D. (2000), Otto H. Jacobs' "Bilanzierungsproblem in der Ertragsteuerbilanz" und dessen Stellung in der Wissenschaftsgeschichte steuerlicher Gewinnermittlung, Der Betrieb, 1241-1245.

Schneider, D. (2002), Steuerlast und Steuerwirkung, Munich/Vienna.

Schön, W. (2004), International Accounting Standards – A "Starting Point" for a Common European Tax Base?, in: European Taxation, 426-440.

Schön, W. (2005), The Odd Couple: A Common Future for Financial and Tax Accounting?, in: Tax Law Review, 111-148.

Schön, W. (2007), Perspektiven der Konzernbesteuerung, in: Zeitschrift für das gesamte Handelsrecht und Wirtschaftsrecht, 409-445.

Schreiber, U. (1992), Die Besteuerung internationaler Kapitaleinkommen, in: Die Betriebswirtschaft, 829-850.

Schreiber, U. (1994), Unternehmensbesteuerung im Europäischen Binnenmarkt, in: Steuer und Wirtschaft, 238-254.

Schreiber, U. (2002a), Die Steuerbelastung der Personenunternehmen und der Kapitalgesellschaften – Ein Beitrag zur Weiterentwicklung der Unternehmensbesteuerung, in: Die Wirtschaftsprüfung, 557-571.

Schreiber, U. (2002b), Gewinnermittlung und Besteuerung der Einkommen, in: Steuer und Wirtschaft, 105-115.

Schreiber, U. (2004), Unternehmensbesteuerung im Binnenmarkt. Angleichung der Gewinnermittlung und des Satzes der Körperschaftsteuer?, in: Steuer und Wirtschaft, 212-226.

Schreiber, U. (2005), Zusammenfassung der Diskussionsrunde, in: Endres, D., A. Oestreicher, W. Scheffler, U. Schreiber and C. Spengel (Eds.), Die internationale Unternehmensbesteuerung im Wandel, Munich, 44-49.

Schreiber, U. and C. Spengel (2006), Allgemeine Unternehmenssteuer und Duale Einkommensteuer, in: Betriebswirtschaftliche Forschung und Praxis, 275-288.

Schreiber, U. and T. Stellpflug (1999), Einkommen oder Konsum als Steuerbasis?, in: Wirtschaftswissenschaftliches Studium, 186-192.

Schreiber, U., C. Spengel and L. Lammersen (2002), Measuring the Impact of Taxation on Investment and Financial Decisions, in: Schmalenbach business review, 2-23.

Schwinger, R. (1992), Einkommens- und konsumorientierte Steuersysteme, Heidelberg.

Slemrod, J. (1996), Which is the Simplest Tax System of Them All?, The Economic Effects of Fundamental Tax Reform, Washington D.C., 355-391.

Slemrod, J. (2001), A General Model of the Behavioral Response to Taxation, in: International Tax and Public Finance, 119-128.

Slemrod, J. (2004), Are Corporate Tax Rates, or Countries, Converging?, in: Journal of Public Economics, 1169-1186.

Slemrod, J. and N. Sorum (1984), The Compliance Cost of the U.S. Individual Income Tax System, in: National Tax Journal, 461-474.

Sørensen, P. B. (2004), Company Tax Reform in the European Union, in: International Tax and Public Finance, 91-115.

Spengel, C. (1995), Europäische Steuerbelastungsvergleiche: Deutschland – Frankreich – Großbritannien, Düsseldorf.

Spengel, C. (2003a), Internationale Unternehmensbesteuerung in der Europäischen Union. Steuerwirkungsanalysen – Empirische Befunde – Reformüberlegungen, Düsseldorf.

Spengel, C. (2003b), International Accounting Standards, Tax Accounting and Effective Levels of Company Tax Burdens in the European Union, European Taxation, 253-266.

Spengel, C. (2004), Einheitliche Bemessungsgrundlage für die laufende Besteuerung der Europäischen Aktiengesellschaft, in: Herzig, N. (Ed.), Besteuerung der Europäischen Aktiengesellschaft (Societas Europaea – SE), Cologne, 101-117.

Spengel, C. (2006a), Besteuerung von Einkommen – Aufgaben, Wirkungen und europäische Herausforderungen, Gutachten F/G zum 66. Deutschen Juristentag, Stuttgart.

Spengel, C. (2006b), IFRS als Ausgangspunkt der steuerlichen Gewinnermittlung in der Europäischen Union- Steuerbelastungskonsequenzen im Länder- und Branchenvergleich, in: Der Betrieb, 681-687.

Spengel, C. (2007), Concept and Necessity of a Common Tax Base, forthcoming.

Spengel, C. and L. Lammersen (2001), Methoden zur Messung und zum Vergleich von internationalen Steuerbelastungen, in: Steuer und Wirtschaft, 222-238.

Spengel, C. and O.H. Jacobs (1994), Ertragsbesteuerung von Konzernen in Deutschland und Frankreich – Eine vergleichende Analyse unter besonderer Berücksichtigung der Behandlung konzerninterner Transaktionen, in: Internationales Steuerrecht, 100-104 (Teil I), 146-151 (Teil II).

Spengel, C. and R.U. Braunagel (2006), EU-Recht und Harmonisierung der Konzernbesteuerung in Europa, in: Steuer und Wirtschaft, 34-49.

Stetter, T. (2005), Computergestützte internationale Steuerbelastungsvergleiche. Bausteinbasiertes Metamodell zur Modellierung von Steuersystemen, Lohmar.

Sutton, T. (2004), Corporate Financial Accounting and Reporting, Harlow.

Theisen, M.R. (1990), Die theoretischen Grundlagen der "neuen Methoden" in betriebswirtschaftlicher Sicht, in: Vogel, K. (Ed.), Verrechnungspreise bei Lizenzen und Dienstleistungen, Munich, 21-37.

Tiebout, C.M. (1956), A Pure Theory of Local Expenditures, in: Journal of Political Economy, 416-424.

Tipke, K. (1981), Steuergerechtigkeit in Theorie und Praxis – Vom politischen Schlagwort zum Rechtsbegriff und zur praktischen Anwendung, Cologne.

Tirole, J. (2003), The Theory of Industrial Organization, Cambridge/London.

United Nations (2006), World Investment Report 2006, FDI from Developing and Transition Economies: Implications for Development, Overview, New York/Geneva.

Utescher, T. (1999), Internet und Steuern, Electronic Commerce und Telearbeit, Düsseldorf.

Vogel, K. (1994), Über „Besteuerungsrechte" und über das Leistungsfähigkeitsprinzip im Internationalen Steuerrecht, in: Kirchhof, P., K. Offerhaus and H. Schöberle (Eds.), Steuerrecht, Verfassungsrecht, Finanzpolitik – Festschrift für Franz Klein, Cologne, 361-376.

Vögele, A., T. Borstell, J. Raab, C. Diessner (2004), Chapter D, in: Vögele, A. (Ed.), Handbuch der Verrechnungspreise, 2nd Edition, Munich, Sections 1-392.

Wagner, F.W. (1995), Leitlinien steuerlicher Rechtskritik als Spiegel betriebswirtschaftlicher Theoriengeschichte, in: Elschen, R., T. Siegel and F.W. Wagner (Eds.), Unternehmenstheorie und Besteuerung, Festschrift zum 60. Geburtstag von Dieter Schneider, Wiesbaden, 724-746.

Wagner, F.W. (2005), Steuervereinfachung und Entscheidungsneutralität – konkurrierende oder komplementäre Leitbilder für Steuerreformen? in: Steuer und Wirtschaft, 93-108.

Wagner, F.W. and H. Dirrigl (1980), Die Steuerplanung der Unternehmung, Stuttgart.

Weichenrieder, A. (1996), Fighting International Tax Avoidance: the Case of Germany, in: Fiscal Studies, 37-58.

Weichenrieder, A. (2006), Profit Shifting in the EU – Evidence from Germany, paper presented at the European Tax Policy Forum Conference "The Impact of Corporation Taxes across Borders, London.

Weichenrieder, A. (2006), Profit Shifting Within the EU: Evidence from Germany. Mimeo, University of Frankfurt, paper presented at the European Tax Policy Forum Conference 'The Impact of Corporation Taxes Across Borders', London.

Wellisch, D. (1999), Finanzwissenschaft II. Theorie der Besteuerung, Munich.

Wellisch, D. (2004), Taxation under Formula Apportionment – Tax Competition, Tax Incidence, and the Choice of Apportionment Factors, in: Finanzarchiv, 24-41.

Wellisch, D. (2004b), Maßstäbe zur indirekten Gewinnaufteilung im Rahmen einer neuen Konzernbesteuerung in der EU: Möglichkeiten und Grenzen, in: Steuer und Wirtschaft, 267-276.

Wenger, E. (1983), Gleichmäßigkeit der Besteuerung von Arbeits- und Vermögenseinkünften, in: Finanzarchiv, 207-252.

Williamson, O.E. (1985), The Economic Institutions of Capitalism, New York.

Williamson, O.E. (1990), Die ökonomischen Institutionen des Kapitalismus. Unternehmen, Märkte, Kooperationen – aus dem Amerikanischen übersetzt von Monika Streissler, Tübingen.

Wilson, J.D. (1999), Theories of Tax Competition, in: National Tax Journal, 269-304.

Wissenschaftlicher Beirat beim Bundesministerium der Finanzen (2007), Einheitliche Bemessungsgrundlage der Körperschaftsteuer in der Europäischen Union, Gutachten, Berlin.

Yeaple, S. (2003), The Role of Skill Endowments in the Structure of U.S. Outward FDI, in: Review of Economics and Statistics, 726-734.

Zeile, W.J. (1997), U.S. Intrafirm Trade in Goods, in: Bureau of Economic Analysis (Ed.), Survey of Current Business Volume 77 No. 2, Washington D.C., 23-38.

Zodrow, G. and P. Mieskowski (1986), Pigou, Tiebout, Property Taxation, and the Underprovision of Local Public Goods, in: Journal of Urban Economics, 356-370.

Zuber, B. (1991), Anknüpfungsmerkmale und Reichweite der internationalen Besteuerung, Eine normative Analyse unter Berücksichtigung der Personensteuern in der BRD und in den USA, Hamburg.

Directives of the European Council

Council Directive 2003/123/EC of 22 December 2003 Amending Directive 90/435/EEC on the Common System of Taxation Applicable in the Case of Parent Companies and Subsidiaries of Different Member States, Official Journal of the European Communities No. L 007, 13/01/2004, 41-44.

Council Directive 2003/49/EC of 3 June 2003 on a Common System of Taxation Applicable to Interest and Royalty Payments made Between Associated Companies of Different Member States, Official Journal of the European Communities No. L 157/49.

Council Directive 2003/51/EC of 18 June 2003 Amending Directives 78/660/EEC, 83/349/EEC, 86/635/EEC and 91/674/EEC on the Annual and Consolidated Accounts of Certain Types of Companies, Banks and other Financial Institutions and Insurance Undertakings, Official Journal of the European Communities No. L 178/16.

Council Directive 2005/19/EC of 17 Februar 2005 Amending Directive 90/434/EEC 1990 on the Common System of Taxation Applicable to Mergers, Divisions, Transfers of Assets and Exchanges of Shares Concerning Companies of Different Member States, Official Journal of the European Communities No. L 58/19.

Council Directive 86/635/EEC of 8 December 1986 on the Annual Accounts and Consolidated Accounts of Banks and other Financial Institutions, Official Journal of the European Communities No. L 372, 1-17.

Council Directive 90/434/EEC of 23 July 1990 on the Common System of Taxation Applicable to Mergers, Divisions, Transfers of Assets and Exchanges of Shares Concerning Companies of Different Member States, Official Journal of the European Communities No. L 225/1.

Council Directive 90/435/EEC of 23 July 1990 on the Common System of Taxation Applicable in the Case of Parent Companies and Subsidiaries of Different Member States, Official Journal of the European Communities No. L 225/6, amended by Official Journal of the European Communities No. L 266/20.

Council Directive 91/674/EEC of 19 December 1991 on the Annual Accounts and Consolidated Accounts of Insurance Undertakings, Official Journal of the European Communities No. L 374, 7-31.

Fourth Council Directive 78/660/EEC of 25 July 1978 Based on Article 54 (3) (g) of the Treaty on the Annual Accounts of Certain Types of Companies, Official Journal of the European Communities No. L 222, 11-31.

Seventh Council Directive 83/349/EEC of 13 June 1983 Based on Article 54 (3) (g) of the Treaty on Consolidated Accounts, Official Journal of the European Communities No. L 193, 1-17.

WWW.GABLER.DE

MIX
Papier aus verantwortungsvollen Quellen
Paper from responsible sources
FSC® C105338

If you have any concerns about our products,
you can contact us on
ProductSafety@springernature.com

In case Publisher is established outside the EU,
the EU authorized representative is:
Springer Nature Customer Service Center GmbH
Europaplatz 3, 69115 Heidelberg, Germany

Printed by Libri Plureos GmbH
in Hamburg, Germany